# THE INSTITUTIONAL FRAMEWORK OF THE EUROPEAN COMMUNITIES

After more than a decade of British membership of the European Community there is still a widespread lack of appreciation of what goes on within the Community institutions, and of its significance for UK political and legal processes. This book aims to provide a concise introduction to the institutions and law making processes of the Community, and to set them in their proper perspective as part of UK public law. The prime focus is upon the Community institutions and their inter-relations, however, reference is also made as appropriate to the effects which Community decision-making has on Westminster and Whitehall and in the English courts. In particular the book examines and explains the sources of Community law, the organisation and composition of the main institutions after the accession of Spain and Portugal, and the decision-making processes involved in the enactment of Community legislation. There are also chapters on the budgetary process and on the role of the European Court of Justice. Despite the UK emphasis some comparative material is used to put the UK approach into perspective. To enhance its value to readers coming to the subject for the first time, the book also contains the text of selected articles of the Treaty of Rome.

D.A.C. Freestone and J.S. Davidson are both lecturers in law at the University of Hull.

# THE INSTITUTIONAL FRAMEWORK OF THE EUROPEAN COMMUNITIES

D.A.C. FREESTONE and J.S. DAVIDSON

CROOM HELM
London & New York

Croom Helm Ltd, Provident House, Burrell Row,
Beckenham, Kent, BR3 1AT

Croom Helm Australia, 44-50 Waterloo Road,
North Ryde, 2113, New South Wales

Published in the USA by
Croom Helm
in association with Methuen, Inc.
29 West 35th Street
New York, NY 10001

British Library Cataloguing in Publication Data

Freestone, D. (David)
The institutional framework of the European Communities.
1. European Economic Community Law
I. Title II. Davidson, S.J. (Scott J)
341'.094

ISBN 0-7099-1048-7
ISBN 0-7099-4908-1 (Pbk)

**Library of Congress Cataloging-in-Publication Data**

Freestone, David.
The institutional framework of the European communities.

Published in the USA in association with Methuen.
Includes index.
1. Law — European Economic Community countries.
2. European Economic Community — Great Britain.
I. Davidson, Scott. II. Title.
KJE947.F74 1988 341.24'2 87-16176
ISBN 0-7099-1048-7
ISBN 0-7099-4908-1 (pbk.)

# Contents

# Abbreviations

| | |
|---|---|
| A.J.I.L. | American Journal of International Law |
| Bulletin EC | Bulletin of the European Communities |
| CAP | Common Agricultural Policy |
| C.L.J. | Cambridge Law Journal |
| C.M.L. Rev. | Common Market Law Review |
| EEC | European Economic Community |
| ECJ | European Court of Justice |
| E.C.R. | European Court Reports |
| ECSC | European Coal and Steel Community |
| ECU | European Currency Unit |
| ELRev | European Law Review |
| EP | European Parliament |
| ESC | Economic and Social Committee |
| EURATOM | European Atomic Energy Community |
| EUT | Draft Treaty on European Union |
| FIDE | International Federation for European Law |
| GATT | General Agreement on Tariffs and Trade |
| G.A.O.R. | Official Records of the General Assembly of the United Nations |
| G.N.P. | Gross National Product |
| H.C. Deb. | House of Commons Debates (Hansard) |
| I.C.J. Reports | Reports of Judgments, Advisory Opinions and Orders of the International Court of Justice |
| I.C.L.Q. | International and Comparative Law Quarterly |
| I.L.M. | International Legal Materials |
| J.C.M.S. | Journal of Common Market Studies |
| J.O./O.J. | Official Journal of the European Communities |
| L.Q.R. | Law Quarterly Review |
| MCR | Modern Law Review |
| MEP | Member of the European Parliament |
| UKAEL | United Kingdom Association for European Law |
| U.K.T.S. | United Kingdom Treaty Series |
| UN | United Nations Organisation |
| UNC | Charter of the United Nations Organisation |
| U.N.T.S. | United Nations Treaty Series |
| Y.E.L. | Yearbook of European Law |

# Table of Cases

## I. Court of Justice of the European Communities

## II. National Courts: United Kingdom

*Rustomjee v. Queen* (1876) 1 Q.B.D. 487. 22–3
*Shields v. Coomes* [1979] 1 All ER 456; [1978] 1 W.L.R. 1408. 164
*Waddington v. Miah* [1974] 1 W.L.R. 683. 24

## III. United States of America

*Edye v. Robertson* 112 US 580 (1884). 17–18
*Foster v. Neilson* 2 Pet. 253 (US 1829). 18n26
*Sei Fujii v. State of California* 217 P. (2d) 481 (1950). 18–19
*Ware v. Hylton* 3 US 199 (1796). 17

## IV. France

*Cohn-Bendit* [1980] 1 C.M.L.R. 543. 15, 43

## V. International Court of Justice

*Reparation for Injuries Suffered in the Service of the United Nations* I.C.J. Reports (1949), p. 174. 11n4, 12n10

# Table of Articles: Treaty of Rome

To
Jenny
and to
Olivia

# Preface

The purpose of this book is to provide first year public law students with an introduction to the institutions and law of the European Community. The origins of the book lie in our experience of teaching Community law within the context of an integrated public law course which perceives Community law not as some specialised and esoteric system but as part of the fabric of UK public law. Our aim in this book has been to emphasise the nature and interrelationship of the Community institutions, their powers and their procedures. The legislative process (which is in the process of amendment by the Single European Act at the time of writing) and the Community Budget are areas to which particular attention is devoted. But perhaps naturally in a book which is intended primarily for new law students, a great deal of emphasis is placed upon the role of the Court of Justice of the European Communities. The Court, through its predominantly teleological approach to interpretation, has been one of the primary actors in the integration process of the Community; we examine its composition, its jurisdiction and its techniques. Finally, we consider the impact of Community law on the UK courts not simply in terms of the doctrinal constitutional issues such as reception of Community law, its direct effect and supremacy, but also from the perspective of the enforcement of Community law at national level and the relationship between the UK courts and the European Court of Justice. Despite the fact that we have unashamedly written the book for law students, we hope that students of other disciplines, particularly political science and European studies will also find it of interest.

In writing this book we have received encouragement and assistance from a number of people. In particular we would like to thank Richard Corbett of the Secretariat of the European Parliament's Committee on Institutional Affairs for his valuable comments on Chapter 5 (The Budget) and Dr Juliet Lodge, Senior Lecturer in Politics at the University of Hull, for her useful comments on a number of issues. Our thanks are also due to Enid Allen who produced a very fine typescript from a *mélange* of our untidy manuscript and bad typing. Finally, we thank our families for their forebearance and understanding while this book was being written.

David Freestone and Scott Davidson
Faculty of Law, University of Hull

# 1

# Introduction

In February 1986 the Heads of the governments of the twelve Member States of the European Communities signed the Single European Act[1] - a treaty which introduced important reforms into the European Community system. By this Act, they declared themselves to be 'moved by the will to continue the work undertaken on the basis of the Treaties establishing the European Community and to transform their relations as a whole among their States into a European Union'.[2] The signing of the Single European Act provoked letters of protest to *The Times* and talk in Parliament of 'a fundamental surrender of sovereignty'. In other quarters mostly outside Britain, however, the Single European Act was denounced for not doing enough to promote European union, and Jacques Delors, the President of the Commission of the European Communities described the Single European Act as a 'compromise for progress'.[3]

What is clear from these diverse reactions is that after more than a decade of UK membership of the European Community there is still in the UK a considerable amount of misunderstanding, as well as misgiving, about the nature of the system established by the European Community Treaties. The fact that the UK is a member of the European Community means that for lawyers in Britain, as for lawyers in all Community Member States, European Community law is not an esoteric specialisation; it is a system which provides an important source of rights and obligations which affect all levels of society - from small businesses and individuals in a range of capacities including those of employer, employee, consumer, traveller or simply European citizen. It is, in short, an important part of United Kingdom public law.

The importance which Community law has to the contemporary

study of public law is not restricted to a debate about parliamentary supremacy or to the occasional conflict with national law, or even to what goes on in the courts. The law and institutions of the Community provide a further dimension to the whole process of democratic decision-making and accountability, and to government under the law. Indeed, the premise upon which this book is based is that an understanding, albeit at a basic level, of the way that the European Community works, and the way that Community laws are made and promulgated, is indispensable to an understanding of contemporary UK public law.

Before looking at the institutions in detail, however, it is necessary to put the European Communities into perspective: first, by distinguishing them from the other international institutions which exist in Europe (and with which they are often confused), and second, by a brief account of the political circumstances of their establishment and evolution. Not only is this perspective of importance in its own right, but it is also necessary for an appreciation of the political premises upon which much of Community law is based and according to which it is interpreted. The EEC may be a European *Economic* Community, but its original signatories intended that through economic integration would come political integration. This objective may have become somewhat obscured in recent years - particularly since the first enlargement of the Communities in 1973 with the accession of Denmark, Eire and the UK - but it still informs much of the work of the Community institutions, notably the case law (or jurisprudence) of the European Court of Justice. English judges are nowadays prepared publicly to acknowledge that they make law, but ever since its inception the European Court has been an explicit advocate of the teleological or 'policy-oriented' approach to the judicial function - whereby, from a choice of interpretations or possible courses open to it, the Court will choose that which is most likely to achieve the goal, or policy, desired - and the goal of the European Court has always been European integration.

## EUROPEAN INTEGRATION SINCE 1945[4]

At the end of World War Two the time was ripe for international cooperation within Europe. Within 30 years Europe had been the main battle-ground for the two most devastating wars the world had known. Its states could no longer rate themselves alongside the US and the USSR as world superpowers and there was a strong political conviction among the victorious allies that a new political system would have to be established to ensure that global war did not happen again. The first manifestation of this was the establishment of the United Nations in 1945, but within Europe a large number of institutions were established which were dedicated to forging closer links between the nation states of Europe.

From the plethora of institutions so created, three main groups have emerged as the most influential. The first group derived their impetus directly from transatlantic cooperation. The Organisation for European Economic Cooperation (OEEC) was inspired by the US plan to provide financial assistance for united European efforts to restructure Europe after World War Two (the Marshall Plan). In 1960, the OEEC was extended to include the US and Canada and renamed the Organisation for Economic Cooperation and Development (OECD). Similarly the North Atlantic Treaty Organisation (NATO) was set up in 1949 as a military alliance between the US, Canada and the majority of the major Western European states. NATO is primarily a defensive pact, providing a permanent secretariat, integrated military command structure and a collective decision-making system.

The Council of Europe, with 21 members, provides a major impetus for inter-governmental cooperation in a number of different fields and represents the second main institutional grouping. Its main decision-making body is the Committee of Ministers, where unanimity is required for substantive decisions, although a consultative Parliamentary Assembly meets regularly to discuss issues of common concern. The Council of Europe institutions have no direct legislative powers, and the Council relies principally on the traditional treaty-making system to attain its objectives. It has promoted treaties on a wide spectrum of issues from data protection to the suppression of terrorism. Its most significant achievement has been the 1950 European Convention for the Protection of Human Rights and Fundamental Freedoms, and its various protocols.[5] This treaty provides for the establishment of a Commission on Human Rights and a Court of Human Rights, which are both based in Strasbourg, and their work has had a major impact on the development of human rights protection in all the Member States. It has also had an indirect effect on the development of European Community law, but the Commission and the Court of Human Rights should not be confused with the institutions of the European Communities which represent the third major group of European institutions.

## THE ESTABLISHMENT OF THE EUROPEAN COMMUNITIES

The origins of the three European Communities - the European Coal and Steel Community (ECSC), the European Atomic Energy Community (EURATOM) and the European Economic Community (EEC) - also lie in attempts to rebuild Europe after 1945. However, the path taken by the drafters of these Treaties differed markedly from that of the previous two groups. The European Communities are based upon the explicit aim of integration.[6] The institutions have autonomous legislative powers (envisaging decision by majority vote in certain circumstances) and Community legislation can take effect directly in national legal systems without the need for prior approval by national parliaments.[7]

Such a system holds the seeds of a form of federal structure, where the participating states surrender certain of their powers to the central 'federal' authorities, and this is no accident. In 1946 in Zurich, Winston Churchill had called for a United States of Europe to unite France and Germany, and in 1950 the French Foreign Minister Robert Schuman proposed (the Schuman Plan) that further conflict between France and Germany could be prevented by the uniting of their coal and steel production under the auspices of a High Authority. The result of the Schuman initiative was the 1951 European Coal and Steel Community Treaty, which established a Council of Ministers, a High Authority, a consultative Assembly and a Court of Justice, and which was signed in Paris by Belgium, Germany, France, Italy, Luxembourg and the Netherlands.

The success of the ECSC, which had limited aims and objectives, led to the proposal that a similar 'functionalist'[8] approach should be adopted for a wider range of activities. The 1956 Spaak Report[9] proposed that the aim of further European integration could most readily be realised by the integration of the economies of the six Member States of the ECSC.

Explicit in the Spaak strategy was the idea that through economic integration would come political integration. Indeed, this very approach had been vindicated by the failure of the more ambitious proposal for a European Defence Community which had foundered as a result of the refusal in 1954 of the French National

Assembly to agree to the surrender of political sovereignty involved. Hence, at the beginning of the preamble to the EEC Treaty, signed by the six in March 1957, the parties declare themselves 'determined to lay the foundations of an ever closer union among the peoples of Europe'.[10] The EURATOM Treaty was signed on the same day and both Treaties came into effect on 1 January 1958.

## ENLARGEMENT OF THE EUROPEAN COMMUNITIES

Despite the fact that Churchill had proposed a United States of Europe, the United Kingdom had held back from membership of the ECSC in 1951 and was initially opposed to the ideas underpinning the EEC, preferring instead a European Free Trade Area. It pioneered the European Free Trade Association, which was formed in 1959. No surrender of sovereignty was involved in membership which comprised Norway, Sweden, Denmark, Austria, Portugal, Iceland, Switzerland and the UK (with Finland having associate status). The members agreed to free trade between themselves, but unlike the EEC there was no external barrier to goods entering the Free Trade Area from non-member states.

The early success of the EEC persuaded the UK to apply for membership, which it did first in 1961. However, its application was blocked by the French veto as a result of the opposition of President de Gaulle. His opposition also blocked a second application by the UK in 1967, but after he resigned from office in 1969 the negotiations were able to proceed, resulting in the Treaty of Accession being signed on 22 January 1972. On 1 January 1973 the UK, together with Denmark and Eire, became members of the European Communities; Norway having dropped out at the last minute as a result of a referendum which showed 53.49% of voters opposed to membership.

In 1975 the newly democratic Greece applied for membership and from 1 January 1981 became the tenth Member of the Communities. In the meantime Spain and Portugal, both newly returned to democracy, had also applied. These negotiations proved more difficult, largely as a result of the worry of the effect that the accession of two more largely agricultural states would have on the functioning of the already troubled Common Agricultural Policy, but in June 1985 the terms of accession were agreed and the European Community became a community of twelve on 1 January

1986.[11]

## REFORM AND DEVELOPMENT OF THE EUROPEAN COMMUNITIES

When the EEC and EURATOM Treaties came into effect on 1 January 1958, a further convention also became effective. This was the Convention on Certain Institutions Common to the European Communities, which provided that a single Parliamentary Assembly and a single Court of Justice should serve all three Communities. However, this still left each Community (ECSC, EEC, EURATOM) with its own Council of Ministers and its own Commission (or in the case of the ECSC, High Authority). This diversity of institutions with the resultant lack of coordination was remedied by the 1965 Treaty Establishing a Single Council and a Single Commission of the European Communities. This Treaty, known as the 'Merger Treaty', unified the executive and legislative functions of the three Communities and since it came into force in 1967 there has been a growing tendency, even in official circles, to describe the three Communities, which are still technically separate bodies, as the European Community.

As we have seen, the drafters of the Treaty of Rome envisaged further integration between the Member States, indeed certain devices are written into the Treaty itself to expedite progress to this end. For example, Article 138(3) envisages a directly elected Assembly (Parliament) elected by 'direct universal suffrage in accordance with a uniform procedure in all Member States'. Proposals to introduce such a system, made as early as 1960 by the Assembly foundered on the argument that until the Assembly had real powers it was unnecessary for it to be directly elected - and vice versa! Continued pressure from the Assembly (which since 1962 has called itself the European Parliament - EP) and from certain of the Member States resulted in the introduction of increased budgetary powers for the EP by treaty amendments in 1970 and in 1975.[12] Proposals by the Vedel Committee in 1972[13] that the Community should have a bi-cameral legislative system, with the EP having a power of co-decision with the Council of Ministers on certain key issues, and a delaying power (similar to that of the UK House of Lords) on other issues, were never taken up. Nevertheless, the increase in budgetary powers seemed to break the vicious circle, and on 20 September 1976 the Council of Ministers agreed to the holding of direct elections to the Assembly. By the time the proposals had received the approval of national parliaments of each of the Member States (as Article 138(3) requires), the first elections to the EP (which were the first ever direct elections to an international assembly) could not be held until July 1979. At the expiry of its five-year term, the second direct election was held in 1984. However, no agreement as to a uniform electoral system as envisaged by Article 138(3) seems to be forthcoming - largely as a result of the opposition of the UK to any of the systems of proportional representation used in any other Member State. It looks, therefore, as if the third direct election due to be held in 1989 will, like the previous two elections, be held according to national voting procedures.

Proposals to realise the aspiration of the preamble of the Treaty of Rome to move towards an 'ever closer union' have had an equally stormy passage. Summit Meetings of the Heads of State and Government of the Member States in 1972 and again in 1974 approved in principle progress towards European Union, and after the 1974 Summit, Leo Tindemans, the Belgian Prime Minister, was asked to prepare a report on European union. This he presented in 1975.[14] His proposals for completion of the European union by 1980, envisaged reform of the Community institutions, a move towards economic and monetary union, implementation of common regional and social policies and a common foreign policy. Although his report was shelved, many of the proposals that he made reappeared in the 1979 Report on European Institutions, the so-called 'Three Wise Men' Report,[15] which also proposed that the Community institutions be reformed so as to speed up decision-making and that foreign policy cooperation (political cooperation) which had taken place outside the auspices of the Community since 1972, be brought within the Treaty. However, even this report did not result directly in reform.

The 1980s have seen a number of attempts to recapture the spirit of the founding fathers, and to rekindle some excitement for the 'European adventure' so obvious in the 1960s. In 1983 the Council of Ministers approved a Solemn Declaration on European Union, which was a shallow reflection of original proposals for European Union put forward by the German and Italian Foreign Ministers Genscher and Colombo in 1982. However, more significant in the longer term was the proposal approved by the European Parliament on 14 February 1984 for a new treaty on European Union to replace the Treaty of Rome. This draft Treaty was the work of a specially created Institutional Affairs Committee of the EP inspired by the Italian federalist, Altiero Spinelli, who died in 1986. Drafted with the assistance of four distinguished Community lawyers the proposed European Union Treaty (EUT) envisaged a new treaty structure with overtly federalist overtones. The power of the Member States within the decision-making process was to be reduced, the power of the EP expanded, the Court was to be given wider powers, and more areas of activity, such as economic and monetary policy, social policy, including health and welfare, foreign policy including security, suppression of terrorism and disarmament, were to be brought within the sphere of competence of the Treaty - taking over many new areas which are currently within the exclusive powers of national governments.[16] Somewhat predictably some of the heads of member governments were opposed to such a major change in both the structure and power of the Communities and after the Fontainbleau Summit in June 1984 the Dooge Committee[17] was set up to investigate institutional reform. This committee recommended the holding of a major Inter-Governmental Conference to consider reforms.

The result of the Inter-Governmental Conference held in Luxembourg in December 1985 was not a European Union Treaty to replace the Treaty of Rome as advocated by Spinelli and the European Parliament, but amendments to the Treaty of Rome approved under the treaty-amendment procedure set out in Article 236.[18] These amendments constituted the Single European Act which will come into force once it has received the approval of the national parliaments of the twelve Member States. The most important aspect of the Single European Act is that its signatories pledge themselves to achieve the completion of the internal market (i.e. a complete free market between the Member States) by the end of 1992.[19] However, it also amends the EEC Treaty so as to provide a clear legal authority for Community programmes on economic and monetary policy, social policy, research and technical development and the environment.[20] It lays down as an aim of the Treaty the achievement of a common foreign policy and brings the political cooperation procedures within the scope of the Treaty for the first time.[21] A new legislative procedure, involving both the Council of Ministers and the EP - called the Cooperation Procedure - is intended to increase the political influence of the EP, although it goes nowhere near the power of co-decision envisaged by Vedel as long ago as 1972.[22] The Single European Act also uses the term Parliament[23] to describe what has previously been called the

Assembly, and gives official recognition to the European Council - the regular Summit Meetings of Heads of State or Government of the Member States - even though its decisions will still need to be formally approved by the Council of Ministers before they can have the force of Community law.[24]

Critics have argued that the achievement of the internal market set for 1992 should already have been achieved under the EEC Treaty, nevertheless, the Single European Act does represent an important commitment by the Member States to achieve certain objectives by a definite date. Rigorous time schedules have been set. Only time will tell whether the Single European Act does indeed represent, as its advocates suggest, a new lease of life for the European Community.

## NOTES

1. Done at Luxembourg 17 February 1986, and at The Hague, 28 February 1986. Reproduced in Bulletin EC, Supplement 2/68.
2. Single European Act, Preamble, para.1.
3. Bulletin EC 11 - 1985, point 1.1.2.
4. On the quest for European integration see e.g. K.D. Borhardt, *European Unification: The Origins and Growth of the European Community* (Office for Official Publications of the European Communities, Luxembourg, 1986). A useful account of the historical background to European integration may also be found in R. Pryce, *The Politics of the European Community* (Butterworths, London, 1973), pp.1-27. An assessment of the various integration theories may be found in J. Lodge, 'Integration Theory' in J. Lodge (ed.), *The European Community: Bibliographical Excursions* (Frances Pinter, London, 1983), pp.6-23.
5. On the European Convention for the Protection of Human Rights and Fundamental Freedoms see further R. Beddard, *Human Rights and Europe*, 2nd edn. (Sweet and Maxwell, London, 1980).
6. On integration theories generally see J. Lodge, 'Integration Theory'.
7. See below, pp.28-44.
8. For a description of the functionalist approach to integration see J. Lodge, 'Integration Theory', pp.12-16.
9. *Rapport des Chefs de Délégations aux Ministres des Affaires Etrangères* (Secretariat of the Inter-Governmental Conference, Brussels, 1956).
10. EEC Treaty, Preamble, para.1.
11. Note, however, that Greenland, which obtained a status of limited autonomy from Denmark by the Home Rule Act of 1979, left the Community on 1 January 1985. See F. Weiss, 'Greenland's Withdrawal from the European Communities' (1985) 10 *E.L.Rev.*, p.173.
12. See below, Chapter 5.

13. See below, p.8.

14. L. Tindemans, *European Union: Report to the European Council* (Brussels, December 1985), Bulletin EC, Supplement 1/1975.

15. *Report on the European Institutions: Presented by the Committee of Three to the European Council* (October 1979).

16. On the EUT see generally, J. Lodge (ed.), *European Union: The European Community in Search of a Future* (Macmillan, London, 1986). On the legal aspects of the EUT see *ibid* D. Freestone and S. Davidson, 'The EUT: Legal Problems', pp.125-50.

17. *Ad Hoc Committee on Institutional Affairs.*

18. On the Conference see R. Corbett, *The 1985 Inter-Governmental Conference* (European Community Research Unit, University of Hull, 1986).

19. Single European Act, Article 8A.

20. Single European Act, Title II, Chapter II, Section II, Subsections II, III, IV, V and VI.

21. Single European Act, Title III. See D. Freestone and S. Davidson, 'Community Competence and Part III of the Single European Act' (1986) 23 *C.M.L.Rev.*, p.793.

22. G. Vedel, *The Enlargement of the Powers of the European Parliament* (1972), Bulletin EC Supplement 4/72. On the cooperation procedure see below, pp. 76-7 and pp. 98-106.

23. Single European Act, Preamble, para.4 and *passim.*

24. Single European Act, Article 2.

# 2

# Sources of European Community Law

The EEC Treaty is first and foremost an agreement governed by international law. The legal regime that it creates, however, is unique among international agreements in a number of respects - notably the way that its rules penetrate the legal systems of its members. In the famous *Van Gend en Loos* case[1] the European Court of Justice (ECJ) declared that it created a 'new legal order'.[2] Nevertheless, as a treaty it derives its binding force from international law, and many of the constitutional problems which Member States have encountered in implementing its obligations have arisen from traditional thinking about the status of international treaties in national legal systems.

What is a treaty and what is its status in national law?

## TREATIES UNDER INTERNATIONAL LAW

A treaty is a form of contract. Indeed the word treaty is an obsolescent term for contract which is still used in the contractual concept of 'invitation to treat' and in property sales 'by private treaty'. Unlike such contracts, however, a treaty is not between individuals but between international persons, that is any entity which is capable of being the subject of rights and duties at an international level.[3] The most obvious international person is a state, but an international organisation - itself set up by treaty - may also qualify.[4] The other main distinction between a contract and a treaty is that whereas a contract will be governed by, and interpreted subject to, national law - usually the national law of the country where it is entered into - a treaty is governed by international law.[5]

International law is very different from national or, as international lawyers call it, municipal law. It does not have the same centralised law-making institutions as national legal systems; there is no international legislature, no world parliament. Instead, international law is created by treaty and by custom - the established practice of law-abiding states.[6] Nor is there a court system similar to national courts. When a legal dispute arises between states it can only be submitted to an international tribunal or to the International Court of Justice at the Hague if both parties agree, by treaty, to accept its jurisdiction.[7] Otherwise the dispute must be resolved by diplomacy, by negotiation, by the use of political or economic pressure or even, in the last resort, by the use of armed force.[8]

Treaties, or conventions, charters, protocols, pacts, alliances, agreements as they are also called, have to perform functions in international law which are done by a wide variety of national law mechanisms. They may be bilateral (an example would be the Anglo-Irish Agreement over Northern Ireland of 1985) or multilateral (such as the United Nations Charter) and they may cover trade, defence, extradition or any of the multitude of issues with which international relations are concerned. They are used to make law in the sense of laying down rules for future conduct of their parties - e.g. the Vienna Convention on Diplomatic Relations 1961,[9] or to establish international institutions with competence to enter into international legal relations. Indeed the same treaty may perform both functions: the UN Charter not only lays down rules for the peaceful conduct of relations between states, it also sets up the UN Organisation which has an international personality independent of the states setting it up. In the *Reparations* case,[10] which arose from the assassination of Count Bernadotte the UN Truce Negotiator in Palestine in 1948, the International Court of Justice said that the 50 states which originally created the UN in 1945 'representing the vast majority of the members of the international community, had the power, in conformity with international law, to bring into being an entity possessing objective international personality and not merely personality recognised by them alone ...'[11] Membership of the UN is open to all 'peace-loving states'[12] of which there are now 157, but some treaties, although multilateral, have membership restricted to certain classes of states (e.g. geographically: Nordic states; economically: the Organisation of Petroleum Exporting Countries; or culturally: the Arab League). The EEC Treaty is such a multilateral treaty. It has economic and political aims and objectives; it establishes institutions which it endows with international personality and although its membership can, with the unanimous approval of existing members, be extended, it is only open to European states.[13]

**Signature and Ratification**

A treaty does not usually come into force when it is signed.[14] Once the text of a treaty has been negotiated there is often a well-publicised signing ceremony. However, unless the treaty itself provides to the contrary, there will usually be a further requirement of ratification before it comes into force.[15] Indeed at the conclusion of some major international negotiations, such as the Third United Nations Conference on the Law of the Sea which took nine years to complete, a further stage is introduced and the participating states sign the Final Act of the conference. There is then a subsequent opportunity to sign, and ultimately to ratify, the treaty itself.

**What does Ratification entail?**

The break between signature and ratification provides a breathing space for the signing state to ensure that the obligations of the treaty do not take effect until it has made the preparations or taken the measures necessary to ensure that it will be able to honour them. Constitutions often give the executive the power to negotiate treaties but make their ratification subject to the approval of the legislature. This is to ensure that there is democratic control over the activities of the executive in the conduct of a state's international relations. For example, in the US the President has the power to negotiate treaties but the assent of two-thirds of the Senate (the Upper House) is required before ratification. The French Constitution of 1958 gives the President the power to negotiate and ratify treaties (Article 52) but the most important treaties -

> ... peace treaties, commercial treaties, treaties or agreements relative to international organisation, those that imply a commitment for the finance of the state, those that modify provisions of a legislative nature, those relative to the status of persons, those that call for the cession or addition of territory may be ratified or approved only by law ... (Article 53)

- and laws require the approval of parliament (Article 36). Apart from formal constitutional requirements it may be that a treaty requires money to be made available or for national law to be amended before the signatory state can be confident that it can meet the obligations the treaty requires. Even then the treaty may not come into force immediately upon ratification. A multilateral treaty will usually specify how many states need to ratify it before it comes into force, and after what period. For example, the 1982 Law of the Sea Convention comes into force one year after the deposit of the sixtieth instrument of ratification.[16] The EEC Treaty with only six original signatories required the ratification of all six before it came into force. The Treaty was signed in Rome on 25 March 1957 but Article 247 specified that 'This Treaty shall come into force on the first day of the month following the deposit of the instrument of ratification by the last signatory state to take this step'.

By a similar procedure, future amendments under Article 236, such as the Single European Act of 1986, only come into force 'after having been ratified by all the existing Member States in accordance with their respective constitutional requirements'.

### The Status of Treaties under National Law

Although treaties are governed by international law, many of them confer obligations upon states which require national or domestic application. A trade agreement, such as the General Agreement on Tariffs and Trade[17] may require abolition of tariffs or quotas. A treaty which lays down basic standards for employment or for the protection of human rights, e.g. the European Convention on Human Rights,[18] will have as its prime object the protection of those standards and rights by the legal systems of the contracting states. Nevertheless, the way that these objectives are actually achieved, the way in which the guaranteed rights are protected, is a matter for the national constitutional law of the ratifying states. It is achieved by as many methods as there are constitutions, but it is possible to distinguish two broadly different approaches to the issue: the monist and the dualist.

## Monism and Dualism

Using a 'broad brush' it can be said that a *monist* constitution accepts that international law obligations are of the same nature as, or are even superior to, national law obligations. So that a rule of customary international law or a rule established by an international treaty to which the state is a party becomes automatically part of national law. Therefore, once such a state has concluded a treaty guaranteeing certain rights for its nationals, for example, equal pay for men and women, then those rights are automatically protected by national law. The French Constitution can again be used as an example. Article 55 provides that treaties and agreements 'have an authority superior to that of laws'.

Similarly, the Dutch Constitution provides that international treaties and agreements shall be 'the supreme law of the land' (Article 68). To reinforce the practical effects of this rule Article 66 provides that:

> legal regulations in force within the Kingdom shall not apply if this application should be incompatible with provisions - binding on anyone - of agreements entered into either before or after the enactment of the regulations.

These constitutional provisions are quite remarkably receptive to international law, even if, as Lasok and Bridge comment wryly, the power to decide which provisions of treaties are 'binding on anyone' so as to have full internal effect is vested in the Dutch courts.[19]

By contrast, a *dualist* constitution is one which gives only limited status to rules of international law unless and until they have been 'transformed' into national law by some acceptable method of national law-making - such as an Act of Parliament. For historical reasons which are discussed below, the UK has a strongly dualist tradition.

It would be foolish to suggest that one or other approach is 'right' or 'wrong'; indeed it would be difficult to categorise any particular state as being wholly monist or dualist. The decisions of the French *Conseil d'Etat* - the supreme administrative court - show that a dualist tradition can influence the interpretation of even the most monist of constitutions. In *Cohn-Bendit*,[20] for example, it refused to follow the rulings of the ECJ on the direct effects[21] of directives within national law.

Nevertheless, the novel character of the obligations which the EEC Treaty imposes are such that they do present particular difficulties to dualist thinkers and hence to Member States with dualist constitutions.

## THE STATUS OF INTERNATIONAL TREATIES BEFORE MUNICIPAL COURTS: TWO MODELS

This section is devoted to a brief discussion of the reception of treaty law into the legal system of two states (the US and the UK) - one of them not even a member of the EEC. Both are common law states with a shared legal heritage, but the US, with its written, ostensibly monist constitution, provides an alternative and sharply contrasting model to that of the UK. The US also provides a useful model of a federal system. In addition, the contrast should also demonstrate, albeit at a simplified level, the extent to which historical and political factors influence the courts' approach to these, as to other, constitutional issues.

### Model 1 : The US Approach

The US Constitution was drafted by delegates from the states which participated at the Philadelphia Conference of 1797. The delegates were concerned to ensure that the Union constitution would respect the notion of the separation of powers and in particular would deny the executive - the President - access to the uncontrolled powers many European heads of state then possessed.[22] But, as representatives of autonomous states, they were equally concerned to clarify exactly what powers were being conferred upon the new federal authorities. Thus Article I enumerates the areas of federal legislative powers (to raise taxes, coin money, etc.) before Article VI proclaims the principle that federal law is supreme over state law (see text below).

Competence to conduct foreign relations is vested solely in the federal authorities with treaty-making power distributed between the President and the Senate. The conduct of foreign relations and the negotiation of treaties appears to be the preserve of the President but he only has power 'by and with the advice and consent of the Senate, to make [i.e. ratify] treaties provided two-thirds of the Senators present concur' (Article II[2]). This division of competence may seem unwieldy, but it has to be read in conjunction with Article VI which gives a duly ratified treaty the same status as federal legislation:

> The Constitution and the Laws of the United States which shall be made in pursuance thereof; and all Treaties made or which shall be made under the Authority of the United States shall be the supreme law of the land; and the judges in every state shall be bound thereby, anything in the Constitution or the laws of any state to the contrary notwithstanding.

The treaty is thus a potentially important legislative device, which the Supreme Court ruled in 1796 would prevail over state law. 'A treaty cannot be the supreme law of the land', it said in *Ware v. Hylton*,[23] 'if any act of a state legislature can stand in its way'. But treaties share this special status of supreme law with federal legislation (i.e. 'the Laws of the US'). What then is the result of a conflict between the provisions of a treaty and those of a federal statute?

This issue was confronted by the Supreme Court in *Edye v. Robertson*,[24] one of the 'Head Money' cases. A federal statute had required the master of every ship bringing immigrants into a US port to pay a tax of 50 cents per head. The plaintiff alleged that this inhibited immigration and thus was contrary to a number of pre-existing treaties of friendship between the US and foreign states. Two main questions emerged. First, was the federal statute inferior to the earlier treaties? The court found that in conflicts between rules of equal status (i.e. treaties and federal law) the normal constitutional principle that later laws take precedence over earlier laws was applicable. Hence a treaty provision would cede superiority to a later inconsistent federal rule, and of course vice versa.

The second question is more important for our present purposes, namely, was it, in any event, possible for the plaintiff to rely on the provisions of a treaty with a foreign state so as to question before a US court the applicability of a federal law? Put another way, did the treaty give the same rights to individuals which a federal statute might? This, the Court held, was a matter of interpretation. In each case it was necessary to examine the wording of the treaty in order to decide whether the treaty drafters intended it to give rights to individuals: 'only when [the Treaty] contains provisions which confer rights on citizens or subjects ... which are of the nature of municipal law and which are capable of enforcement will the Constitution place it in the same category as other acts of Congress'.[25]

Applying this principle, take the example of a treaty by which the states party agree to promote friendly relations between themselves or to change their trade laws to facilitate mutual trade. Such a treaty would not be sufficiently precise to confer rights on individuals - for the obligations would require implementation by the authorities: *how* would friendly relations be promoted? *Which* trade laws would need to be changed, and *how*? The rationale for this distinction was explained by the Supreme Court in 1829:[26]

> When either of the parties [to a Treaty] engages to perform a particular act, the treaty addresses itself to the political, not the judicial department; and the legislature must execute the contract before it can become a rule for the court.

On the other hand, when the treaty provisions are precise and clear, then no implementation is required; the legislature does not need to take further action 'to execute the contract' and for this reason such provisions are said to be '*self*-executing'.

To summarise, provisions of duly ratified treaties can have the same status as federal law *provided that* they are self-executing, i.e. they appear to have been intended to confer enforceable individual rights.

A more recent illustration of this important proviso can be seen in *Sei Fujii v. State of California.*[27] Sei Fujii was a Japanese citizen who claimed that the California Alien Land Act - which restricted land ownership rights of aliens ineligible for US citizenship - was discriminatory and thus unconstitutional in that it was contrary to both the letter and the spirit of the United Nations Charter (UNC) - a duly ratified treaty and thus superior to Californian law. The Californian Supreme Court held the Act to be unconstitutional for violation of the principle of 'equal protection of the laws' contained in the 14th Amendment to the Constitution. This it thought reflected the 'spirit' of the UNC provisions, but it was not prepared to accept that the human rights provisions of the UNC itself - Articles 55 and 56 - were self-executing. Gibson CJ argued that 'in order for a treaty provision to be operative without the aid of implementing legislation and to have the effect and force of a statute, it must appear that the framers of the treaty intended to prescribe a rule that standing alone would be enforceable in the courts ...'.[28] Article 55 provides that:

> The United Nations shall *promote* ...
> (c) universal respect for, and observance of, human rights and fundamental freedoms for all without distinction as to race, sex, language or religion.

And by Article 56 'All Members *pledge* themselves to take ... action ... for the achievement of the purposes set forth in Article 55' (emphasis added).

The Chief Justice considered that this wording indicated that the articles were 'framed as a promise of future action' lacking 'the mandatory quality and definiteness which would indicate an intent to create justiciable rights in private persons immediately upon ratification'.[29] He then contrasted the terminology with other articles of the UNC which he thought were sufficiently precise to be self-executing, for example, Article 104 which requires that:

> The organisation *shall* enjoy in the territory of each of its members such legal capacity as may be necessary for the exercise of its functions and the fulfilment of its purposes. (emphasis added)

Although it may be difficult to establish that a treaty article is self- executing, nevertheless the development of the doctrine itself indicates that the US system is potentially highly receptive to rules of international treaty law. Such a model contrasts vividly with the UK constitutional position, considered next, where treaty rules invariably require domestic implementation by statute before they can confer rights on private citizens, whatever the intentions of the treaty makers.

This is not to say that the US system is free from criticism. To the considerable embarrassment of successive Presidents the Senate has refused to ratify a number of important treaties including the Treaty of Versailles (which brought an end to World War One and set up the League of Nations), the 1948 Genocide Convention and a succession of human rights treaties including the 1966 UN Covenants on Civil and Political Rights, and Economic and Social Rights and the 1970 American Convention on Human Rights. As a result of the disruption to foreign policy which this has caused, the executive has evolved the practice of entering into 'executive agreements', which do not require Senate approval but which have the same effect as treaties both inter-nationally and constitutionally.

## Model 2 : The UK Approach

*Treaty Making as a Prerogative Power*

To appreciate the constitutional position of treaties in the UK it is necessary to take a brief historical survey of the constitutional crisis which developed in the late seventeenth century. At this time the Roman Catholic King James II, anxious to increase his power and influence at the expense of the Protestant Parliament, claimed a prerogative power to 'dispense' with Parliamentary statutes designed to keep Catholics out of public office. Such a 'dispensation' granted to Sir Edward Hales was challenged in the famous case of *Godden v. Hales*.[30] Not only did the court hold this to be a legitimate exercise of royal prerogative power, but also that as a prerogative power its exercise was not subject to review by the courts. Encouraged by this and other support from the courts James continued to 'dispense' with and 'suspend' statutes and it was this disregard for Parliamentary authority which precipitated the Glorious Revolution of 1688. The King fled, was deemed to have abdicated, and was replaced with the Protestants William and Mary of Orange. Their accession was subject to certain conditions dictated by Parliament and contained in the Bill of Rights of 1689. Amongst other things this declared that dispensation from parliamentary statutes was illegal. The courts, whose judgment in *Godden v. Hales* had encouraged the King's excesses, now transferred their allegiance and after 1689 accepted without question the doctrine of supremacy of Parliament. However, the prerogative powers untouched by the settlement remained. These included the control of armed forces abroad and the conduct of foreign affairs, including diplomatic relations and the negotiation and conclusion of treaties. This position has not been modified and thus it is that the treaty-making power of the UK is a function exercised by prerogative. As the monarch withdrew from politics, the exercise of this and other prerogative powers was taken over by the executive. It is now therefore the government which negotiates and ratifies treaties. Nevertheless, the courts have maintained their view that the exercise of these powers - even in these radically changed circumstances - is not subject to judicial review. This traditional position was confirmed in 1971 at the time the Heath government was negotiating accession to the EEC. Raymond

Blackburn sought a declaration that, because of the surrender of sovereign parliamentary power involved, accession to the Treaty of Rome would be unconstitutional.[31] Refusing the application Lord Denning MR said:

> the treaty making power of this country rests not in the courts, but in the Crown: that is Her Majesty acting on the advice of Her Ministers. When Her Ministers negotiate and sign a treaty, even a treaty of such paramount importance as this proposed one, they act on behalf of the country as a whole. They exercise the prerogative of the Crown. Their action in so doing cannot be challenged or questioned in these courts.[32]

The courts therefore take the view that neither treaty-making powers nor legislation can be challenged before them. Although both functions are *de facto* exercised by the executive, there is a world of difference between the two. Before legislation is passed, even by a government with a large Commons majority, there is in most cases extensive opportunity for consultation and debate, not least in Parliament itself. For treaty making, however, as a prerogative power, there is no similar constitutional requirement for public debate, not even in Parliament. The anomaly that such an important aspect of state activity should not be subject to public scrutiny in a democracy was recognised some 50 years ago when the so-called 'Ponsonby Rule' was introduced in 1924.[33] Under this rule of procedure the government undertook to inform Parliament of all international agreements, commitments and understandings it had entered into, and to lay the texts of treaties which it had signed on the tables of both Houses for a period of 21 days prior to ratification. It also undertook to allow time for discussion of 'important' treaties, although it would always also be open to individual MPs to raise matters revealed by this practice to the attention of Parliament.

The exact constitutional status of this rule is debatable. Professor de Smith suggested that it might be a 'binding constitutional convention', it has, however, been observed except where there have been 'urgent reasons' for ratifying within the 21-day period.[34] More radical approaches could have been introduced - Ponsonby himself acknowledged this when introducing his rule. Parliamentary approval for ratification of every treaty could have been sought by requiring an affirmative resolution of both Houses,[35] or even an Act of Parliament. As it is, a treaty which the

UK has ratified but not chosen to implement internally by statute remains in a dualist 'limbo': it is binding under international law but has limited status before the UK courts. The political rationale for this position was clearly stated by Sir Robert Phillimore in the *Parlement Belge.*[36]

This case arose from a collision in 1878 off Dover between the steam tug *Daring* and the Belgian packet boat - the *Parlement Belge*. The owners of the *Daring* sought damages from the owner of the other vessel - the King of the Belgians. The Attorney-General intervened to argue that by reason of an Anglo-Belgian Postal Convention of 1876 the mail boat was to be treated as a 'public ship of war' and thus immune from suit. Sir Robert refused to accept the immunity because the 1876 treaty had not been implemented by an Act of Parliament. He said:

> If the Crown had power without the authority of Parliament by this treaty to order that the Parlement Belge should be entitled to all the privileges of a ship of war ... then ... This is a use of the treaty making prerogative of the Crown which I believe to be without precedent, and in principle contrary to the laws of the constitution. Let me consider to what consequences it leads. If the Crown without the authority of Parliament, may by processes of diplomacy shelter a foreigner from the actions of one of Her Majesty's subjects who has suffered injury at his hands, I do not see why it might not also give a like privilege of immunity to any number of foreign merchant vessels or to any number of foreign individuals.[37]

The Ponsonby rule does, of course, acknowledge and attempt to counteract the accusations of unfettered treaty-making power which Sir Robert Phillimore makes in this passage. Nevertheless, the consequences of this view of the contrasting international and internal effects of treaties remain.

In the absence of implementing legislation, the Crown may not be able to use its treaty-making power to take away the rights of individuals but neither can it confer rights upon them.

A well-known line of cases confirms that where the government, or more accurately the Crown, receives compensation under a treaty for losses suffered by British subjects, it cannot be held accountable for that money in the UK courts. In *Rustomjee v. Queen*[38] the plaintiff claimed that money paid by the Emperor of China to compensate British subjects, like himself, for losses relating from the Anglo-Chinese War of 1838 was held by the Crown as agent for those injured. 'A treaty is an act of the prerogative', said Lush J. 'In making and negotiating and perfecting that treaty the Crown acts of its own inherent authority, and not by the authority, actual or supposed of any subject; and I think that all that is done under the treaty is as much beyond the domain of municipal law as the negotiation of the treaty itself.'[39] The House of Lords upheld this view in a similar case brought after World War One.[40]

*Presumption that UK legislation is not contrary to International Law*

Although UK law requires treaties to be implemented by statute beforeindividuals can derive rights and duties from them, this does not mean that the texts of the treaties themselves will be ignored by the UK courts. There is a general judicial presumption that Parliament does not intend to legislate contrary to international law and this presumption extends to obligations imposed by treaty as well as by general principles of international law. Hence:

(1) A treaty will be used as an aid to the interpretation of a statute which purports to implement it nationally. Indeed, the text of relevant articles of the treaty are sometimes included as schedules to the implementing act to reinforce this point, e.g. the 1961 Vienna Convention on Diplomatic Relations is annexed as a schedule to the 1964 Diplomatic Privileges Act.[41] Of course where Parliament has clearly chosen not to follow the strict treaty regime in the way that it is implemented then the statute must take precedence. For example the 1978 Suppression of Terrorism Act[42] purports to implement the 1977 European Convention on the Suppression of Terrorism (ECST)[43] which, *inter alia*, removes the political defence in extradition proceedings between Member States.[44] Membership of the ECST is restricted to Member States of the Council of Europe but section 5 of the 1978 Act quite clearly permits the Secretary of State to extend the ambit of the Act to *any* state.[45]

(2) Where a treaty has been ratified but no implementing statute passed the presumption will still apply in relation to the interpretation of relevant acts. A particular example is provided by the European Convention for the Protection of Human Rights and Fundamental Freedoms (ECHR)[46] which by definition is drafted so as to confer rights on individuals. The UK is a party to the ECHR but it has not, for a number of reasons, enacted it as a statute.[47] Its

obligations are of course binding on the UK and the courts have been able to use its provisions to aid statutory interpretation. For example, in *Waddington v. Miah*[48] the defendant was convicted of two offences under the 1971 Immigration Act relating to events which took place between October 1970 and September 1973. The 1971 Act did not come into force until 1 January 1973. Upholding the decision of the Court of Appeal to quash the conviction, Lord Reid referred to Article 11(2) of the UN General Assembly's Universal Declaration of Human Rights[49] and to the similar provisions of Article 7 of the ECHR which declare that

> No one shall be held guilty of any criminal offence on account of any act or omission which did not constitute a criminal offence under national or international law at the time when it was committed ...

So, he concluded in a phrase perhaps tinged with irony, 'it is hardly credible that any government would promote or that Parliament would pass retrospective criminal legislation.'[50]

This approach was taken even further by Lord Denning MR in the unreported case of *Birdi*[51] when he said 'If an Act of Parliament did not conform to the Convention I might be inclined to hold it invalid'. In *Bajhan Singh*[52] he later retracted this statement saying he 'went too far', but commented in relation to Article 12 of the ECHR (which guarantees the right to marry) 'It is to be assumed that the Crown in taking its part in legislation would do nothing which was in conflict with the treaties'. So the court should now construe the Immigration Act 1971 so as to be in conformity with the Convention and not against it ... If an Act of Parliament contained any provisions contrary to the Convention, the Act of Parliament must prevail. But I hope no Act will ever be contrary to the Convention. So the point should not arise.'[53]

Other examples could be adumbrated, but these few cases should demonstrate that as a matter of statutory interpretation and construction, treaties which have not been implemented may still have considerable significance before the UK courts. This is particularly true of the ECHR. Although the courts are constitutionally constrained, there have been indications of a willingness to take a wider view of the concept of legality than that dictated by parliamentary supremacy.

## THE SOURCES OF COMMUNITY LAW

1. The Treaties.
2. Community Legislation, i.e. Regulations, Directives and Decisions.
3. Decisions of the Court of Justice.

Each of these will be examined in turn.

### The Treaties

The primary sources of Community law are the founding Treaties: the ECSC, EEC and EURATOM Treaties. These establish the basic obligations for Member States and also provide a basis for future development by amendment and by Community legislation. Amendment is possible under various articles of the EEC Treaty. The procedure is fundamentally the negotiation of a supplementary treaty which comes into force once ratified by all Member States 'in accordance with their respective constitutional requirements' (Article 236). Such amendment can entail:

Accession of new Member States under Article 237.

First Accession Treaty of 1972 (UK, Eire and Denmark), second of Greece in 1981 and third of the Iberian countries in 1986.

Amendments to the Treaty regime.

The Merger Treaty 1965 which created a single Council and Commission for the three Communities; 1970 Budgetary Treaty; 1975 Brussels Treaty increasing the European Parliament's Budgetary Powers (for details see Chapter 5) and the Single European Act 1986 which modifies, *inter alia*, the decision-making process of the EEC.

Other treaties too may affect the legal regime of the Communities. Pre-existing treaties to which all Member States were party such as GATT;[54] treaties guaranteeing human rights (the UN Covenants and the ECHR); and treaties between the EEC and third states can give rise to rights which Community law may enforce directly or indirectly.[55]

## Community Legislation

The legally binding acts of the EEC's institutions are enumerated in Article 189:

*(a) Regulations*

> A regulation shall have general application. It shall be binding in its entirety and directly applicable in all Member States.

The Council and the Commission are empowered to issue regulations. The regulation is the most novel of the methods of legislation created by the EEC. Once a regulation is adopted it becomes automatically part of the national legal system of all the Member States, without the need for legislative or administrative implementation. This is what is meant by *direct applicability*. Having said that, however, regulations do occasionally require Member States to take legislative implementing measures as was the case of Regulation 543/69 which introduced, *inter alia*, the tachograph system.[56]

*(b) Directives*

> A directive shall be binding, as to the result to be achieved, upon each Member State to which it is addressed, but shall leave to the national authorities the choice of form and methods.

The obligations a directive imposes are rather similar to those of a treaty - the obligations must be complied with but there is a discretion in the method of national implementation. Note also that Article 189 clearly envisages that a directive - unlike regulations - may not be directed at all the Member States. The main function of directives is to enable Member States to harmonise or bring into line their domestic legislation and thereby give effect to Community standards.

*(c) Decisions*

> A decision shall be binding in its entirety upon those to whom it is addressed.

Decisions may be addressed to individuals, to firms, to an individual Member State, or to them all, as, for example, the Council Decision of 1976 approving direct elections to the European Parliament.[57]

It can be seen that directives, and usually decisions, impose obligations of *result* (i.e. to achieve the desired result by a choice of means) whereas regulations impose obligations of *form* (i.e. the requirement that the regulation becomes automatically part of the national legal system is an integral part of the obligation that the regulation imposes, see *Slaughtered Cow case* (No 2)[58] (below p. 38)). As if in recognition of this distinction, Article 191 requires that regulations, but not directives or decisions, shall be published in the Official Journal. The latter are in fact published in the Official Journal under the title of 'Acts which are not required to be published'. The way in which the obligations of Article 189 have been interpreted by the ECJ is considered in detail below.

## DEVELOPMENT OF COMMUNITY LAW BY THE ECJ

Having looked at the basic sources of Community law it is important now to examine the way in which they have been interpreted by the ECJ. The significance of judicial interpretation will become apparent throughout this book, but the analogy of the ECJ as a constitutional court merits further consideration here. The judgments of the ECJ cannot be reversed by legislation, but only by the complicated and politically difficult process of treaty amendment. Hence its judgments and its interpretations of the Treaties and Community laws are definitive and final, and bear many of the hallmarks of a constitutional court operating only within the constraints of a constitution, of which it provides the final interpretation.[59]

There is a strong temptation to compare the ECJ with a federal supreme court such as the US Supreme Court. Indeed many comparisons are made in this book but it should be stressed that they are only *comparisons*. The EEC is *not* a federal system, nor is the ECJ a federal court even if many of its judgments have advanced further down the federal road than might have been expected. In general it has interpreted the spirit of the Treaties. Its views on the status of and effect of the Treaties and Community legislation are therefore definitive statements of Community law.

As the previous discussion of the way that national systems have dealt with international treaties will have demonstrated, there is no right or wrong approach to the subject and a nation's constitution and, indeed, the approach of its courts, is largely dictated by its political system and traditions. Nowhere is this more true than in the approach to the interpretation of Community law taken by the ECJ. From an early stage it has been clear that ECJ has been intent upon developing the aspirations of the Treaty drafters; thus *policy* has been a more obvious aspect of its case law than is usual in the approach of national judges. Hartley has described the process by which a new principle is introduced 'perhaps in an inoccuous case, or in a case where the principle is not applied, and gradually that principle is developed; the qualifications around it are gradually whittled away, until the full effect of the doctrine can be seen'.[60] If this excellent description can be criticised, it is only in its implicit suggestion that the Court maps out its approach in advance. Judicial development dictates an opportunist philosophy. Given a policy objective, each case has to be considered within its own context and on its own merits. After all, courts can only consider the cases put to them and they are therefore essentially responsive.

The development of the concepts of direct effect and direct applicability must be seen within this context. In the important judgment of *Van Gend en Loos*[61] it is clear that the Court did not have the current state of the law in mind but grasped the opportunity to introduce a doctrine of considerable potency. The law has developed organically; hostile state reactions have caused certain doctrines to be foreshortened, while the enthusiastic support of litigants has extended others. This responsive approach has meant that terminology used in earlier cases is inappropriate at a later stage of the Court's development of the law and nowhere is this truer than in the distinction between the concepts of direct applicability and direct effect. This distinction is very much based on a retrospective, *ex post facto* analysis of the state of the law and the distinction is accepted in the following discussion on the basis that it does distinguish between two important aspects of the reception of Community law, particularly into a dualist system. But it should be borne in mind that although the distinction is derived from the case law and terminology of the court it has never been accepted *as such* by the Court.

## Direct Applicability and Direct Effect

### *Terminology*

Direct applicability denotes the ability of a provision of Community law to become part of the domestic legal system of a Member State automatically without the need for formal enactment by national means. If a provision is *directly effective* then it may be relied upon by an individual in an action before the national courts. The concept of direct applicability is, of course, to be found in the text of Article 189 EEC in relation to the effect of regulations. The development of direct effectiveness, or enforceability, of Community law, however, is a judicial creation, a product of the policy- oriented approach of the ECJ. Its first appearance was in *Van Gend en Loos.*[62] The plaintiff, a haulage company, had imported the chemical ureaformaldehyde from Belgium to Holland. The Dutch tax classification of this had been changed by an agreement between the Benelux countries. As a result of this change in tax classification being put into effect by the Dutch authorities there was an increase in customs duty, which Van Gend claimed violated Article 12 of the EEC Treaty. This provides:

> Member States shall refrain from introducing between themselves any new customs duties on imports or exports or any charges having equivalent effect, and *from increasing those which they already apply in their trade with each other.* (emphasis added)

The Dutch government argued a traditionally dualist position that Article 12 was a treaty obligation any violation of which (if it had taken place) could only be invoked at an international level (i.e. by an action against Holland by the Commission or by another Member State).[63] The plaintiffs argued, however, that a violation of the EEC Treaty was a violation of Dutch law which could consequently be invoked before the Dutch courts. On a reference from the Dutch court under Article 177 the ECJ in a famous ruling (which has been called the 'cornerstone' of its jurisprudence) adopted a radically monist position examining the 'spirit of the general scheme' of the Treaty as well as its wording:

> The objective of the EEC Treaty, which is to establish a Common Market, the functioning of which is of direct concern to interested parties in the Community, implies that this Treaty is more than an agreement which merely creates mutual obligations between the Contracting States.[64]

After pointing out that the Treaty refers to peoples as well as governments, that it creates institutions which have the power to affect individuals as well as governments and that individuals take part in the EP and ESC, the Court pointed out that its own power (under Article 177) to rule on issues of Community law referred to it by national courts indicated that Community law was intended to be invoked by national courts. It went on:

> The conclusion to be drawn from this is that the Community constitutes a *new legal order* of international law for the benefit of which the states have limited their sovereign rights, albeit within limited fields, and the subjects of which comprise not only Member States but also their nationals. Independently of the legislation of Member States, Community law therefore not only imposes obligations on individuals, but is also intended to confer upon them *rights* which become part of their legal heritage. These rights arise not only when they are expressly granted by the Treaty, but also by reason of obligations which the Treaty imposes in a clearly defined way upon individuals as well as upon Member States and upon the institutions of the Community.[65] (emphasis added)

Community law rights could therefore be implied from obligations imposed on Member States, provided, however, that they were 'clear and unconditional'[66] which the categorical prohibition on all increases in customs duties contained in Article 12 (above) certainly was. The ECJ therefore concluded 'Art 12 must be interpreted as producing *direct effects* and creating individual rights which the national courts must protect'.[67]

The *Van Gend en Loos* case presents an excellent example of the policy approach in action. By adopting this 'new legal order' the ECJ had clearly in mind the overall objective of compliance with the Treaty. By encouraging individuals to base actions in the domestic courts on the basis of *what the ECJ itself has decided* to be directly effective provisions of the Treaty, the Court is able to exercise considerable influence over the development of Community law at national level - despite the fact that Article 177 only gives it a role of *interpretation*. As the ECJ commented, the 'vigilance of individuals to protect their rights would amount to an effective form of supervision of Member States acting in breach of the provisions of the Treaty'.[68] For example, if the UK for short-term national reasons imposes a ban on the importation of poultry from other EEC countries in breach of Article 30 EEC, then importers of poultry adversely affected, would be able to rely on the direct effect of Article 30 in order to challenge this ban in the UK courts.[69] Not only would the government face the prospect of being ruled to have acted illegally by its own courts, but the ruling is likely to take place quicker and without the likelihood of political compromise which surrounds an action brought by the Commission or a fellow Member State.

*Which Articles of the Treaty are directly effective?*

Building on *Van Gend en Loos* the ECJ has developed a large case law on the tests to be applied. Again, we see that the tests are not applied with the rigid formality which a national court might adopt. Indeed Professor Van Gerven has suggested that 'the direct effect of a provision depends mainly on whether the courts and finally the Court of Justice, feel able and sufficiently equipped to apply the provision without any further act by the authorities of the Communities or of its Member States'.[70]

This captures the essence of what the ECJ means when it requires that to be directly effective a provision must be 'complete and legally perfect', i.e. it must *in itself* be legally self-sufficient. In deciding whether a provision meets this requirement the following tests are applied:[71]

1. The obligation it establishes must be 'clear and precise' or 'clear and unambiguous'.
2. The obligation must be unconditional.
3. The obligation must not be dependent upon further action by either the Community or national authorities.

*1. 'Clear and precise' or 'clear and unambiguous'*. This means that the obligation must be formulated in such a way that it is capable of being applied with precision. Article 12 completely prohibits all new custom duties between Member States. The clarity of this prohibition - which brooks of no qualification or exception - means that it may easily be utilised by individuals even though the obligation itself is imposed upon Member States. Similar prohibitions on, for example, the use of quotas to restrict trade (in Article 30) have been held to have direct effects, but positive obligations too can confer rights on individuals, *provided* that they are formulated with precision.

Consider Article 11:

> Member States shall take all appropriate measures to enable Governments to carry out, within the periods of time laid down, the obligations with regard to customs duties which devolve upon them pursuant to this Treaty.

What are appropriate measures? How wide does this obligation extend to assist the governments of other states? Without looking at these issues in detail it should be apparent that although it binds Member States it is not drafted with the sort of precision which would enable a national judge to rule that a breach has occurred. It is the sort of obligation which falls more obviously to be considered in a much wider context; in an action between Member States or by the Commission against a Member State.

The very generality of an obligation may mean that it is not sufficiently precise to have direct effects. See, for instance, Article 5 which provides:

> Member States shall take all appropriate measures, whether general or particular to ensure fulfilment of the obligations arising out of this Treaty or resulting from action taken by the institutions of the Community. They shall facilitate the achievement of the Community's task.
>
> They shall abstain from any measure which would jeopardise the attainment of the objectives of this Treaty.

The same arguments would apply here. Although it could perhaps be argued that the second paragraph when read against a specific obligation elsewhere in the Treaty is sufficiently precise. Nevertheless, in *Schlüter*[72] the ECJ held that even when read with Article 107, Article 5 was not directly effective.

2. *Unconditional.* There is obviously an overlap between each of these. The most common form of condition in the Treaty is that which requires implementation or further enactment by national or Community action (see 3 below). Time scales too (e.g. 'by the end of the transitional period') may mean that there is no clear obligation upon Member States until the specified time has elapsed; or the obligation itself may permit Member States to retain a degree of discretion, thus imposing a condition and upsetting the requirement of precision.

A good illustration of all these problems can been seen in Article 48:

1. Freedom of movement of workers shall be secured within the Community by the end of the transitional period at the latest.

2. Such freedom of movement shall entail the abolition of any discrimination based on nationality between workers of the Member States as regards employment, remuneration and other

conditions of work and employment.

3. It shall entail the right, subject to limitations on the grounds of public policy, public security or public health:

(a) to accept offers of employment actually made;

(b) to move freely within the territory of Member States for this purpose;

(c) to stay in a Member State for the purpose of employment in accordance with the provisions governing the employment of nationals of that State laid down by law, regulation or administrative action;

(d) to remain in the territory of a Member State after having been employed in that State, subject to condition which shall be embodied in implementing regulations to be drawn up by the Commission.

4. The provisions of this Article shall not apply to employment in the public service.

In general, the Article is clearly drafted so as to confer rights on individuals. Nevertheless, Article 48(1) contains a time condition which had to elapse before the whole Article became directly effective. Similarly, Article 48(3)(d) contains a right which only became complete once the implementing regulation had been passed.[73] More problematic, however, is Article 48(3) for it subjects all the specific rights to a general condition - that they may be 'subject to limitations justified on the grounds of public policy, public security or public health'. These are well-known concepts in national public law and are usually construed to give wide and often unchallengeable discretion to governments.[74] However, in 1964 the Council adopted Directive 64/221[75] which limited the way that governments could use this discretion when deciding to exclude or deport non-nationals. For example, Article 3 of the directive required that:

> Measures taken on the grounds of public policy or of public security shall be based exclusively on the personal conduct of the individuals concerned.

In *Van Duyn v. Home Office*,[76] the plaintiff was a Dutch scientologist who was given a job at the Church of Scientology[77] at East Grinstead in Sussex. When she arrived at Dover to take up her job she was refused admittance by the British immigration authorities. The reason for this refusal was that in 1968 the Home

Secretary had announced that the government was concerned at the spread of Scientology which it regarded as harmful and had made the following announcement:

> The Government are [sic] satisfied that Scientology is socially harmful. It alienates members of families from each other and attributes squalid and disgraceful motives to all who oppose it; its authoritarian principles and practice are a potential menace to the personality and well-being of those so deluded as to become its followers; above all its methods can be a serious danger to the health of those who submit to them.[78]

The Minister of Health went on to say that although the government had no power under the law to ban Scientology it did, however, have the power to prevent foreign nationals who wished to take up employment at a Scientology establishment from entering the UK. In order to effect this, he declared that work permits and vouchers would not be issued to such foreign nationals attempting to enter the UK in order to work at the Church of Scientology in East Grinstead.

Miss Van Duyn sought a declaration from the English court that her exclusion was unlawful because Article 48 conferred a right '(a) to accept offers of employment actually made' and '(b) to move freely within the territory of Member States for this purpose' and that although that right was conditional (in that it was subject to public policy limitations) it was nevertheless directly effective because the limitations could only be utilised in certain clear and precise circumstances set out in Directive 64/221, e.g. when based 'exclusively on the personal conduct of the individual concerned' (Article 3).

Membership of the Church of Scientology or indeed any organisation, the argument continued, was not 'personal conduct' for these purposes, therefore her exclusion was unlawful. These issues were referred to the ECJ which upheld the general tenor of the argument, ruling that the discretion left to Member States did not prevent Article 48(3) having direct effects because the Directive had laid down strict criteria by which the exercise of this discretion could be reviewed by the courts. It did not, however, agree with the substantive argument that membership of an organisation was not personal conduct for these purposes. Hence Van Duyn's exclusion was lawful under EC law.

*3. Not dependent upon further action by either the Community or national authorities.* An obligation which is dependent upon further action by legislation will obviously not be sufficiently precise to be relied upon. An example can again be taken from Article 48(3)(d) (above) which confers a right to remain in the territory of a Member State *after* having been employed in that state 'subject to conditions which shall be embodied in implementing regulations to be drawn up by the Commission'. Such a provision could not produce direct effects until the conditions attached to the right had been clarified by the legislation.[79]

It is unusual that Article 48(3)(d) does not impose a time limit on the passing of that clarifying legislation for, as part of its programme of integration for the transitional period, the Treaty does in many cases lay down strict timetables for legislative action. For example, Article 16 requires that 'Member States shall abolish between themselves customs duties on exports and charges having equivalent effect by the end of the first stage'. In *Eunomia*[80] the ECJ decided that once the first stage of the transitional period had passed (i.e. 1962) the obligation to phase out duties on exports was complete, and although it remained apparently dependent on Member State action to take measures to comply with the obligation, nevertheless, having been completed by the passage of time Article 16 became directly effective. Thus export duties levied after that date could be challenged by individuals before their national courts. This demonstrates the important policing effect which direct effect provides. Individuals will readily detect breaches of the Treaty affecting them, and for a national court to rule that its own government's export duty is illegal is a more effective and directly relevant remedy than a general declaration by the ECJ.

More radical still is the approach the ECJ has taken in other areas. For example, in relation to freedom of establishment, i.e. the right to set up and manage business in another Member State without discrimination on the ground of nationality. Here the Treaty (Articles 54-57) obliges the Commission and Council to embark upon a programme of legislation by directive to ensure that restrictions on this right are progressively abolished. At a basic level, however, Article 52 provides that, within the framework of this programme 'restrictions on the freedom of establishment of nationals of a member state shall be abolished by progressive stages in the course of the transitional period ...'

In *Reyners v. Belgian State*[81] the plaintiff was a law graduate of

Dutch parents, born and educated in Brussels, who had retained his Dutch nationality. After qualifying as a lawyer under Belgian law he applied for admission to practise as an *advocaat* in Belgium. He was refused because he was not a Belgian national. When he appealed to the Belgian *Conseil d'Etat* a reference was made to the ECJ which held that, despite the fact that the political organs of the EEC had not embarked upon their legislative programme, the primary obligation of non-discrimination in Article 52(1) became complete at the end of the transitional period. For, said the ECJ:

> By laying down that the freedom of establishment shall be attained at the end of the transitional period, Article 52 imposes an obligation to achieve a *precise result*, the fulfilment of which had to be made easier by, but not dependent upon, the implementation of progressive measures ... After the expiry of the transitional period the directives provided for by the chapter on the right of establishment have become superfluous with regard to implementing the rule of nationality since this is henceforth sanctioned by the treaty itself with direct effect[82]

Here we see the Court giving direct effect to certain aspects of a provision which appears to require action *both* by Member States and the Community. The policy approach of the court can be seen even more clearly in *Defrenne v. Sabena.*[83] Gabrielle Defrenne, an air hostess, was compulsorily retired from her job with the Belgian national airline Sabena when she reached the age of 40. Male colleagues were permitted to remain in office until the age of 50. She argued that this practice was discriminatory (which it clearly was) but she could not find a rule of Belgian or Community law outlawing such discrimination. She then brought a series of test cases in the Belgian courts and one of her arguments was that this practice contravened Article 119 of the EEC treaty which provides:

> Each Member State shall during the first stage ensure and subsequently maintain the application of the principle that men and women should receive equal pay for equal work.

The case was referred to the ECJ by the Belgian court, seeking a ruling as to whether it extended to Defrenne's situation. The British and Irish governments intervened[84] in the case to argue that if Article 119 were to be declared directly effective then it would be open to all those who thought themselves victims of pay discrimination on the grounds of sex to claim back-pay from the time that Article 119 became binding upon them.[85] Notice too the wording of Article 119. It is a classic example of a conditional obligation which has become unconditional with the passing of time. But that is not the end of the difficulties it poses. Equal pay for equal work involves a number of difficult concepts - not the least of which is: what is equal work? It would clearly cover the same job being done by a man and a women, but how deep does discrimination run - are certain jobs for example undervalued, purely because they are seen as 'woman's work', for example, repetitive jobs requiring a high degree of manual dexterity. Such issues, which are now being addressed by job evaluation schemes, involve highly complex issues and are difficult to resolve in a court room.[86] The ECJ took the view, however, that none of these problems was an insuperable obstacle to Article 119 being ruled to be directly effective. But it made two limitations. First, it was only directly effective in relation to complaints which could be settled by purely *legal means* (e.g. without the aid of job evaluation schemes) and second, that in an obvious move to stem disquiet among Member States about huge sums of back-pay, it held that Article 119 would be directly effective prospectively (i.e. from the date of the *judgment*) except in relation to claims currently pending before the courts.

The decision involves an input of policy, of judicial lawmaking, which is outside the contemplation of most national courts (see e.g. the criticism of Professor Hampson).[87] But it has laid the foundation for the subsequent development of a large body of important case law on sex discrimination and probably also provided the necessary political impetus for a legislative programme in this field covering not only equal pay but also equal treatment conditions relating to employment and also social security matters.

## VERTICAL AND HORIZONTAL DIRECT EFFECT

Another important aspect of the *Defrenne* case is that unlike *Van Gend en Loos*, and *Van Duyn*, the defendant was not an organ of the state but the Belgian Airline Sabena - a separately constituted company. It thus provides a useful illustration of the distinction between what have been called 'vertical' and 'horizontal' direct effects. 'Vertical' direct effect is the ability to invoke an obligation of the Treaty against an organ of the state responsible for implementing it. For example, in *Van Gend en Loos* and *Van Duyn* the Dutch and British governments respectively.[88] However, if a right is to be fully part of the national legal system it should also be capable of utilisation against another individual, i.e. 'horizontally'.

The *Defrenne* case was such an action. Despite the lack of success of the instant case, the principle was established that in 'equal pay' cases employers could be held responsible for what is essentially a breach of obligation by their government - a vivid reminder that the EEC treaty not only confers *rights* on individuals as well as governments, it also confers *duties*.

## Legislation

### *1. Regulations*

Article 189 requires regulations to be of 'general application and directly applicable'. The important supra-national element of regulations is the fact that they become part of the national legal systems of all Member States immediately they are adopted. This system of Community legislation is a vital part of the Community system for regulating such matters as customs tariffs and the control of agricultural products where market structures and prices change rapidly. In order for such a system to work effectively, the legislation must take effect in all Member States at the same time. However, the traditional means of incorporating international or external legal obligation into national law have caused some problems, as *Leonesio*[89] demonstrates. This case arose from the establishment of a scheme to reduce dairy herds and thus Community production of dairy products. Council Regulation 1975/69[90] established a scheme, applicable to all farmers having at least two dairy cows, under which a premium would be paid for the slaughter of such cows. Half the premium was to be met from the EAGGF[91] and half from national budgets. As is normal, the Commission was empowered to produce more detailed regulations for the implementation of this scheme.[92] This it did by Commission Regulation 2195/69[93] which established that the premium would be paid within two months of delivery of the certificate of slaughter. Member States were empowered to enact more detailed *administrative* rules but the Italian government declared that the implementation of the scheme in Italy would be postponed until the necessary budgetary provision had been passed. In the meantime Leonesio slaughtered five cows and claimed 625,000 lire. Faced with the argument that the regulation did not yet apply in Italy, she took her claim to the Pretore - a first instance court similar to the English County court - which referred a number of questions to the ECJ:

1. Are regulations directly applicable in Italy?
2. If so, does provision of regulations create claims which can be enforced against the state?
3. Can national legislation delay such claims?

In what is now a classic judgment the ECJ affirmed the importance of the concept of direct applicability of regulations stressing that without it the schemes established by the Community would not work.

After this situation had been brought to light by Leonesio's complaint, the Commission investigated the case and took action against Italy for a breach of the Treaty under Article 169. The Commission argued that Italy was in breach not only in its attempts to delay the implementation of the regulation but also subsequently in the formal method it had chosen to give effect to the regulation in Italy. What the Italian government had done was to issue a decree dated 22 March 1972 proclaiming 'the provisions of regulations ... are deemed to be included in the present decree'. The Commission claimed that this suggested that the regulation drew its legal force from the Italian government decree rather than from the EEC Treaty. This may seem a somewhat pedantic point to make - could it not be argued that the important objective after all was to make sure that the regulation has effect by whatever means? The court held, however, that the *form* was as important as the *result*.

*2. Directives*

Article 189 confers a different status on directives from that it confers on regulations. They are, of course, binding as to the result to be achieved upon each Member State to which they are addressed, but leave 'to the national authorities the choice of form and methods' of implementing them. They are different from regulations in three important respects:

1. They are not of general application: directives need not be addressed to all Member States simultaneously; some indeed are only addressed to one state, whose practices are, perhaps, out of line with others.

2. They are not directly applicable in the sense explained above, because they *specifically* require implementation.

3. As a corollary to (2) there is a time-limit within which Member States must implement their obligations.

In fact the obligations imposed on a Member State by a directive are similar to those imposed by many Treaty articles, i.e. to achieve certain objectives by certain specified dates. It was therefore inevitable, perhaps, that once the principle of direct effect of Treaty provisions had been established that a similar concept should evolve in relation to directives. In fact the issue was first discussed in a series of cases brought at the end of the transitional period when many of the obligations of the EEC Treaty were being completed by the effluxion of time.

We have seen above that such an example is Article 16 which required the abolition of all customs duties on exports by the end of the first stage. Another is Article 13(2) which provides that:

> Charges having an effect equivalent to customs duties on imports in force between Member States, shall be progressively abolished by them during the transitional period. The Commission shall determine by means of directives the timetable for such abolition. It shall be guided by the rules contained in Article 14(2) and (3) and by the directives issued by the Council pursuant to Article 14(2).

Such a directive was issued by the Commission setting the date as 1 July 1968 (i.e. before the end of the transitional period).[94] The Italian government had not met this deadline. But in *SACE v Italian Ministry of Finance*[95] the plaintiff, in order to challenge charges imposed on his imports *after* that date, argued that Article 13(2) read together with the directive provided a complete and precise legal obligation, i.e. to abolish these charges by the specified dates. This argument was accepted by the ECJ in what is described by Hartley as the first step in the development of the idea of direct effects of directives.[96] It can equally be seen as part of the continuing processes of expounding the doctrine of direct effect of Treaty provisions by delineating the circumstances in which their obligations can be said to be 'precise and legally perfect' or 'complete'. So that, for example, in the case of *Van Duyn* the ECJ had to consider whether Article 48(3) had direct effects when it was subject to a general condition that limitations could be 'justified on the grounds of public policy, public security or public health'.[97] In the same way that in *SACE* the obligation of 13(2) was completed by the directive so in *Van Duyn* a conditional obligation was made complete by the provisions of Directive 64/221 specifying that exclusions on the grounds of public policy or public security should be based exclusively on the conduct of the individual himself. Nevertheless, the importance of these cases is that the ECJ adverted to the issue of whether directives and, indeed, decisions could have direct effects. It said:

> It would be incompatible with the binding effect attributed by a directive by Article 189 to exclude, in principle, the possibility that the obligation which it imposes may be invoked by those concerned. In particular, where the Community authorities have, by directive, imposed on Member States the obligation to pursue a particular course of conduct, the useful effect of such an act would be weakened if individuals were prevented from relying on it before their national courts and if the latter were prevented from taking it into consideration as an element of Community law.[98]

In both cases provisions of directives completing other obligations could be relied upon. The first case, however, where the ECJ accepted that a directive based upon an article of the Treaty which was not *itself* directly effective was that of *Verbond.*[99]

In *Verbond* it was argued that the requirements of the 2nd VAT directive[100] had not been properly implemented by the Dutch government, in that tax-deductable allowances for expenditure on capital goods specifically permitted by Articles 11 and 17 had not been allowed by Dutch law. The plaintiff challenged the Dutch VAT authorities arguing that he should not be financially penalised for improper implementation of Community obligations. The issue was referred to the ECJ which confirmed this interpretation of Articles 11 and 17 of the VAT directive and also the right of an individual to invoke them before his national courts.

Immediately following *Verbond* were a number of cases in which individuals deployed similar arguments, i.e. that they should not be penalised for the improper implementation within national law of obligations imposed on Member States in a clear and unambiguous way. The clearest case is probably that of *Publico Ministero v. Ratti.*[101] Ratti, the accused, was the supplier of paints and solvents affected by two Council directives, one of which,

Directive 73/173[102] on labelling of solvents, had an 18-month implementation period (by 8 December 1974). When at the end of this period Italy had still not passed implementing legislation, Ratti unilaterally complied with the requirements of the directive in his labelling. He was then prosecuted for breach of an existing Italian labelling law of 1963 which imposed different requirements. In his defence he argued that the provisions of the directive were directly effective once the implementation period had elapsed. In response to a reference from the Milan Court, the ECJ confirmed that a national government could not rely on its own breach of EC law to prosecute an individual who had complied with directly effective provisions of EC law. This case is made clearer by the fact that in relation to a second prosecution for the selling of varnishes improperly labelled under the 1963 law the ECJ held that Ratti could *not* rely on a second directive relating to varnishes, Directive 77/728,[103] because the implementation period (up to 9 November 1977) had not then elapsed - the obligation therefore was not yet directly effective.

## Horizontal Effects: Can Directives Impose Obligations on Individuals?

Once this line of cases had established beyond doubt that individuals could rely upon the direct effects of directives, speculation increased as to whether the ECJ was moving towards the view that directives, like certain Treaty articles, could confer rights enforceable not only 'vertically' against the state but also 'horizontally' against individuals. In other words, could impose obligations upon individuals. In the considerable amount of literature which has appeared on this issue the following other arguments emerged for and against the horizontal direct effect of directives.[104]

*Arguments against horizontal direct effects of directives*

*1. Uncertainty.* Directives *require* implementation by national measures. Were directives to be horizontally directly effective then individuals would in Wyatt and Dashwood's words have to 'consult national and Community texts on identical subject matter being ever vigilant for discrepancies between them'.[105]

2. *Directives are not the same as regulations.* Article 189 clearly

distinguishes the legal effects of regulations and directives. Were directives to be enforceable by individuals *inter se* then their effects would be identical to those of regulations - undermining an important distinction in the legislative powers conferred by the Treaty and incidentally encroaching further into the sphere of national law. This latter argument seems to be the dominant view of the French *Conseil d'Etat* in *Cohn-Bendit*[106] which - contradicting the established jurisprudence of the ECJ in relation to Directive 64/221 - held that directives could *not* be relied upon before French national courts because by reason of Article 189 they were not directly applicable. This view has also been taken by the German courts.

*3. Reflex Argument.* This argument suggests that the only reason the court has held provisions of directives to be directly effective is to prevent a state relying on its own faulty implementation or non-implementation of Community obligations to the detriment of individuals.[107] Certainly this theme can be seen clearly in the cases of *Verbond*, *Ratti* and, Hartley suggests,[108] even *Van Duyn*, in that the UK had not implemented the obligation in Article 3 of Directive 64/221 into a provision of UK law therefore the only way the right could be protected was by relying directly upon the directive. The result of this argument is that direct effects will only arise where the *Member State* is in breach of obligation imposed by a directive - hence it must be limited to vertical effects.

*Arguments in favour of horizontal direct effects of directives*

*1. Uncertainty/unequal application.* Paradoxically the argument of uncertainty can also be used by the opposing view, in that the distinction between the state and individuals is not as clear as it may first seem. The degree of state activity varies from one Member State to another. Were a directive in the field of employment law to be held to be vertically directly effective then presumably civil servants and other public employees could utilise it against their employer (the state) whereas employees in the private sector would have to rely upon the imperfectly implemented national legislation. In addition the public sector varies: university teachers are, for example, civil servants in France but not in the UK. Thus discrimination would result both within and between Member States.[109]

*2. Effet Utile.* This argument is briefly that the furtherance of Community policies would be more effectively promoted by holding directives horizontally directly effective. Direct effect has been a major impetus to legal integration; this impetus would be maintained by permitting directives to be used freely in national courts both vertically and horizontally. One of the exciting aspects of Community law is that issues such as this remain at large. The ECJ has yet to make a clear pronouncement either way on this important issue, but given the reluctance of important national courts such as the *Conseil d'Etat* and the German *Bundesverfassungsgericht*[110] to accept this development, there may have been an element of rethinking or consolidation. In a series of cases from the UK courts involving the direct effects of the Equal Pay and Equal Treatment directives,[111] English courts had specifically asked whether these two directives confer horizontally effective rights on individuals so as to be utilised by individuals against their employers. The court has consistently refused to address this issue, preferring instead to base its judgments on an extended interpretation of the concept of equal pay under Article 119 which is already horizontally directly effective. Judge Pescatore has suggested that the debate over direct effect is an 'infant disease' of community law, suggesting that direct effect will be seen in retrospect to be the normal state of the law.[112] Of course infant ailments, if not treated correctly, can cause lasting and even permanent damage.

## IMPLEMENTATION OF COMMUNITY LAW WITHIN THE UK

### European Communities Act 1972

Prior to accession there was considerable speculation as to whether the European Communities Act by which the UK would implement its obligations under the Community Treaties would be a single section or a 1,000-section act. In other words whether it would adopt a highly monist approach and declare the UK to be a member of the European Communities and Community law to be part of the legal system of the UK, leaving the administration and the courts to draw out the detailed implications for themselves, or whether it would take a highly dualist approach and specify to the finest minutiae the changes which would be brought about in the UK legal system. In the event the European Communities Act took a middle path: it had 12 sections, and adopted a procedure for implementation which is as novel in UK law as the obligations it was implementing. The key provisions of the Act are sections 2 and 3, of which S.2(1) is by far the most important in constitutional terms. S.2(1) provides:

> General implementation of Treaties
> 2.(1) All such rights, powers, liabilities, obligations and restrictions from time to time created or arising by or under the Treaties, and all such remedies and procedures from time to time provided for by or under the Treaties, as in accordance with the Treaties are without further enactment to be given legal effect or used in the United Kingdom shall be recognised and available in law, and be enforced, allowed and followed accordingly; and the expression 'enforceable Community right' and similar expressions shall be read as referring to one to which this subsection applies.

**The Novel Approach**

The essential components of this complex section are these:

- it covers present and future rights and obligations;
- it covers not only those rights etc. created *by* the Treaties but also *under* the Treaties, i.e. Community legislation;
- it recognises the principle that the Treaties should determine the extent of these rights in the UK;
- it permits the direct enforcement of these rights in the UK.

These provisions are supplemented by S.3(1):

> 3.(1) For the purposes of all legal proceedings any question as to the meaning or effect of any of the Treaties, or as to the validity, meaning or effect of any Community instrument, shall be treated as a question of law (and, if not referred to the European Court, be for determination as such in accordance with the principles laid down by and any relevant decision of the European Court).

This reinforces the points made above:

1. Community law has the status of *law* before the UK courts - unlike foreign law (e.g. French law) which has the status of fact and must be proved by expert evidence.

2. Questions as to the meaning or effect of the Treaties or Community instruments shall be determined in accordance with *principles*, laid down by the ECJ if not referred to the court under Article 177.

Read together these sections provide that directly effective provisions of Community law will have the effect in the UK that *Community law itself* provides. This is an extremely flexible means of accepting the requirements of Community law as developed by the ECJ. The European Communities Act is, of course, a UK statute which itself derives its authority from Parliament, but it creates what might be called a *legislative gateway* whereby those provisions of Community law which it requires to become part of the national legal system automatically become part of the UK legal system according to the definition of its meaning and effect laid down by Community law. The constitutional doctrine of parliamentary supremacy dictates that the European Communities Act could be repealed but until that happens the *legislative gateway* which it establishes is wedged open to permit new law to enter the system.[113]

## Supremacy of Community Law

In *Costa*[114] and *Simmenthal*[115] the ECJ made clear its own view that in cases of conflict between national law and directly effective Community law, national courts are under a duty to give effect to Community law, even in the face of later rules of national law. To what extent is this basic principle accepted by the European Communities Act? It can be approached in two ways:

1. S.2(1) prescribes that Community rights should be given the effect which *Community* law requires without further enactment and S.3(1) provides that questions according to principles laid down by, and decisions of the European Court - the doctrine of supremacy of Community law and the cases of *Costa* and *Simmenthal* are of course examples of each.

2. S.2(4) contains a provision tucked away in the middle of the paragraph '... and any enactment passed or to be passed, other than one contained in this part of this Act, shall be construed and have effect subject to the foregoing provisions of this section'. There has been considerable speculation as to the extent of this provision in so far as it purports to suggest that both present and *future*

legislation should be 'subject to the foregoing provisions ...' *viz* the enforceable community rights of S.2(1).[116] But what does the phrase 'be construed and take effect' mean? At a minimum it means that in cases of conflict between Community rights and UK legislation there shall be a rule of *construction* that the obligations arising under the European Communities Act should take priority. The issue is, however, whether it is simply that - as Hood-Phillips suggests[117] - or whether it is anything more. The drafters use the phrase *'and take effect'* in addition to the words 'be construed'. This does seem to be an attempt to recognise the principle of superiority of Community law over later conflicting rules of UK statute law.

If indeed this is what was intended, the next question must be, can it be done? Could the 1972 UK Parliament bind its successors? Here Hood-Phillips is, of course, quite right to remind us of the doctrine of supremacy of Parliament.[118] But constitutional theory must be moulded, as it always has been, by practical politics.

Take two situations:

1. If the UK were to withdraw from the EEC, or even to derogate expressly by statute from an obligation imposed by Community law, such action in itself might well engage the UK in legal responsibilities under international and/or Community law, but the UK courts would doubtless give internal effect to the UK legislation.

2. If a clear conflict arose between Community law and a later UK statute which was not expressly intended to derogate from an obligation of Community law, then it is suggested that the doctrine of implied repeal[119] does not apply and that Community law will take priority. This is not simply the operation of a rule of construction, it is recognition of normative superiority within the functioning of the system. The practice of the English courts since 1973 generally supports this view.

*Further implementation*

*(a) By delegated legislation.* In order to enable the obligations imposed on the UK to be implemented swiftly, the European Communities Act also provides powers of delegated legislation to the government, for implementation of decisions of the Council or Commission, or even decisions of the Court.
It reads:

2.(2) Subject to Schedule 2 to this Act, at any time after its passing Her Majesty may by Order in Council, and any designated Minister or department may by regulations, make provision -

(a) For the purpose of implementing any Community obligation of the United Kingdom, or enabling any such obligation to be implemented, or of enabling any rights enjoyed or to be enjoyed by the United Kingdom under or by virtue of the Treaties to be exercised; or

(b) for the purpose of dealing with matters arising out of or related to any such obligation or rights or the coming into force, or the operation from time to time, of subsection (1) above; and in the exercise of any statutory power or duty, including any power to give directions or to legislate by means of orders, rules, regulations or other subordinate instruments, the person entrusted with the power or duty may have regard to the objects of the Communities and to any such obligation or rights as aforesaid.

Note the last paragraph enjoining those who utilise these powers to have regard to the objects of the Communities and to preceding Community obligations and rights. For example, in 1982 the UK was taken before the ECJ by the Commission under Article 169 because its sex and equal pay legislation did not fulfil the full requirements of the Equal Pay Directive.[120] After the ECJ ruling the government introduced regulations under S.2(2).

There are, however, major limitations on this subordinate legislative power, contained in Schedule 2 of the Act. This schedule provides that the secondary legislation should not be used:

(a) to make provisions imposing or increasing taxation; or

(b) to make any provision taking effect from a date earlier than that of the making of the instrument containing the provision; or

(c) to confer any power to legislate by means of orders, rules, regulations or other subordinate instrument, other than rules of procedure of any court or tribunal; or

(d) to create any new criminal offence punishable with imprisonment for more than two years or punishable on summary conviction with imprisonment for more than three months or with a fine of more than £400 (if not calculated on a daily basis) or with a fine of not more than £5 a day.

This does not mean that the UK would not be able to meet such an obligation if Community law required it, it merely means that it cannot be done under 2(4); an Act of Parliament would be required.
*(b) By additions to the Treaties.* S.1(2) sets out the Treaties listed in Schedule I which shall be regarded as the Treaties for these purposes - these include the founding Treaties - ECSC, EEC, EURATOM - and the amending Treaties including the Merger Treaty of 1965 and the Budgetary Treaty of 1970. It also includes any treaties entered into with their states to which the Community was a party.

In relation to new treaties, however, S.1(3) establishes a new procedure. No new treaty may be added to this list unless it has been declared to be one of the Community Treaties by an Order in Council, and that Order in Council requires an affirmative resolution of both Houses of Parliament. This is a considerably more rigorous procedure than the Ponsonby rule requires, but of course, once a treaty joins this list then all the rights and obligations referred to in S.2 may apply.

## NOTES

1. Case 26/62 *Van Gend en Loos v. Nederlandse Administratie der Belastingen* [1963] E.C.R. 1; [1963] C.M.L.R. 105.

2. [1963] E.C.R. 1 at p.12; [1963] C.M.L.R. 105 at p.129. The concept of this 'new legal order' is elaborated upon below pp.30-44.

3. On the question of international personality see below p.12.

4. For example, the United Nations Organisation was held to be an international person by the International Court of Justice in the *Reparation for Injuries Suffered in the Service of the United Nations* case, I.C.J. Reports (1949), p.174. See further below p.12.

5. The most authoritative definition of a treaty is to be found in Article 2(1)(a) of the Vienna Convention on the Law of Treaties 1969:

> 'treaty' means an international agreement concluded between States in written form and governed by international law, whether embodied in a single instrument or in two or more related instruments and whatever its particular designation.

Note that this definition is limited to states and does not cover other international persons. The International Law Commission, which drafted the Convention, felt that agreement on the law relating to treaties involving other international persons would not be practical. Article 3 of the Convention makes clear, however, that its rules do not affect the validity of agreements between other international persons. There is now a Vienna

Convention on the Law of Treaties between States and International Organisations 1986, XXV (1986) *I.L.M.* p.543.

6. The sources of international law are conveniently set out in Article 38 of the Statute of the International Court of Justice. Customary international law, which is created by the uniform action of states together with a sense that they are acting in conformity with a legal obligation (called *opinio juris sive necessitatis*) is arguably the most important source of law. See e.g. M. Akehurst, *A Modern Introduction to International Law*, 5th edn. (George Allen and Unwin, London, 1985), pp.25-34.

7. See Article 36(2) of the Statute of the International Court of Justice, the so-called optional clause, by which states undertake to accept the compulsory jurisdiction of the Court.

8. It should be noted, however, that the use of force by way of self-help in the resolution of a dispute is, except in cases of self-defence, prohibited by Article 2(4) of the UN Charter.

9. This convention deals with such matters as the inviolability of diplomatic personnel and diplomatic premises.

10. *Loc. cit.*, above, note 4.

11. *Ibid.*, 174 at 179.

12. Article 4 of the UN Charter.

13. Article 237 EEC.

14. Although Articles 11 and 12 of the Vienna Convention on the Law of Treaties provide that the consent of state to be bound by a treaty *may* be expressed by signature alone.

15. See Article 14 of the Vienna Convention on the Law of Treaties.

16. Article 308, Law of the Sea Convention 1982.

17. 55 U.N.T.S. 124; Cmnd.7258.

18. U.K.T.S. 70 (1950); Cmnd.8969.

19. D. Lasok and J.W. Bridge, *Introduction to the Law and Institutions of the European Communities*, 3rd edn. (Butterworths, London, 1982), p.270.

20. *Conseil d'Etat*, 22 December 1978; Dalloz, 1979, p.155; [1980] 1 C.M.L.R. 543.

21. See below pp.30-44 for further discussion of the concept and characteristics of 'direct effect'.

22. See e.g. B. Schwartz, *American Constitutional Law* (Cambridge University Press), Ch. 1.

23. 3 U.S. 199 (1796).

24. 112 U.S. 580 (1884).

25. *Ibid.* at p.598.

26. *Foster v. Neilson*, 2 Pet. 253 (US 1829).

27. 217 P. (2d) 481 (1950).

28. 242 P. (2d) 617 (1952) at p.620.

29. *Ibid.*

30. (1689) St. Tr. 1165.

31. *Blackburn v. Attorney-General* [1971] A11 ER 1380; [1971] 1 W.L.R. 1037.

32. [1971] 2 A11 ER 1380 at 1382; [1971] 1 W.L.R. 1037 at 1040.

33. 171 *H.C. Deb.* 2001 (1 April 1924).

34. S.A. de Smith, *Constitutional and Administrative Law*, by H. Street and R. Brazier, 5th edn. (Penguin, Harmondsworth, 1985), p.152.

35. The affirmative resolution procedure, which is normally used to approve delegated legislation, requires either or both Houses to vote in favour of an instrument within a specified period of time. See further de Smith, *Constitutional and Administrative Law*, pp.345-6.

36. (1879) 4 P.D. 129.

37. (1879) 4 P.D. 129 at 154.

38. (1876) 1 Q.B.D. 487.

39. (1876) 1 Q.B.D. 487 at 497.

40. *Civilian War Claimants' Association v. R.* [1932] A.C. 14.

41. 1964 c.81.

42. 1978 c.26.

43. U.K.T.S. 93 (1978); Cmnd.7390.

44. Prior to the entry into force of the European Convention on the Suppression of Terrorism, it was open to a foreign national being extradited from the UK to the place where the alleged offence took place to argue that the offence was of a political character in that it was performed in the course of disturbances in which a political faction was trying to wrest power from the established government. Article 1 of the ECST removes the political defence from a number of 'terrorist' acts such as the use of automatic weapons or letter-bombs.

45. S.5, *loc. cit.*, above, note 42.

46. *Loc. cit.*, above, note 18. Article 1 ECHR provides:

> The High Contracting Parties *shall secure* to everyone within their jurisdiction the rights and freedoms defined in Section 1 of this Convention. (emphasis added)

47. For some of the arguments for and against enacting the ECHR see P. Wallington and J. McBride, *Civil Liberties and a Bill of Rights* (Cobden Trust, London, 1976).

48. [1974] 1 W.L.R. 683.

49. Resolution 217A (III), G.A.O.R., 3rd Session, Part I, Resolutions, p.71.

50. [1974] 1 W.L.R. 683 at 694.

51. *Birdi v. Secretary of State for Home Affairs* (not reported but referred to directly in *R. v. Secretary of State for Home Affairs ex parte Bhajan Singh* [1976] Q.B. 198.

52. *Loc. cit.*, above, note 51.

53. [1976] Q.B. 198 at 207.

54. *Loc. cit.*, above, note 17.

55. See, for example, Cases 51-54/71 *International Fruit Company v. Produktschap voor Groenten en Fruit* [1971] E.C.R. 1107 in which the question of the direct effect of Article 11 of GATT (concerning the removal of quantitative restrictions on the import of goods) was raised. The ECJ, however, found that although in theory a treaty provision could produce direct effects, in the case of Article 11 of GATT there was too much flexibility and, hence, uncertainty to allow it to confer individual

rights. See further T.C. Hartley, *The Foundations of European Community Law* (Clarendon Press, Oxford, 1981), pp.176-9.

56. J.O. 1969 L77/49. The tachograph is an instrument placed in the cabs of commercial vehicles to record the time, speed and distance which a driver has done. It enables the authorities in Member States to ensure that drivers of commercial vehicles take adequate rest periods.

57. Council Decision 76/787, 0.J., 1976, L278/1.

58. Case 93/71 *Leonesio v. Ministry for Agriculture* [1972] E.C.R. 287; [1973] C.M.L.R. 343.

59. This analogy is explored more fully by E. Stein, 'Lawyers, Judges and the Making of a Transnational Constitution' (1981) 75 *A.J.I.L.* p.1.

60. Hartley, *Foundations*, p.60.

61. *Loc cit.*, above, note 1.

62. *Ibid.*

63. See Articles 169 and 170 EEC.

64. [1963] E.C.R. 1 at 12; [1963] C.M.L.R. 105 at 129.

65. *Ibid.*

66. *Ibid.*

67. *Ibid.*

68. *Ibid.*

69. Article 30 EEC was, in fact, held to be directly effective in Case 74/76 *Ianelli v. Meroni* [1977] E.C.R. 557.

70. W. van Gerven, 'De niet-contractuele aansprakelijkheid van de Gemeenschap wegens normatieve hondelingen' [1976] *Sociaal Economische Wetgeving* 28. Translated and cited by H.G. Schermers, *Judicial Protection in the European Communities*, 3rd edn. (Kluwer, Deventer, 1983), para.175.

71. These tests were most clearly articulated by A-G Mayras in Case 2/74 *Reyners v. Belgian State* [1974] E.C.R. 631; [1974] 1 C.M.L.R. 305.

72. Case 9/73 *Schlüter v. Hauptzollampt Lörrach* [1973] E.C.R. 1135.

73. Regulation 1251/70. O.J. Special Ed., 1970 (II), 402.

74. Public policy is known as *ordre public* in French administrative law. The French concept is closer to the meaning of the term in the EEC Treaty than the English notion of public policy.

75. O.J. Special Ed., 1963-4, 117.

76. Case 41/74 [1974] E.C.R. 1337; [1975] 1 C.M.L.R. 1.

77. Scientology was described by the Minister of Health as a 'pseudo-scientific cult'. *H.C. Deb.*, vol.769, col.189.

78. *Ibid.*

79. This has been done by Regulation 1251/70, *loc. cit.*, above, note 73.

80. Case 18/71 *Eunomia v. Italian Ministry of Education* [1971] E.C.R. 811; [1972] C.M.L.R. 4.

81. Case 2/74 [1974] E.C.R. 631; [1974] 2 C.M.L.R. 305.

82. [1974] E.C.R. 631 at 635; [1974] 2 C.M.L.R. 305 at 327.

83. Case 43/75 [1976] E.C.R. 455; [1976] 2 C.M.L.R. 98.

84. Under the Rules of Procedure of the ECJ, Member States have a right to intervene in any case before the Court in order to make their position known.

85. In the UK this would have been January 1973, whereas in the case of Belgium it would have been January 1962.

86. See further de Smith, *Constitutional and Administrative Law*, pp.453-6.

87. *Reports of the Judicial and Academic Conference* (Luxembourg, 1976), p.II-3.

88. In *Marshall v. South West Hampshire Area Health Authority (Teaching)* [1986] 2 All E.R. 584 it was held by the ECJ that directly effective rights were enforceable vertically against any emanation of the state, i.e. any body established by governmental authority. In this case it was the Area Health Authority established by the National Health Service Act 1977 as amended by the National Health Service Act 1980.

89. Case 93/71 *Leonesio v. Ministry for Agriculture* [1972] E.C.R. 287; [1973] C.M.L.R. 343.

90. J.O. 1969, L252/1.

91. European Agricultural Guidance and Guarantee Fund.

92. This is a good example of subordinate EEC legislation. See below p. 66.

93. J.O. 1969, L278/6.

94. Directive 68/31, 1968, J.O., L12/8.

95. Case 33/70 [1970] E.C.R. 1213; [1971] C.M.L.R. 123.

96. Hartley, *Foundations*, pp.204-5.

97. For an elaboration of the concepts see Directive 64/221 *loc. cit.*, above, note 75.

98. [1974] E.C.R. 1337 at 1348.

99. Case 51/76 *Verbond der Nederlandse Ondernemingen v. Inspecteur der Invoerrechten en Accijnzen* [1977] E.C.R. 113; [1977] 1 C.M.L.R. 413.

100. Directive 69/463, 1969, O.J., Special Edition, 551.

101. *Publico Ministero v. Ratti* [1979] E.C.R. 1629; [1980] 1 C.M.L.R. 96.

102. 1973, O.J. L189/7.

103. 1977, O.J. L303/23.

104. See e.g. A.J. Easson, 'Can Directives impose obligations upon Individuals?', (1979) 4 *E.L.Rev.* p.67; A.J. Easson, 'The "Direct Effect" of EEC Directives', (1979) 28 *I.C.L.Q.* p.319; D. Wyatt, 'The Direct Applicability of Regulations and Directives' [1977] *C.L.J. p.216.*

105. D. Wyatt and A. Dashwood, *The Substantive Law of the EEC* (Sweet and Maxwell, London, 1980), p.40, note 81.

106. *Loc. cit.*, above, note 20.

107. See e.g. Easson (1979) 28 *I.C.L.Q.* p.319, and Hartley, *Foundations*, p.207.

108. Hartley, *Foundations*, p.207.

109. See the *Marshall* case where this point was pleaded specifically by the UK.

110. This is the highest German constitutional court.

111. See below Ch. 6 and also D. Freestone, 'Equal Pay before the European Court', (1982) *M.L.R.* p.82.

112. P. Pescatore, 'The Doctrine of "Direct Effect": An Infant Disease', (1983) 8 *E.L.Rev.* p.155.

113. It is generally accepted in English constitutional law that one parliament may not bind either itself or its successor by attempting to entrench legislation, i.e. make the repeal of an act contingent upon some

particular circumstance or procedural requirements. See e.g. de Smith, *Constitutional and Administrative Law*, pp.73-101.

114. Case 6/64 *Costa v. E.N.E.L.* [1964] E.C.R. 585; [1964] C.M.L.R. 425.

115. Case 106/77 *Minister of Finance v. Simmenthal* [1978] E.C.R. 629; [1978] 3 C.M.L.R. 263.

116. See e.g. de Smith, *Constitutional and Administrative Law*, pp.92-4.

117. See O. Hood-Phillips, 'Has the "Incoming Tide" Reached the Palace of Westminster?' (1979) 95 *L.Q.R.* p.167. See *contra* D. Freestone 'The Supremacy of Community Law in National Courts' (1979) 42 *M.L.R.* p. 220.

118. *Ibid.*

119. The doctrine of implied repeal is reflective of the generally accepted legal principle that the later in time prevails over the earlier. For a consideration of the doctrine of implied repeal in English law see e.g. de Smith, *Constitutional and Administrative Law*, p.83.

120. Case 61/81 [1982] E.C.R. 2601.

# 3

# The Community Institutions

The primary institutions of the European Community are:

The Council of Ministers
The Commission
The European Parliament (EP)
The European Court of Justice (ECJ)

Together, these four institutions, whose powers are conferred upon them by the Community Treaties, carry out the functions of the legislature, executive and judiciary. They do not, however, fit into the classic 'separation of powers' mould. The most obvious example of this is the European Assembly - or Parliament as it has called itself since 1962 and as it is now termed by the single European Act - which has no legislative capacity in its own right, but which is primarily a consultative body.

The threefold division of powers may have been in the minds of the drafters of the Treaty of Rome, not as something which would take immediate effect, but rather as an ideal towards which to work. Within the framework of the Treaty, it is arguable that there is the germ of a bicameral legislature with the EP as the assembly of the peoples of Europe and the Council as the assembly of the Member States. The existing balance of Community institutions, however, is characterised by the Commission and the Council of Ministers which represent the Community and the national interests respectively. The Commission provides the initiatives for Community development and integration, whereas the Council, which consists of the representatives of the Members States, ensures that the rate of progress is acceptable to the governments of the Member States. Over the years it has become clear that it is the

Council which is the dominant force in the Community and that the Community's progress is dictated by the speed at which the Member States' governments wish to travel. Often that is the speed of the slowest and least enthusiastic.

In addition to the four major institutions there are a number of other Community bodies: the Economic and Social Committee (ESC), the Court of Auditors and the European Investment Bank. These are dealt with briefly at the end of this chapter.

The European Council, which should not be confused with the Council of Ministers, is the 'summit' of the Member States' Heads of State or Heads of Government which meets three times a year. The emphasis in the European Council had traditionally been upon broad issues of policy often relating to matters outside the sphere of Community competence. However, the Single European Act (Article 2) accords, for the first time, official recognition within the Treaty of the existence of the European Council. Although the European Council's decisions do not represent Community law, they have, nevertheless, always had significant influence on the Community and its policies.

## THE EUROPEAN COUNCIL AND EUROPEAN POLITICAL COOPERATION

The European Council is given formal recognition as a Community institution for the first time by Article 2 of the Single European Act. This is a limited recognition of the *status quo*, for the Heads of State or Government have regularly held Summit Meetings to discuss matters of common concern. Until now these meetings have been outside the ambit of the Treaties, in that they are not formally constituted meetings of the Council of Ministers, and the subjects discussed are certainly not restricted to issues regulated by the Treaties. Any decisions taken, which have usually been on broad policy issues, were not part of Community law.

At the 1972 Paris Summit it was agreed to hold these meetings on a regular basis, and since then Heads of Government, accompanied by their Foreign Ministers have met three times a year as the European Council. Loose rules of procedure for these meetings were agreed in 1977.

Despite the fact that important policy decisions, such as the settlement of the British budgetary complaints and the decision to increase the resources of the Community, have been taken at these meetings, the meetings themselves have remained outside the Community framework, as have the parallel meetings of the Foreign Ministers discussing issues of political cooperation. These latter discussions, termed European Political Cooperation (EPC), have been relatively successful, facilitating the adoption of common positions at various times on the Middle East, occasionally on matters such as terrorism, and on sanctions against Argentina in the first month of the Falkland Islands conflict.

The Single European Act recognises that both the European Council (Article 2) and the EPC procedures (Article 1) take place, but their deliberations are specifically excluded from the jurisdiction of the ECJ (Article 30). This means that the meetings now take place under the umbrella of the Communities for the first time, but that the decisions reached there have no enforceable status under Community law. What this will mean in practice is as yet uncertain. Both the European Council and the Foreign Ministers will continue their discussions with the aim of achieving agreement and common positions on a wide variety of international topics. However, decisions on matters which effect the Community will require, as at present, to be formally agreed at a subsequent Council of Ministers' meeting before they give rise to enforceable obligations under Community law.

## THE COMMISSION

### Composition

The Commission has 17 members.[1] All must be nationals of the Member States, one at least from each state.[2] By convention the largest states, France, Germany, Italy and the UK, have an extra member. Once a Commissioner is appointed, he or she (although to date all have been male) is required to renounce national allegiances and to give a solemn undertaking to be completely independent in the performance of duties and not to seek or take instructions from any government or any other body.[3] Member States, for their part, undertake not to influence members of the Commission in the performance of their tasks.[4]

A further undertaking is also required from Commissioners, that they will behave with integrity and discretion during and after their term of office 'as regards the acceptance after they have ceased to hold office of certain appointments or benefits'.[5] Breach of these undertakings can result in compulsory resignation or deprivation of pension and other rights.[6]

## Appointment of Commissioners

Commissioners are appointed by the 'common accord' of the Council (i.e. unanimously) for a four-year term.[7] The Merger Treaty envisages that the President be elected from the ranks of the Commission by the same procedure.[8] In fact, the President plays such a key role in formulating and guiding the programme of the Commission through its four-year term that in 1975 the Tindemans Report[9] proposed that he be appointed first by the Summit of Heads of State or Government - the European Council as it is now called - and that the choice be then endorsed by the Council of Ministers. This procedure was first used for the appointment of Roy Jenkins in 1976. Tindemans also suggested that the President should then play a key role in choosing the rest of the Commission, thus ensuring a unified approach to the four-year term. This, however, has not proved practicable. Member States continue to insist on the right to choose which of their nationals should serve in the Commission. Indeed in the UK the practice has arisen that a Commissioner should be chosen from each of the two major political parties - hence the nomination of the current Commissioners, Stanley Clinton Davies and Lord Cockfield. The President may, however, play some small role behind the scenes before final agreement is reached on the composition of the Commission, but when in 1976, Roy Jenkins, the president-elect, expressed public disapproval of one of the two potential German candidates, in an attempt to influence the German nomination, a major political row broke out, and Jenkins was then forced to work with a man about whom he had publicly expressed reservations. Needless to say, no such overt attempts at influence have been made since.

However, in the allocation of responsibilities, or portfolios, within the Commission the President may have greater influence, for these are agreed amongst themselves by the new Commissioners. Considerable lobbying takes place, especially for the prestigious portfolios such as External Affairs. Indeed in 1981 Mrs Thatcher was reported to have telephoned the President about the responsibilities to be given to the British Commissioners. As we have seen, the President does not have these within his gift, but the effectiveness of his Commission may depend upon which Commissioner takes which portfolio, and as Henig comments,[10] it represents an early test for the effectiveness of the new President.

**Dismissal**

The Commission can be dismissed *en bloc* by the EP under Article 144 EEC, if a motion of censure is carried by two-thirds majority of votes cast. The fact that individual Commissioners cannot be singled out for censure severely undermines the political usefulness of this procedure, but reflects the collegiate nature of Commission decision-making, in that the whole Commission is accountable for every decision it takes. Although four motions have been tabled they have never achieved the two-thirds majority necessary.[11]

If it is alleged that any Member of the Commission no longer fulfils the conditions required for the performance of his duties, or has been guilty of serious misconduct, then either the Council or the Commission (which acts by majority vote) can apply to the ECJ to have him 'compulsorily retired'. This procedure has never been invoked.

**Internal Organisation**

The internal organisation of the staff of the Commission is centred around 20 Directorates-General covering all the sectors for which the EC has any responsibility. The Head of each DG, as they are known, is responsible to the Commissioner who holds that particular portfolio. The Commission has a total staff of about 13,000, of whom some 3,000 are involved in research and a third of whom are involved in translating the mountain of documents which the use of nine official working languages necessitates. As the Commission itself is fond of reminding visitors, this is considerably less than the staff of most major national ministries and even some local authorities.

Each Commissioner has a small inner office or *Cabinet* of officials - usually of the same nationality - whose task is to keep their Commissioner well briefed on current developments. The Spierenberg Report[12] was highly critical of the power which the *Chef* or Head of this *Cabinet* wields, often, it alleged, obstructing communication between the Commissioners and the staff of the

Directorates-General for which they are responsible.

Decisions of the Commission are taken collegiately. This means that the whole Commission bears responsibility for every decision taken. To enable such a decision-making system to work, a written procedure is used whereby proposals are circulated to all Commissioners, and if no objections are received within the stated period, it is deemed to have received assent. In the case of objections or queries the matter is referred to a full Commission meeting where decisions are taken by majority vote.[13]

**The Role of the Commission**

The powers and functions of the Commission are set out in general terms in the paragraphs of Article 155. These will be examined in turn. 'In order to ensure the proper functioning and development of the common market', Article 155 provides:
'The Commission shall:

*(a) Ensure that the provisions of this Treaty and the measures taken by the institutions pursuant thereto are applied.'*

This is the 'watchdog' or policing role in which the Commission acts as guardian of the Treaty. It has two aspects: first, the monitoring of compliance with the Treaty and detection of breaches; and second, the enforcement of the Treaty against defaulters, be they individuals, businesses or states.

*(i) Detection of breaches of Community law.* Article 213 gives the Commission supervisory powers to collect information and carry out necessary checks. Although these actions must be carried out within the authority of Community law this is generally interpreted widely to include, for example, the collection of general statistical information for reports to Council. But the Commission is generally responsible for ensuring that the obligations imposed by Community law are adhered to. Hence it collects information about alleged breaches of Community law. Is, for example, a UK ban on the import of turkeys and turkey parts which have been vaccinated against Newcastle disease (a contagious disease affecting poultry) a genuine health measure or is it intended as a method of restricting imports of turkeys from other Member States for economic reasons?[14]

More specific investigative powers are given by Community

legislation. The best example is the powers given to the Commission by Regulation 17/62[15] to investigate possible breaches of competition rules. Article 4 of regulation 17/62 authorises it to 'undertake all necessary investigations into undertakings and associations of undertakings'. This includes power:

(a) to examine the books and other business records;
(b) to take copies of or extracts from the books and business records;
(c) to ask for oral explanations on the spot;
(d) to enter any premises, land and means of transport of undertakings.

The Commission's responsibility extends to ensuring that Community legislation is properly implemented and adhered to. It has computerised systems for monitoring the implementation of directives at a procedural level, i.e. have the Member States taken the necessary action within the time-limits laid down by a directive? But it also has the more difficult job of checking whether national measures purporting to meet the requirements of directives do so in fact. Information about substantive breaches in this latter sense is brought to the Commission's attention in a number of ways including private letters of complaint from members of the public, questions from MEPs and even Article 177 references to the ECJ from national courts.[16] Once a violation is detected then enforcement action may take a number of forms.

*(ii) Enforcement of Community law against Member States.* The Commission has primary responsibility for taking legal action against Member States in breach of the Treaty. A number of articles of the Treaty permit enforcement action against Member States but by far the most common procedure is that of Article 169:

> If the Commission considers that a Member State has failed to fulfil an obligation under this Treaty, it shall deliver a reasoned opinion on the matter after giving the State concerned the opportunity to submit its observations. If the State concerned does not comply with the opinion within the period laid down by the Commission the latter may bring the matter before the Court of Justice.

The use of the words 'considers' and 'may' indicates the wide discretion that the Commission is given. States do not relish being arraigned in public for acting illegally, hence the Commission, as the representative of the Community interest, is given this role so that Member States are not left to police each other. This ensures that a consistent policy can be pursued and avoids the political damage that can be done to Community relations by inter-state actions.

However, the Article 169 procedure itself is designed to ensure that the maximum opportunity is given to a Member State to remedy an infringement before being taken to court. First, formal notice is given that the Commission considers an infringement to have occurred. The offending state will be asked to submit its observations on the suggestions that it has, for example, violated Community law by imposing a ban on the import of particular goods, or that it has failed to meet the requirements of a directive. The Commission then considers these observations and if it persists in its view that an infringement has occurred, then the second stage is for it to issue a 'reasoned opinion' which sets out the detailed argument and requires the offender to take remedial action within a specified period, usually six months. If this action is not taken the third stage is for the state to be taken before the ECJ. Only about one-third of the reasoned opinions issued result in court action, and a number of cases are removed from the register before the hearing because the offending state has taken remedial action. On a strict view of the law all such cases could be pursued, for the ECJ has clear authority to rule that an infringement of the Treaty has occurred in the past as well as that an infringement is continuing. However, if the offending state does comply with the Commission's reasoned opinion before the Court hearing, it seems that the Commission often takes the pragmatic view that the object of the procedure has been accomplished.

The role of the Commission as 'honest broker' between the states is also reflected in the procedure of Article 170 under which Member States may initiate action against each other if a Treaty violation is suspected. Article 170(2) obliges the complainant state first to 'bring the matter before the Commission' and the Commission then has three months to issue a reasoned opinion after allowing both complainant and respondent states to submit their observations. The result may well be that the violation is then taken over by the Commission as an Article 169 action, thus avoiding the political problems which might result from a confrontation between two member states. As a result only one Article 170 action has been before the ECJ: *France v. UK* (Fisheries case).[17]

If the ECJ finds that violation of the treaty has occurred, then its judgment to that effect will be declaratory; there are no sanctions for such a violation. Nevertheless, with rare exceptions, Member States do comply with rulings of the ECJ, often, as we have seen, before the matter comes to court; sometimes with bad grace afterwards (see e.g. the British compliance with the Sex Equal treatment directive after *Commission v. UK.*[18]) Although the French refusal to comply with the ECJ's condemnation of the French ban on British lamb imports attracted a great deal of publicity in 1979,[19] such cases are surprisingly rare.

The Treaty also permits the Commission direct access to the ECJ without the preliminary procedure if it considers there has been a violation of the ban on state aids to industry (Article 93) or where a state has taken action obstructing the conditions of free competition in the market for improper reasons (Article 225). These reflect the central importance the drafters of the Treaty attributed to safeguarding the internal market.

*(iii) Enforcement against individuals.* The watchdog role of the Commission is primarily concerned with the risks of breaches of the Treaty by states - after all the Treaty imposes the majority of obligations upon them. There is, however, one major area of EEC policy where the main actors are not states but individuals and business undertakings; this is competition policy. Distortions of competition may be engineered by contractual policy and other arrangements between undertakings, and an effective competition policy requires policing at that level. As we have seen, the basic competition regulation, Regulation 17/62, empowers the Commission to collect relevant data and to require individuals and businesses to supply data to it. Violations of the Treaty's competition provisions (Articles 85 and 86) may be punished by substantial fines not in excess of one million units of account or 10% of annual turnover. All decisions taken by the Commission are subject to review by the ECJ. This centralised policing of a common policy is not only unique within the EEC it is also unique in the world.

*(b) Formulate recommendations or deliver opinions on matters dealt with in the Treaty, if it expressly so provides or if the Commission considers it necessary.*

Article 189 EEC makes it clear that recommendations and opinions have no binding force, nevertheless this power is an important aspect of the Commission's role as initiator and formulator of policy. In specific cases the Treaty makes the opinion of the Commission a specific prerequisite for Council action. A prominent example is Article 237 which concerns the admission of new members to the Community. Although the decision on admission is taken unanimously by the Council, it may only be done 'after obtaining the opinion of the Commission' on the matter. Its opinions are not always followed. The Commission expressed views favourable to British accession in 1965, 1967 and 1969, but its opinion in favour of Greek accession and also of the Iberian countries was highly persuasive.

In general terms the power to recommend and give opinions to the Council provides the Commission with the means to sustain momentum towards integration and to improve institutional relations. In February 1984, for example, in the context of a long-standing dispute over the budgetary procedure, the Commission on its own initiative proposed improvements to the procedure to impose more discipline on spending. Its proposals included the important principle that agricultural spending should not increase at a faster rate than general EC 'own resources', and were, in general, accepted by the Council in December 1984.[20]

This general discretionary power also permits the Commission to suggest areas of policy change and expansion and to formulate legislative programmes utilising, e.g. Article 235, where the Treaty does not provide explicit powers.[21]

The formulation of policy and recommendations and opinions is a major preoccupation of the Commission. In 1986 it sent to the Council 739 proposals, recommendations and drafts for instruments, and 214 communications, memoranda and reports.[22]

*(c) Have its own power of decision and participate in the shaping of measures taken by the Council and the Assembly in the manner provided for by this Treaty.*

There are two aspects to this paragraph:

(i) *The Commission's power of decision.* It is true to say that the preponderance of instruments emanating from the Commission (in total 12,081 in 1986)[23] are issued under the direct authority of Council legislation, nevertheless, a number of Treaty articles do give the Commission power to pass legislation on its own initiative - a 'primary' rather than a derived power. For example, Article

13(2) empowered the Commission to determine by directive the timetable for the abolition of 'charges having an effect equivalent to customs duties' - the subject of the famous SACE case (see above p.40); Article 90 (concerned with the application of competition rules to nationalised and state-financed industries) empowers the Commission 'to address appropriate directives or decisions to Member States'. In *France, Italy and UK v. Commission*[24] (1982) it was argued that a directive based on Article 190 should be annulled on the ground, *inter alia*, that the Commission had no right of primary legislation. This argument was firmly dismissed by the ECJ.

*(ii) The right of participation in the shaping of legislative measures.* This is probably the most important aspect of the Commission's role as the main promoter of integration. The normal method of legislation envisaged by the majority of Treaty articles is for the Council to act on a proposal of the Commission. The right to make proposals for legislation or, in other words, the right of legislative initiative, rests with the Commission, and the weighted voting procedure of Article 148 is specifically designed to ensure that decisions may be taken more easily on proposals from the Commission than in other cases. Similarly, the Council can only make amendments to Commission proposals by unanimous vote, whereas the Commission may amend its own proposals at any time before they are adopted by the Council. It may, for example, feel that changes would make a proposal more likely to be approved by the Council, or perhaps it wishes to take account of a view expressed by the EP during consultation (see further below at pp. 90-2 and pp. 99-100). In addition to the right of proposal, the view of the Commission must also be sought formally by the Council before the latter can take action on a number of specific issues.

The Commission is specifically given the right to be physically present at meetings of the EP. There is no corresponding right to be present at Council meetings but in practice the Commission is always represented.

*(d) Exercise the powers conferred upon it by the Council for the implementation of the rules laid down by the latter*

This is the truly executive role of the Commission. The Council is given the primary responsibility to 'take decisions' by Article 145 but it does not have, nor was it ever intended to have, the necessary administrative machinery to carry those decisions into practice; this is the task envisaged for the Commission.

The range of tasks so delegated by the Council may be loosely classified into administrative and legislative powers:

*(i) Administrative tasks.* These will normally involve the supervision of established policies, and the role of the Commission as administrator will overlap with its watchdog role discussed above. For example, the Commission is given a major role in the implementation and policing of EC competition policy. Although the Treaty itself envisages such a role for the Commission, its duties are crystallised by the terms of Council Regulation 17/62. It is this basic regulation which specifically gives the Commission the power to grant exemptions from Article 85(1) (as envisaged by Article 85(3)), to investigate complaints and to impose fines.

Similarly in the agricultural sector, Council regulations often envisage that the Commission should have the power to take 'safeguarding' decisions if there is a disturbance in the markets, and immediate action is necessary to prevent damage to the CAP objectives.[25]

*(ii) Legislative powers.* This is the area of the Community where its legislation can truly be said to be subordinate or secondary, in the sense that the Council expressly delegates to the Commission the task of detailed implementation of policy - which the Commission will then carry out by 'secondary' legislation. It is now a firmly established practice that in the implementation of these policies, particularly in the sphere of agriculture, that a 'management committee' should be established to ensure that the implementing legislation is in line with Council guidelines. The management committee procedure is dealt with in detail below (Chapter 4).

## THE COUNCIL OF MINISTERS

### Composition

The Council of Ministers is constituted by the Ministers of the Member States.[26] Each Member Government is obliged to delegate one of its Ministers to attend Council meetings.[27] Which Minister actually attends depends upon the issues under discussion. So, for example, the UK Minister of Agriculture, Food and Fisheries will attend discussions on fisheries and the Minister of Transport will attend discussions of transport policy. When general Community policy issues are under discussion it is normal for the Foreign Ministers to attend. However many representatives a state may have at a Council meeting, it is only entitled to one vote, and in the absence of a person of ministerial rank from one country that vote may be exercised by proxy through the Minister of another state (only one proxy vote may be exercised by any one state: Article 150 EEC). The office of President of the Council is held in strict rotation by the Member States according to an 'absolute' alphabetical order thus Belgie, Danmark, Deutschland, Ellas, Espagne, France, etc, for a six-month period. Although this short period results in a lack of continuity in the office, it does at least mean that each state holds the presidency at least once every six years. The short period of office also means that Member States are keen to achieve the maximum amount of political capital from their period in office - thus providing a strong impetus for agreement and compromise on important issues. Unsatisfactory though this system of rotation may appear, it is difficult to devise a satisfactory alternative.

*Voting*

There is considerable discrepancy between the Treaty provisions relating to voting at Council and actual practice.

*The Treaty*

The Treaty sets out three methods of decision-making
(a) Simple majority. Article 148(1) envisages this as the norm.
(b) Qualified majority. A system of weighted voting is set out by Article 148(2):

| | | | | | |
|---|---|---|---|---|---|
| Belgium | 5 | Spain | 8 | Luxembourg | 2 |
| Denmark | 3 | France | 10 | Netherlands | 5 |
| Germany | 10 | Ireland | 3 | Portugal | 5 |
| Greece | 5 | Italy | 10 | United Kingdom | 10 |

Where the Council is acting on a proposal from the Commission then it will require at least 54 votes in favour. Other cases require the 54 votes to be cast by at least 8 members. These two requirements indicate the somewhat favoured position the drafters envisaged for Commission proposals, and the need to protect the interests of the small states from block voting by the larger states in other cases.

(c) Unanimity. Numerous articles require a unanimous vote. Article 237 requires unanimity on the admission of new Members as do the supplementary legislative powers of Article 235. If the Council is considering a Commission proposal and wishes to amend it, this may only be done unanimously - again protecting the integrity of Commission proposals.

*Voting in practice*

Despite the elaborate voting procedures envisaged by the Treaty, the overwhelming majority of Council decisions are in fact taken by consensus. In part this reflects a wish to act on a broad basis of agreement, but more significantly it reflects the practice envisaged by the so-called Luxembourg Accords or Compromise. After a constitutional crisis in 1965 during which for six months France refused to participate in Council meetings, the Council issued the following statement:

> *Majority Voting Procedure*
> I. Where, in the case of decisions which may be taken by majority vote on a proposal of the Commission, very important interests of one or more partners are at stake, the Members of the Council will endeavour, within a reasonable time, to reach solutions which can be adopted by all the Members of the Council while respecting their mutual interests and those of the Community, in accordance with Article 2 of the Treaty.
> II. With regard to the preceding paragraph, the French delegation considers that where very important issues are at stake the discussion must continue until unanimous agreement is reached.
> III. The six delegations note that there is a divergence of views on what should be done in the event of a failure to reach complete agreement.
> IV. The six delegations nevertheless consider that this divergence does not prevent the Community's work being resumed in accordance with the normal procedure.

The crucial aspects of this are that 'very important interests' are not defined and may, it seems, be interpreted unilaterally, i.e. each state is free to decide what its 'very important interests' are. Hence a *de facto* 'veto' has been introduced into virtually all Community decision-making. Majority voting is used in only about 5% of decisions and the real importance of the weighted voting system is primarily in relation to the management committee voting structures discussed below.

The Luxembourg Accords, or Compromise, have no formal legal status. It is not an amendment of the Treaty - indeed the texts issued in 1966 manifest a clear lack of agreement. All the major reports on Community procedures - Vedel,[28] Tindemans[29] and the Three Wise Men[30] - have called for a return to majority voting, as too did Genscher and Colombo in their 'European Act'.[31] Nevertheless, it is now a settled convention of Council procedures. The accession of the new member states was negotiated on the basis of its existence, and the 'veto' formed a part of the case put for continued UK membership of the EC in the 1975 referendum.[32] In May 1982, however, when Britain attempted to use the 'veto' to block an increase in farm prices until agreement had been reached on its contribution to the Community Budget, the Council over-rode the British objection, taking the farm price increase on a majority vote.[33] Immediately afterwards, the French delegation, with Italian support, declared that the Luxembourg Compromise still stood, arguing that as the farm prices rise did not affect Britain's 'vital interests', the situation was not covered by the Compromise.[34] Denmark and Greece, luke-warm Europeanists, anxious to maintain the 'veto', abstained. The British, protesting about this 'change of the rules', instigated an unsuccessful attempt to amend the Treaty to formalise the 'veto'.[35] It appears that there has only been a practical limitation of the circumstances in which the plea of 'vital interests', or in the 1966 terminology 'very important interests', may be used in the future. The Single European Act has also added a new dimension to the question of voting in the Council in that it introduces new majority voting procedures into a large number of Treaty provisions which previously required unanimity in voting. It is hoped by the supporters and drafters of the Act that this will ensure more rapid progress in certain fields of Community legislation and less reliance on the 'veto'.

### The Powers of the Council

The Council is primarily the legislative authority of the Community. Article 145 requires it to 'ensure that the objectives set out in this Treaty are attained' and *'in accordance with the provisions of this Treaty*' (emphasis added) the Council is to: 'ensure co-ordination of the economic policies of the Member States; have power to take decisions and confer on the Commission, in the acts which the Council adopts, powers for the implementation of the rules which the Council lays down ...'. Note the words in italics, for they stress the point that the Council does not have unfettered legislative powers; they may only be exercised within the constraints imposed by the Treaty itself. Each legislative act must be based upon one or more Treaty articles and each article which authorises legislation will specify both the procedure which must be followed - consultation with EP and/or ESC, majority or unanimous approval - and also the type of legislative act which it permits - regulation, directive or decision. So, for example, Article 43(2) permits the Council, acting by majority vote to enact regulations, directives or decisions in the field of the Common Agricultural Policy, but only on a proposal from the Commission after consulting the EP.

These legislative constraints reflect the idea of the Treaty as a form of constitutional document which provides a framework within which the legislative system must operate. On occasions this scheme has restricted Community activity. Admittedly, some legislative powers are wide. Article 100 permits harmonisation of any national laws or administrative practices which 'directly affect the establishment or functioning of the common market' and a wide residual legislative power is contained in Article 235 which permits 'appropriate measures' where action is necessary in the course of the operation of the common market to achieve one of the objectives of the Community where the Treaty has not provided the necessary powers. But even Article 235 does not provide a *carte blanche* for legislative action. All proposed legislation based upon Article 235 must show how and why the proposed action is necessary to attain one of the objectives of the Common Market. This may permit the Community to initiate action in important areas not envisaged by the original Treaty drafters - such as environmental policy, energy policy or even, arguably, fisheries policy - but it has meant that the Council has sometimes been forced to base quite laudable legislative measures upon somewhat spurious grounds. A notable example is the attribution of economic significance to the conservation of migrating birds, in Directive 79/409.[36] Indeed, the difficulties of establishing a legal basis for legislative programmes in new areas was recognised by the drafters of the proposed European Union Treaty (EUT) as one of the major reforms needed within the Communities.[37] The Single European Act goes some way to meeting the proposals of the EUT by including several new areas of Community activity within the Treaty. Legal bases are established for Community action in the fields of *inter alia*, research and technological development and the environment. This means that rather less reliance will need to be placed on either straining the meaning of Articles 100 and 235 or hoping for developments within the context of political cooperation.

Paradoxically, the existence of the residual legislative powers of Article 235 - and the possibility of amendment of the Treaty itself under Article 236 - have possibly inhibited the development in Community law of the doctrine of *implied powers*. In international institutional law and the law of federal constitutions the doctrine of implied powers - whereby powers deemed necessary to achieve the objectives of the constitutional document but not specifically conferred are deemed to have been given - has been an important dynamic, often ensuring that the purpose of a constitutional provision is not frustrated by technicalities. Despite the generally expansive interpretation of the Treaty by the ECJ it is only in one field - that of external relations - that the doctrine of implied powers *per se* has been employed extensively. Relatively early in its case law the ECJ ruled that the initiation of a common Community legislative programme in a specific area, e.g. regulation of transport or fisheries, carried with it an implied exclusive common external competence.[38]

## THE EUROPEAN PARLIAMENT

Since 1962 the Assembly, as it is called in the EEC Treaty,[39] has called itself the European Parliament (EP). This term, which is now given official recognition by the Single European Act, will be used in this book, although it is important to realise at the outset that the EP is not a parliament in the sense that Westminster is a parliament. It does not pass legislation, nor is the executive chosen from its members. As we have seen, the legislative and executive functions are performed by the Council and the Commission. The Treaty only gives it restricted 'advisory and supervisory powers'. The French text uses the expressions *'pouvoirs de deliberation'* and *'pouvoirs de contrôle'*, this term *'contrôle'* is stronger than the English 'supervisory' and is probably now a more accurate description; it will be used here in conjunction with the English word. Built into the Treaties are specific powers which indicate that the drafters intended the EP to provide an important element of democratic accountability within the legislative and executive system. These elements have been strengthened by a number of Treaty amendments granting the EP increased budgetary powers, and the democratic element has been substantially increased by the holding of direct elections in 1979 and 1984. The EP is now in its second term as a directly-elected institution and with a democratic mandate behind it. Members of the European Parliament (MEPs) are increasingly assertive in their demands for increased influence over, and indeed share in, the legislative and executive processes of the Community. It is against this background that the powers set out below should be viewed.

## Composition

Since 1958 the EP has progressively increased in size. The original Assembly consisted of 142 delegates chosen from the six national parliaments. This was increased to 198 at the first accession in 1973. The introduction of direct elections in June 1979 raised the size of the EP to 410 and this number was itself increased to 434 by the accession of Greece in 1981 and to 518 by the accession of Spain and Portugal in 1986. The allocation of MEPs is as follows:

| | | | | | |
|---|---|---|---|---|---|
| Belgium | 24 | Greece | 24 | Luxembourg | 6 |
| Denmark | 16 | Spain | 60 | Netherlands | 25 |
| France | 81 | Ireland | 15 | Portugal | 24 |
| Germany | 81 | Italy | 81 | United Kingdom | 81 |

Article 138(3) EEC envisages that direct elections will be held according to a 'common code', i.e. by the same procedure in each state. However, successive British governments have been opposed to any form of proportional representation, and largely for this reason agreement on the uniform electoral code has not been forthcoming. The 1976 Council of Ministers Direct Elections 'Act' represents a compromise: pending the conclusion and entry into force of a common code, MEPs will be elected by existing national procedures, i.e. 'first past the post' in Britain, and differing systems of proportional representation elsewhere, including Northern

Ireland.

MEPs are elected for a five-year term.[40] They may simultaneously be members of national parliaments - the so-called 'dual mandate' - but they may not be members of national governments nor hold office in any EC institution, related body or committee.[41]

## Organisation

The EP is primarily organised upon political lines with MEPs being organised into nine transnational groups. This practice is encouraged by the rules of procedure, which give special privileges and rights to official groups. To form a group the rules require 21 MEPs from one member state, or 15 from two, or eleven from three or more.[42] The party groups are: the Socialist Group, the European People's Party (EPP), the European Democratic Group, the Communists and Allies, the Liberal and Democratic Group and the European Democratic Alliance, the Rainbow Group and the European Right Group. Seven MEPs are unattached.

Party affiliations are particularly important in the election of the formal officers of the EP, who are elected by the MEPs themselves. The President - elected for a 2-year term - has a role rather like that of the Speaker of the House of Commons, and once elected is required to act for the EP with complete impartiality.[43] It is the President who takes the chair at plenary sessions. In addition twelve Vice-Presidents are elected, who with the President make up the Bureau - the body responsible for organising the business of the EP. In fact the Bureau usually meets in an enlarged form with the leaders of the political groups present and this is the body which is responsible for determining the membership of the various committees and for appointing chairmen and women and support staff. The EP also elect a College of at least three, but in practice they elect five Quaestors whose task is to look after MEPs' working conditions.

The main work of the EP is done in the 18 standing committees. In 1986 these met a total of 407 times to prepare for plenary debates.[44] Rather like the House of Commons committee structure which shadows the various national ministries, the EP committees mirror the responsibilities of the Commission as reflected in its various Directorates-General. In 1984 these committees were: Political Affairs (45 members); Agriculture, Fisheries and Food

(45); Budgets (42); Economic and Monetary Affairs and Industrial Policy (42); Energy, Research and Technology (30); External Economic Relations (25); Legal Affairs and Employment (30); Regional Policy and Regional Planning (28); Transport (30); Environment, Public Health and Consumer Protection (31); Youth, Culture, Education, Information and Sport (24); Development and Cooperation (42); Budgetary Control (30); Rules of Procedure and Petitions (25); Institutional Affairs (30); Women's Rights (25); Verification of Credentials (9).[45]

## The Seat of the EP

Article 216 empowers the governments of the Member States to fix the seat of the institutions of the Community by common accord. Unfortunately, the Member Governments have never definitively resolved where the seat or seats of the institutions will be. When the EEC Treaty came into force the Council decided that, in the absence of a definitive or provisional seat being fixed, the Commission should meet in Brussels and Luxembourg, the Council wherever the President may appoint, and the Assembly in Strasbourg. The Secretariat of the ECSC Assembly had already been established in Luxembourg where the ECSC High Authority and the ECJ had met and thus the division of places of work which is such a distinctive feature of the current EP began. The Secretariat was based in Luxembourg, the plenary sessions were held in Strasbourg and with the establishment of the Commission offices in Brussels, the EP committees began to be held in Brussels. After the holding of an emergency plenary session in Luxembourg in 1967 the practice arose of holding short plenary sessions (or part-sessions) in Luxembourg. In April 1965, after the signing of the Merger Treaty, the Member States did decide that 'Luxembourg, Brussels and Strasbourg shall remain the provisional places of work of the Communities' and that 'the General Secretariat of the Assembly and its departments shall remain in Luxembourg'.[46]

After the signing of the Direct Elections Act in 1976, the EP expressed concern about the need for a hemisphere building to house the plenary sessions of the enlarged EP, and the result was the erection of two buildings, one ostensibly to house the Council of Europe Assembly - the *Palais de l'Europe* in Strasbourg and the other in Luxembourg - both put up like 'cargo cult' attractions with a view to the final fixing of the permanent site for the EP.

Once the directly elected and much enlarged EP was returned, it began immediately to demand an improvement in its working conditions and in November 1980 asked the member governments to reach a final determination on the seat of the EP 'by 15 June 1981 at the latest', declaring that if a decision had not been taken by that date 'it would have no option but to take the necessary steps to improve its working conditions'. However, the European Council meeting in Maastricht in March 1981 decided unanimously to confirm the *status quo* with regard to the provisional places of work. On 15 June 1981 the EP therefore passed a resolution in which it asserted its right to 'meet and work where it chooses' and called once again upon the member governments to meet their obligation to fix a single seat for the institutions.[47]

The Luxembourg government, alarmed that its newly-built hemicycle would no longer be used even for part-sessions, and concerned that the movement of permanent staff from Luxembourg to Brussels envisaged in Article 3(c) presaged the ultimate movement of all EP staff to Brussels, brought an action in the ECJ challenging the right of the EP to make such a determination. The action was brought under Article 38ECSC because the EEC and EURATOM Treaties do not give a clear right of review of EP acts. In its judgment in February 1983[48] the ECJ held that the EP had not acted illegally. It confirmed the right of the member governments to fix the seat of the EP. It observed that the holding of plenary half-sessions in Luxembourg had not received the approval of the member governments and was done in the face of protest from the French government, hence a decision to hold all future plenary sessions in Strasbourg was not contrary to the member governments' views. It also confirmed the right of the EP to move a small proportion of its staff (some 300 of its 3,000 in 1982) in order to provide support for meetings held quite legitimately in Brussels.

The judgment does perhaps provide some comfort to Luxembourg in that the ECJ did emphasise that the 1965 provisional decision required the EP Bureau and its departments to remain in Luxembourg, but it provides little comfort to the MEPs and their staff condemned to a nomadic existence between three sites. Its plight has been compared to dividing the UK Parliament's work between London, Edinburgh and Cardiff. It is extremely expensive, time-consuming and wasteful. In staff terms the time taken packing and unpacking documents and travelling occupies some 244,700 hours annually, which, when added to the time spent on organisation, results in some 154 'man years' annually. When extra telex, telephone and postage costs as well as duplication of facilities are also taken into account the total cost was set in 1982 at 4.5 million units of account per annum.[49]

## Advisory Powers

The advisory powers which the EP possesses are both formal - conferred by the Treaty itself - and informal - those that have arisen by practice in response to MEPs demands.

*Consultation on draft legislation.*

Seventeen articles of the EEC Treaty require that the EP be consulted on draft legislation prepared by the Commission before the draft is considered for adoption by the Council.[50] In fact, the overwhelming majority of all Commission proposals, whether based upon a Treaty article which requires consultation or not, are submitted by the Commission to the EP for its opinion.

Once the draft is received by the EP it is passed to one of the 15 specialist committees which will analyse it in detail (in discussion with the relevant Commissioner if necessary) and then report to the EP plenary. In its report the committee will indicate whether it feels the EP should support, oppose or suggest amendments to the Commission's draft. The plenary session will then consider its Committee's report. It has the option of accepting, rejecting or amending the proposal, or even of referring it back to the Committee for further consideration. If, however, the plenary does pass a resolution, this will be conveyed to the Council as the EP's opinion. This procedure permits the EP to examine proposals and to express its opinion on their acceptability in political terms.

Following the amendment of the EEC Treaty by the Single European Act (SEA) 1986, the consultative role of the EP in the formulation of certain legislation has been strengthened. Article 6 of the SEA introduces for the first time a cooperation procedure between the Council and the EP in respect of the adoption of acts based on certain of the EEC Treaty's articles.[51] Article 7 of the SEA, which amends Article 149(2) EEC, establishes a fairly complex system of consultations and references between the Community institutions.

Under Article 149(2) where the Council acts 'in cooperation' with the EP, it is required to adopt a common position on the basis of a qualified majority. This common position is then transmitted to the EP together with a full statement of the reasons which led to its adoption by the Council. The Commission's position is also communicated to the EP. If within three months the EP approves the common position or fails to act upon it, then the act in question is definitively adopted by the Council. Within the three-month period, however, the EP may by an absolute majority of MEPs (i.e. 51% of those entitled to vote) propose amendments to the Council's common position or reject it altogether. The three-month decision period may be extended by a further month by common agreement between the Council and the EP. If the common position is rejected by the EP, then unanimity is required from the Council to allow it to act on a second reading of the proposed act. After rejection of the common position by the EP, the Commission must, within one month, re-examine the proposal on which the Council adopted its common position, taking into account the EP's proposals. The Commission then forwards to the Council its re-examined proposal and any EP amendments which it has not accepted. The Council may, nevertheless, adopt these amendments unanimously if it thinks fit. If the Council wishes to adopt the Commission's re-examined proposal it may do so on the basis of a qualified majority, but if it wants to amend the re-examined proposal, unanimity is required.

On the basis of this new legislative procedure, the EP's formal powers are considerably enhanced; it has a much more active and potentially constructive role to play in the Community's legislative activities. Although the Council still remains firmly in control of the legislative process, its susceptibility to direct democratic influence from the EP through the cooperation procedure is much greater.

The EP's powers in the legislative process have also been enhanced by the rulings of the ECJ in the *Isoglucose* cases.[52] Here the ECJ held that where a Treaty article requires the opinion of the EP, a legal act is not validly adopted in the absence of such an opinion. This does not give the EP a power of veto on legislation, but, insofar as it prevents the Council from approving legislation while the EP is actively considering a proposal, it gives the EP a *de facto* delaying power. The EP has capitalised upon this by amending its rules of procedure to permit continued reference between committee and plenary session in cases where there are reservations about a draft proposal. In many cases even a short delay may render draft legislation obsolete hence the EP has considerably improved its bargaining position with the Commission, for if the latter does amend its proposals in the light of the EP's view, then this will speed the passage of the draft through to the Council.

These developments indicate the way the relatively meagre formal powers of the EP can be exploited by the use of political pressures. Three other developments also indicate the way that the EP has been able to increase its general input into Community decision-making.

*Conciliation procedure*

In response to the increase in budgetary powers of the EP, the Council and the EP have jointly established a conciliation procedure to deal with disagreements they may have over 'acts having substantial financial implications'. Although this has not been a great success, as the discussion below will indicate, nevertheless, it does provide the EP with a forum for its views to be put forcibly to the Council.

*Endorsement of the incoming Commission and its programme*

In January 1985 for the first time the President of the newly appointed Commission appeared before the EP, outlined the problems it faced and its priorities and sought a vote of confidence.[53] Although there was some misunderstanding among MEPs as to the significance of this request, which is not required by the Treaty, this voluntary acceptance by the Commission of the principle of its accountability to the EP, must surely increase the EP's credibility.

*'Luns-Westerterp' Procedure.*

In the field of external relations the drafting of the Treaty itself has given rise to confusion as to the role of the EP. Article 238 requires consultation with the EP before an agreement between the Community and a third state is 'concluded' by the Council. There is some disagreement as to what the drafters meant by 'concluded'. Is a treaty 'concluded' when it comes into force (i.e. after it is ratified) or when the text is finalised (i.e. at the point that it is signed but before it is submitted to national constitutional procedures prior to ratification)? In 1962 the Council adopted the first interpretation, presenting the Greek Association Agreement to the EP immediately prior to its coming into force - at which point no changes could be made.[54] MEPs' protests that such an interpretation of Article 238 rendered the consultation provision meaningless resulted in the adoption of the 'Luns-Westerterp' procedure[55] whereby the Commission keeps an EP committee constantly informed of the progress of the negotiations. The EP is now pressing, to date unsuccessfully, for the negotiating mandate to receive its approval before the negotiations begin.

### Powers of Control or Supervision

*Dismissal of the Commission*

Article 144 obliges the Commission to resign as a body if a motion of censure is tabled in the EP and in an open vote on the motion at least three days later the motion is carried by a two-thirds majority of the votes cast. The two-thirds who vote in favour must themselves represent a majority of the MEPs (i.e. 260). This power of censure is similar to the powers of national parliaments to require the resignation of the government in office once it fails to maintain a majority, and it is clearly intended to impose upon the Commission that same element of democratic accountability. Four such motions have been tabled to date but none has been carried.[56] This may be explained by the number of limitations in the procedure itself. First, the Commission must resign *en bloc*. This reflects the collegiate nature of Commission decision-making and responsibility, but it does make the censure motion something of a 'blunt weapon'. Most national systems have a procedure whereby individual ministers may be singled out for censure or dismissal, but the same is not possible for individual Commissioners under Article 144, hence it is unlikely to be used in anything but drastic circumstances. Second, the EP has no formal power over reappointment. Its endorsement of an incoming Commission carries no legal force, thus in theory it would be open to the member governments to reappoint the censured Commission. While such an action might be unlikely, the prospect of a second Article 144 motion and the ensuing political crisis may also act as a deterrent. Third, MEPs' complaints are more often directed at the Council of Ministers as the main legislature, than against the Commission as the executive. In three of the four motions tabled to date, the object of complaint was as much the behaviour and policies of the Council as the Commission. The exception was a motion tabled in December 1976 prompted by the refusal of the Commission (which was reaching the end of its term of office) to show an internal

Commission document to the EP control sub-committee. It was heavily defeated (95 to 15), but the new Commission in 1977 did release the document subject to the complaint.[57]

Nevertheless, the censure motion procedure of Article 144 does provide the EP with an important political power, second only to its power to reject the budget, and it formally expresses a democratic notion of the public accountability of the executive, which is reinforced by some of the other powers discussed below.

*Reports to the EP*

By Article 143 the EP is obliged to discuss the annual general report of the activities of the Community submitted to it by the Commission. It may seem strange at first sight that a whole Treaty article be devoted to such an obligation, but it should perhaps be read in the light of the power of censure of the Commission contained in the Article which immediately follows (Article 144). A loose analogy could be made to the tradition of annual executive reports which are a feature of some national constitutions, e.g. the US President's 'state of the Union' speech or the German Chancellor's 'state of the Nation' report. An opportunity to review the achievements or failures of the last year could provide an important opportunity for the EP to make a political judgment upon them, but in fact, although they underline the Commission's accountability to the EP, these retrospective debates tend to be rather low key. More significant in the long term are the regular reports which the Council of Ministers and the Foreign Ministers make to the EP, which recognise its increasing political importance.

Three times a year a Council representative makes an oral report to the plenary session of the EP on the activities of the Council, and the President of the Council - who holds office for six months - makes a statement of 'the programme of the Presidency' at the beginning of each term, and a report six months later on the achievements of the term. Each year the EP meets the President of the Council, with the Commission, for a 'colloquy' to discuss issues of interest currently outstanding on the Council's agenda. Also yearly are the reports made by the Foreign Ministers of the Member States who report on activities in the sphere of political cooperation - outside the terms of the Community treaties. These reports are followed by a debate.

*Question time*

Under Article 140 both the Commission and the Council have the right to be heard in the EP, but it is only the Commission which is obliged to reply either orally or in writing to questions put by MEPs or the EP itself. This right to question members of the executive has close parallels with national parliaments and the idea of a specific time set aside for such questions is most closely associated with the British House of Commons which has had such a 'question time' since 1849. Indeed, the EP question time was only introduced as a regular feature of EP procedure in January 1973 after pressure from the Legal Affairs Committee since 1971, and British MEPs have played a leading role in its development and exploitation. Only the Commission is formally obliged to answer questions put by MEPs, but since 1958 the Council has agreed to answer questions, both orally and in writing, and since 1976 Foreign Ministers too have consented to answer questions about political cooperation.

The procedural rules regarding question time which are designed to stop MEPs using it for speech-making are complex. The answers made, particularly by the Council and the Foreign Ministers, are often evasive or nebulous. There is very little that the EP can do if the answers that it is given are unsatisfactory. Apart from censure of the Commission - a somewhat drastic response - the rules of procedure permit the holding of an immediate debate on an answer given by the Commission. In the final analysis there is no formal power of complaint against unsatisfactory answers from the Council or the Foreign Ministers. Having said that, however, the questions and their answers are printed in the Official Journal. They do provide an important source of information on Community activities and aspects of Community policy. The fact that the Council and the Foreign Ministers take part in question time must surely indicate a recognition, albeit grudging, that the EP has a legitimate right to make demands of them, and this is perhaps the beginning of accountability.

*Judicial review*

The power to challenge before the ECJ the legality of action or inaction by the other Community institutions can be an important power to a political institution like the EP which is continually pressing for increases in its powers and in the level of accountability to it. Skilfully used, it provides another weapon in the armoury of pressures which can be brought to bear upon the other institutions. However, the position of the EP under the EEC Treaty regime of judicial review is anomalous.

Article 175 confers upon the EP a general power to take legal proceedings against either the Council or the Commission for failing to act in a manner required by the Treaty. This is sometimes called the 'appeal against inaction'. Article 175(1) reads:

> Should the Council or the Commission, in infringement of this Treaty, fail to act, the Member States and the other institutions of the Community may bring an action before the Court of Justice to have the infringement established.

Before such proceedings can be brought the institution concerned must be 'called upon to act' - i.e. the complainant must first formally notify that institution of the nature of the alleged infringement of the Treaty (e.g. failure to take a decision or enact legislation required by the Treaty). Secondly, if the institution has not 'defined its position' within two months of being so called upon to act, then proceedings must be brought within a further period of two months - a fairly short time period but normal in the Treaty regime and in civil law systems generally. If the ECJ finds that an infringement of the Treaty has taken place then it has the power to order the offending institution to take 'necessary measures' to comply with this ruling.

In *EP v. Commission and Council*[58] the EP sought and was granted, for the first time, by the ECJ, *locus standi* to bring an action under Article 175 against the Council for failure to make progress in implementing the Community's Common Transport Policy. There had been considerable doubt about whether the EP was one of the other 'institutions' referred to in Article 175(1), but the ECJ observed in this case that the right to initiate proceedings could not be limited with regard to any institution since this would jeopardise its institutional position within the structure of the Treaty.

This case clarifies the importance of this procedure in permitting the EP to obtain a clear condemnation of the Council. However, the exact extent of the power in Article 175 is still unclear. The phrase 'infringement of this Treaty' clearly covers breaches of obligations contained in Treaty articles. Does it also include breaches of Community legislation, which is itself based upon provisions of the Treaty? Commentators seem agreed that the ECJ would take a liberal interpretation of these powers and be prepared to permit the use of the Article 175 procedure in such a case - for example, where a regulation required specific action to be taken by the Council or the Commission in designated circumstances.[59]

More radical still is the suggestion that 'infringement of the Treaty' should be deemed to include the general principles of Community law developed by the ECJ as principles 'relating to the application of the Treaty'. These include the concepts of lack of discrimination, proportionality, and protection of human rights. Such a view would support the suggestion that proceedings could, for example, be instituted against the Commission where its inaction endangered human rights.

As we have seen, there is little judicial authority on Article 175 and this highlights the anomalous position that the EP occupies within the general scheme of judicial review under the EEC Treaty; for the EP seems to have been deliberately excluded from the main avenue for review of the legality of Community acts - namely Article 173. Under Article 173(1) the ECJ has power to review the legality of 'acts of the Council or the Commission other than recommendations or opinions', but only in actions brought by 'a Member State, the Council or the Commission'. The EP is mentioned neither as a possible complainant nor defendant. This cannot have been an accidental omission, for there is a precedent in Article 38 of the earlier ECSC Treaty which provides for the review of the legality of acts of, *inter alia*, the Assembly on the application of the High Authority (now the Commission) on the grounds of 'lack of competence' or 'infringement of an essential procedural requirement'. The most popular explanation for this omission from the EEC Treaty is that under the original EEC regime (i.e. prior to the budgetary amendments dealt with in Chapter 5) the only specific power given to the EP was the right of dismissal of the Commission under Article 144 - an overtly political power which the drafters perhaps felt was not properly made subject to review by the ECJ. If this is the case, and it does perhaps indicate a narrow conception of the role of judicial review, the position no longer pertains. Since 1975 the EP has had a number of budgetary rights - notably the right to 'adopt' the Budget and indeed to reject it. Not surprisingly this anomalous position has received a great deal of attention in the directly elected EP. Professor Pescatore, former President of the ECJ, has argued that the ECJ already possesses a sufficiently general mandate under Article 164 (which enjoins it to 'ensure that in the interpretation and application of this Treaty the law is observed') to allow it to review the legality of the EP's acts, notwithstanding the wording of Article 173.[60] However, in the case of *Luxembourg v. EP* (1981),[61] brought under Article 38 ECSC, Luxembourg complained that the EP had no right to move part of its staff from Luxembourg to Brussels, as the right to fix the seat of the institutions was vested solely in the member governments. In dismissing this action the ECJ accepted that it would have been impossible to disentangle the work of the three Treaty regimes making up the Community, hence a decision that the complaint was admissable under the ECSC Treaty meant that the instant proceedings related 'simultaneously and indivisibly to the spheres of the three Treaties'.[62] The Court declined, however, to rule on the further question of whether the EP could be a party to proceedings under Article 173 EEC. The issue is therefore still at large.

*Budgetary powers*

It is in the sphere of the Budget that the EP has the most extensive formal powers. Because of the importance of the Budget to the whole Community decision-making process Chapter 5 is devoted entirely to the issue. However, the main powers that the EP possesses should be mentioned here. First, the EP as a member (with the Council) of the Budgetary Authority is given the final word on whether or not the Draft Budget should be approved, and in December 1980 the newly elected EP rejected the Draft Budget in total. Secondly, the EP is also given the last word - within certain limits - on the approval of all non-compulsory expenditure, i.e. areas of the Treaty where expenditure is not specifically required by the Treaty, e.g. social and regional policy.

Once the Budget has been adopted and the money spent, the Commission is required to render its account to the Budgetary Authority. It is then investigated by the Court of Auditors. In the light of the Court of Auditors' report the EP, on the recommendation of the Council, then decides whether or not to grant a 'discharge' to the Commission for its implementation of the Budget. The treaty provides no specific sanction for failure to grant discharge, but in 1979 Christopher Tugendhat, then Commissioner for Budgets, did suggest that the Commission would regard such a vote as a vote of no confidence and feel itself obliged to resign. Nevertheless, the Commission did not feel obliged to resign in 1984 when the EP refused to grant it a discharge in relation to the 1982 Budget.[63]

## THE ECONOMIC AND SOCIAL COMMITTEE

The Economic and Social Committee (ESC) is a purely advisory body. Its members are appointed by unanimous vote of the Council of Ministers for four-year renewable terms from a list of candidates produced by the Member States. Each Member State is required to produce a list containing twice as many candidates as that State is allocated. The candidates, like the composition of the ESC itself, must include representatives of 'the various areas of economic and social activity' and the Treaty singles out representatives of 'producers, farmers, carriers, workers, dealers, craftsmen, professional occupations and members of the general public'.[64] In making its selection from these national lists the Council must consult the Commission and may also ensure that the composition of the ESC adequately represents the 'various categories of economic and social activity'. Once chosen the members may form themselves into groups which represent these 'categories' - and in effect this means employers, workers and 'others'.

The ESC has a current membership of 188 with members allocated as follows:

| | | | | | |
|---|---|---|---|---|---|
| Belgium | 12 | France | 24 | Netherlands | 12 |
| Denmark | 9 | Ireland | 9 | Portugal | 12 |
| Germany | 24 | Italy | 24 | Spain | 21 |
| Greece | 12 | Luxembourg | 6 | United Kingdom | 24 |

Unlike the EP, the ESC is not autonomous. Its rules of procedure must be approved by the unanimous vote of the Council and sessions of the ESC may only be called at the request of the Council or the Commission. The Members do, however, elect their own chairman for a two-year term. The ESC is obliged to constitute sections with special responsibilities for specific areas, notably agriculture and transport, and sub-committees to prepare opinions on specific issues or in specific fields. Neither may be approached directly for their opinion, but the opinions of the specialised sections may be submitted together with the opinion of the full Committee.

The Treaty specifically requires consultation with the ESC in a number of instances. In the light of the *Isoglucose*[65] judgments it may be presumed that failure to comply with this 'essential procedural requirement' would result in an act subsequently adopted being liable to annulment. It is also open to either the Council or the Commission to consult the ESC on such other matters as they see fit, and since 1974 the ESC has also had the power to prepare and give opinions on its own initiative, a right that it has used quite extensively. It is difficult to assess the importance of the ESC in EC decision-making. In its Annual Report the ESC published the number of times its opinions have been taken into account 'in some respects', 'to a large extent' and 'ignored'.[66] These figures seem to suggest that the ESC, although not a powerful institution (indeed it has no formal powers at all under the Treaty), does provide a useful forum for discussion and its views appear to be given some, albeit limited, credence by the Commission and the Council.

## THE COMMITTEE OF PERMANENT REPRESENTATIVES (COREPER)

Article 4 of the 1965 Merger Treaty authorises a committee consisting of permanent representatives of the Member States to be responsible for 'preparing the work of the Council and for carrying out the tasks assigned to it', although such a body had been in *de facto* existence previously.

It is a body composed of career diplomats, whose primary responsibility is to sieve through the agenda of the Council and separate those items on which political agreement is likely to be difficult from non-contentious business. The committee members are employees of the Member States and the composition, presidency and voting patterns of COREPER mirror those of the Council itself. Composed as it is of national civil servants, COREPER has no independent right of decision and its place in EC decision-making is discussed more fully in Chapter 4.

## COURT OF AUDITORS

The Court of Auditors was established by the 1975 Budgetary Powers Treaty. It has twelve members appointed by common accord of the Governments of the Member States after consulting the EP. Members are elected for six-year renewable terms and those eligible for election must have 'belonged to external audit bodies' or must be 'especially qualified for this office'. Once appointed its members are entitled to the same privileges and immunities as Members of the ECJ.

The primary tasks of the Court of Auditors are to conduct an annual audit of the accounts and records of the Community institutions and of any other body created by the EC and to assist the Budgetary Authority (the EP and the Council) in exercising their control over the implementation of the EC Budget. Its task is to ensure not only that expenditure has been legal, but also that it is based upon sound principles. For example, in the 1979 report the Court was critical of a number of issues resulting from the lack of a permanent single site for the EC institutions, notably the cost of diverse meeting places, unfavourable rentals and so on. In conducting its general audit the Court of Auditors has power to conduct on-the-spot investigations within the Community institutions, and also, in liaison with national bodies within Member States. The Court of Auditors may also submit observations on specific questions and has the power to deliver opinions in response to requests from any of the institutions.

## NOTES

1. Merger Treaty, Article 10(1).
2. *Ibid.*
3. Merger Treaty, Article 10(2).
4. *Ibid.*
5. *Ibid.*
6. *Ibid.*
7. Merger Treaty, Article 11.
8. Merger Treaty, Article 14.
9. Leo Tindemans, *European Union: Report to the European Council* (Brussels, December 1975), Bulletin EC, Supplement 1/1975.
10. S Henig, 'The European Community's Bicephalous Political Authority', in J. Lodge (ed.), *Institutions and Policies of the European Community* (Frances Pinter, London, 1983), pp.10-20.
11. See V. Herman and J. Lodge, *The European Parliament and the European Community* (Macmillan, London, 1978), pp.48-56.
12. D. Spierenburg, *Proposals for Reform of the Commission of the European Communities and its Services* (The Commission, Brussels, 1979).
13. See Henig, 'Bicephalous Political Authority', p.10.
14. See Case 40/82 *Commission v. UK* [1982] E.C.R. 2793.
15. J.O. 1962, 204.
16. On Article 177 references see pp.152-61 below.
17. Case 141/78 [1979] E.C.R. 2923; [1980] 1 C.M.L.R. 6.
18. Case 61/81 [1982] E.C.R. 2601.
19. Case 232/78 *Commission v. France* [1979] E.C.R. 2729.
20. See *Eighteenth General Report on the Activities of the European Communities 1984* (Office for Official Publications of the EC,

Luxembourg, 1985), p.59. (Hereafter cited as *Eighteenth General Report*.)

21. Article 235 provides:

If action by the Community should prove necessary to attain, in the course of the operation of the common market, one of the objectives of the Committee and this Treaty has not provided the necessary powers, the Council shall, acting unanimously on a proposal from the Commission and after consulting the assembly, take the appropriate measures.

22. *Twentieth General Report on the Activities of the European Communities 1986* (Office for Official Publications of the EC, Luxembourg, 1987), p.40. (Hereafter cited as *Twentieth General Report*.)

23. *Ibid*.

24. Cases 188-190/80 [1982] E.C.R. 2545.

25. See further *Parry and Hardy: EEC Law*, 2nd edn. by A. Parry and J. Dinnage (Sweet and Maxwell, London, 1981), pp.15-17.

26. Merger Treaty 1965, Article 2.

27. *Ibid*.

28. G. Vedel, *The Enlargement of the Powers of the European Parliament* (1972), Bulletin EC, Supplement, 4/72.

29. *Loc. cit*., above, note 9.

30. Committee of Three (B. Bishevvel, E. Dell, R. Marjolin), *Report on European Institutions* (1979).

31. On the Genscher-Colombo proposals see J. H. H. Weller, 'The Genscher-Colombo Draft European Act: The Politics of Indecision', *Journal of European Integration*, vol.6 (1983), pp.129-53.

32. On the 1975 UK referendum see R. E. M. Irving, 'The United Kingdom Referendum' (1975) 1 *E.L.Rev*., 1.

33. See *Europe*, no.3049, 5/6 January 1986 and no.3059, 19/20 January 1986.

34. *Europe*, no.3049, 5/6 January 1986.

35. *Ibid*.

36. O.J. 1979, L 103/1. See A. J. Easson, 'EEC Directives for Harmonization of Laws' (1981) 1 *Y.E.L.* p.1.

37. On the EUT and its proposed changes see D. Freestone and S. Davidson, 'The EUT: Legal Problems' in J. Lodge (ed.), *European Union: The European Community in Search of a Future* (Macmillan, London, 1985), p.125.

38. See Case 22/70 *Commission v. Council* (ERTA Case) [1971] E.C.R. 263; [1971] C.M.L.R. 335.

39. Articles 4 and 137 EEC. It is noteworthy that the Single European Act refers to the Assembly as the European Parliament throughout.

40. Council Decision and Act on Direct Elections, Article 1.

41. *Ibid*., Article 4(1).

42. Rules of Procedure of the EP, Rule 36.

43. *Ibid*., Rule 5. The current President of the EP is a Briton, Sir Henry Plumb. He is a member of the European Democratic Group and he will hold office until June 1989 when the next direct elections are due to be held.

44. *Twentieth General Report*, p.39.

45. *Eighteenth General Report*, p.29.

46. J.O. 1967 152/18, Article 4.

47. See Case 230/81 *Luxembourg v. European Parliament* [1983] E.C.R. 255 at 262.

48. *Ibid.*

49. See the *Zagari Report*, European Parliament Working Documents 1981-1982, Document 1-333/81.

50. Articles 7, 14, 43, 54, 56, 57, 63, 75, 87, 100, 126, 127, 201, 228, 235, 236, 238.

51. The cooperation procedure applies to acts based on Articles 7, 49, 54(2), 56(2) second sentence, 57, except the second sentence of paragraph 2 thereof, 100 A, 100 B, 118 A, 130 E and 130 Q (2) of the EEC Treaty. Single European Act, Article 6(1).

52. Case 138/79 *SA Roquette Freres v. Council* [1980] E.C.R. 3333; Case 139/79 *Maizena v. Council* [1980] E.C.R. 3393.

53. See Bulletin EC 1-1985, p.7.

54. See P. M. Leopold, 'External Relations Power of the EEC in Theory and in Practice' (1977) 26 *I.C.L.Q.* 54, and K. R. Simmonds, 'The Evolution of the External Relations Law of the European Economic Community' (1979) 28 *I.C.L.Q.* p.644.

55. See Hartley, *Foundations*, p.150.

56. See above, note 13.

57. See Bulletin EC 12-1976, p.81.

58. Case 13/83 [1986] 1 C.M.L.R. 138.

59. See Hartley, *Foundations*, p.394 and the literature cited there, especially H. G. Schermers, *Judicial Protection in the European Communities*, 2nd edn. (Kluwer, Deventer, 1979), para. 251.

60. P. Pescatore, 'Reconnaissance et contrôle judiciaire des actes du Parlement européen' [1978], *Revue Trimestrielle du Droit Européen*, p.581.

61. Case 230/81 [1983] E.C.R. 255.

62. *Ibid.* p.282.

63. See Bulletin EC 11-1984, pp.71-73.

64. Article 193 EEC.

65. *Loc. cit.*, above, note 52.

66. See e.g. *ESC Annual Report 1985*.

# 4

# Community Decision-making

The last chapter dealt with the organisation and powers of the Community institutions. In two major spheres of Community activity the inter-relationships of these institutions can be seen most clearly: the Community legislative process, and the Community Budget. In the first process the principal actors are the Commission, as initiator of policy, and the Council, as the decision-making body. In the second the Council and the EP make up the Budgetary Authority. The reality, however, is not so clear cut. Since direct elections were held in 1979, the EP has been anxious to increase its influence in the legislative process. It has discovered afresh that, although it has constitutional powers over the Commission, it has no formal control over the Council, which at present dominates the whole process. It is therefore intent upon devising methods of exercising indirect influence, primarily through the Commission, on the Council. The introduction of the cooperation procedure by the Single European Act into the legislative procedure will, as indicated in Chapter 3, enhance the degree of influence which the EP may exercise over the Council, but it is not yet clear how potent this influence will be. National parliaments, too, have an interest in the decisions reached by the Council. National MPs are often uneasy at the legislative power which the Treaty of Rome has conferred on the Council, and fully appreciate the limited control which they can exercise over their respective ministers meeting in secret session in the Council. Yet Council meetings commonly result in the passing of regulations, directly applicable in national law, or directives that will require implementation by the national legislature.

Similarly, the budgetary process is complicated by important power struggles between the institutions. The Brussels Budgetary

Treaty of 1975 gives the EP the right to reject the Budget *in toto*. This is a major constitutional power, but not one of much subtlety if there is no corresponding power to influence the major contents of the Budget. MEPs are therefore seeking to use the EP's budgetary power to increase their general influence over the content of Community decisions, both budgetary and otherwise. This has been done, for example, by using the prospect of total rejection as a sanction if the Council fails to meet the EP's demands over the content of the Budget, as in the rejection of the 1980 draft Budget in 1979, or by concentrating on one major area of expenditure. Caught between the Council and the EP is the Commission, and the inter-institutional pressures throw interesting light on the present role of the Commission. The budgetary process will, however, be dealt with in the next chapter.

The purpose of the present chapter is to explain briefly the Community legislative process from the initiation of policy to the passing of legally binding acts. After looking at the role of the Commission as initiator of legislation, and discussing the possible future role of the European Parliament, there is an examination of the consultation requirements of the Treaty. This is followed by an examination of the Council's decision-making procedures, an assessment of the role of national parliaments (particularly the Westminster Parliament) in the process and a discussion of the underestimated legislative role of the Commission.

## THE INITIATION OF POLICY

The Treaty of Rome places the role of initiation of policy on the shoulders of the Commission. By Article 155 the Commission is required to 'formulate recommendations or deliver opinions on matters dealt with in this Treaty, if it expressly so provides or if the Commission considers it necessary', while it is the Council of Ministers which is given the major role of enacting legislation. The clear intent of the Treaty drafters was that the tension between the Commission, with its primary concern for Community interests, and the Council, with its concern for national interests, would result in a continued pressure for further investigation. In the words of Spinelli and Ippolito in the first *Crocodile* newsletter '... Jean Monet had ingeniously thought that the Ministers would debate projects in which the European factor should have priority because they had been prepared by the Commission and judged by the

European Parliament'.[1]

The first programme of legislative action for the Commission was written into the Treaty itself. In the major policy areas specific targets were laid down to be reached by the end of one or other of the three four-year stages of the transitional period: 1962, 1966 and 1970 (although customs duties were abolished by 1968 under the acceleration decisions of 1966). So, for example, Article 48 provides that 'Free movement of workers shall be secured within the Community by the end of the transitional period at the latest', and work on this objective is directed to begin 'As soon as this Treaty enters into force' (Article 49). Similar detailed instructions are to be found in other areas. The intention was that if the programme set by the Treaty was followed the integration process would proceed at such a pace in the first twelve years that it would have generated its own momentum by the time the detailed instructions of the Treaty had been met. This is the essence of the functionalist approach underlying the Treaty regime.

In fact, the initial momentum did result in some of the targets of the transitional period, like the abolition of customs duties being met 18 months early, but that momentum has now dissipated. The Council of Ministers, and hence the individual interests of the Member States, has now assumed such a dominant role in the Community legislative process that the Commission has not been able to counter-balance its influence in the way the Treaty drafters had intended. In general terms there are three loosely related reasons for this. The first is that, with the end of the transitional period, the specific Treaty obligations agreed to by the original Member States came to an end; the Commission has therefore had to devise a legislative programme acceptable to the Council. Second, this period has coincided with the accessions in 1973, 1980 and 1986 of six new Member States. In addition to problems caused by the transitional arrangements, there is in most of the new states significant and vocal opposition to the idea of further integration, on which the Treaty is based. Third, the successive enlargements of the Communities also coincided with a period of western economic decline and recession, which has made the economic objectives of the Treaty of Rome ring hollow. Article 2 proclaims that the economic task of the Community is 'to promote throughout the Community a harmonious development of economic activities, a continuous and balanced expansion, an increase in stability' and 'an accelerated raising of the standard of living'.

For these reasons, amongst others, the Council has been

unwilling to accept proposals leading to major steps in political, legal or economic integration. The Commission has felt itself obliged to play down its policy-making role and to project itself with a more bureaucratic or technocratic image, concentrating in the early 1970s on technical - although not entirely uncontroversial - matters such as the harmonisation of national law. The Presidents of the last three Commissions have attempted to reverse this trend. Roy Jenkins was, on his appointment as President in 1978, one of the most experienced national politicians to have held the post - having been British Home Secretary and Chancellor of the Exchequer. He immediately committed himself and his Commission to a programme of European social policy under the slogan 'Europe with a human face'. His successor, Gaston Thorn - a former President of the Council of Ministers as well as an MEP - adopted on his appointment in 1980 an even more specific approach. He drew up the so-called '30th May Mandate' setting out the programme of action of his Commission, which he then submitted to both the Council and the European Parliament for approval. This idea of an initial policy statement was also followed by Jacques Delors in 1982. Both these moves were prompted by the same intention: to re-introduce clear objectives into the legislative programmes which the Treaty obliges the Commission to initiate.

## THE INITIATION OF PROPOSALS

The Commission, as a collegiate body, is responsible *en bloc* for the initiation of policy; the actual process of devising and crystallising proposals is the work of the Departments within the Commission. Once a policy proposal has been formulated in outline within a Department, it will be the subject of informal consultation with governments, national experts and relevant pressure groups. After this informal consultation, a draft proposal in general terms will be submitted by the relevant Directorate-General for the approval of the Commission. If the Commission itself is agreeable in principle to the proposal then a working conference will often be held to consider the problems likely to arise from the detailed implementation of the policy. Member governments are invited to send representatives for discussions held under the chairmanship of Commission staff. The object of this procedure is solely consultative, and the proposal may well be dropped at this stage if it encounters a great number of obstacles or unexpected opposition.

Thus participants in this process are most commonly state employees, expert in the relevant field, although there are discrepancies in national practice. In France, for example, where university teachers and research workers are state employees, senior academics commonly contribute to these discussions. In the UK, it is a task which is sometimes allocated to junior career civil servants, often, it is alleged, embarrassingly ill-briefed.

It is, however, from the deliberations of the working conference that the Commission's detailed proposals emerge. Because of the collegiate nature of Commission decisions, all drafts must be formally submitted for the consideration of the Commission as a whole. This is usually done by means of the written procedure, by which documents are circulated to all the Commission members and deemed to be formally adopted unless objections are received within a specified time. Controversial proposals will be considered at a full meeting.

Such a procedure is inevitable if one considers the scale of work involved. In 1986, with a staff of under 10,000 (including some 1,400 in the language service), the Commission submitted to the Council 739 proposals, recommendations or drafts for Council acts and 214 other communications and reports.[2] It also drafted and adopted itself 12,081 instruments (which will be discussed in more detail below).

## A RIGHT OF LEGISLATIVE INITIATIVE FOR THE EUROPEAN PARLIAMENT?

The importance which the Treaty authors attributed to the Commission's role as legislative initiator can be deduced from the voting structures of the Council. Under Article 148, where the Council is acting by qualified majority (see above Chapter 3) on a proposal from the Commission, 54 votes are required to secure adoption of the proposal, whereas on any other proposal there is a more stringent requirement (54 votes including the votes of eight Member States). Similarly, where the Council wishes to amend a Commission proposal then it requires a unanimous vote (Article 149(1)). This bias in favour of Commission proposals does not, however, prevent the Commission itself withdrawing or amending a proposal. Before it was amended by the Single European Act 2, Article 149 permitted this 'in particular where the Assembly has been consulted on that proposal'.

This latter provision had been read by MEPs as an indication that the Treaty imposed on the Commission a responsibility to take into account the EP's opinions, and to amend its proposals accordingly. This interpretation was not based solely on the wording of the original Article 149(2), which was, after all, not phrased in obligatory terms (it permitted change, it did not require it) but also on the general way in which the Treaty makes the Commission politically accountable to the EP. It will be remembered that it is the EP which has the sole right to censure - and hence require the resignation of - the Commission (Article 144). The Commission must also answer the written and oral questions of the EP (Article 140) which has the right to discuss, and thus assess, the Annual General Report (Article 142). It is the EP too which has been given, with the Council, the right to grant a discharge to the Commission for its implementation of the Budget (Article 206(b)). This will be discussed below (Chapter 5), but in 1977 Commissioner of Budgets Tugendhat was of the view that a Commission censured by a failure to discharge the Budget would be forced to resign.

In the light of these Treaty provisions, it is perhaps inevitable that the directly elected EP should wish to take advantage of what appears to be Commission accountability to it. At a time when MEPs are sensitive to the accusation that they possess no formal power to influence the content of Community legislation, they have become jealous of the Commission's right of legislative initiative. It is, however, worth reflecting that although legislative power is usually seen as the prime attribute of a parliament, political scientists have for some time made the point that the role of individual MPs in initiating legislation in national parliaments is extremely restricted - squeezed out by increased pressure from government legislative programmes. In Westminster, where a ballot is held each session for the right to present private members' bills, very few have much chance of becoming law (e.g. seven out of 20 in 1976-7) and Government 'advice against' the bill is usually enough to guarantee its failure.[3] In other words, the right of legislative initiative of MPs - as opposed to Government (the executive) - is very limited. Nevertheless, MEPs do seek a role in policy initiation and in 1981 on a proposal from their Political Affairs Committee (the Van Miert Report)[4] passed a resolution on 'the right of legislative initiative and on the role of the European Parliament in the legislative process of the Community'. This resolution has no legal force, but is of considerable interest in so far as it demonstrates the particular nature of the relationship between the EP and the Commission, and the methods by which the EP is seeking to exploit its powers to the full. The Van Miert resolution called upon the Commission to agree to a *Joint Declaration* under which the Commission would undertake to submit to the Council any reports adopted by the EP which were intended to be the basis for Community legislation (these are what the EP calls its 'own initiative' reports, see above). Should the Commission fail to submit such a proposal to the Council, then the Commission should undertake to appear before the EP to explain why, and 'where Parliament decide nonetheless to call upon the Commission to submit the legislative proposals to the Council, *the Commission should undertake to comply with such a decision without delay*' (emphasis added). The latter phrase reveals that the purpose of such a declaration would be to wrest from the Commission the exclusive right of legislative initiative in as much as it would require the Commission to be answerable to the EP for submitting Parliament's legislative proposals to the Council. The only sanction against the Commission for non-compliance with the terms of such a declaration would be, it should be stressed, the political one of censure and hence dismissal (under Article 144). Obviously MEPs would have to feel very strongly about the issue to take such a step, but they do feel very strongly about their absence from the legislative table.

Legally it can be argued that such a joint declaration would upset the balance of the legislative process and hence the balance of the Treaty. The ECJ has ruled on a number of occasions that procedures which distort the structures of the Treaty are contrary to Community law.[5] In response, however, it can be pointed out that the current dominance of the legislative process by the Council does itself create a similar imbalance which the EP might legitimately seek to redress. Nevertheless, it seems unlikely that a Commission would voluntarily agree to fetter its exclusive right of legislative initiative by participating in such a joint declaration.

## CONSULTATION

Once the draft proposal has been submitted to the Council, the Treaty specifically provides for consultation with either the EP or the Economic and Social Committee, or on occasions both. There are, however, important differences between the consultation procedures with the two institutions. Article 198 empowers the

Council to consult the ESC in 'all cases where they consider it appropriate'. There is no similar provision in relation to the EP, although the opinion of the EP has in the past been sought in circumstances where the Treaty does not expressly require it. For example, Directive 64/221 and Regulation 1612/68 passed under Article 49 to facilitate the free movement of workers. Article 198 allows the Council to require that the ESC give its opinion within a time-limit of not less than ten days from notification. There is no similar provision in relation to the EP, presumably as a recognition of the more overtly political nature of such consultation.

The endemic problem of all provisions requiring consultation is that they can become a pure formality, with the consulter going through the formal motions of consultation yet, in fact, paying no heed to the opinion expressed by the consulted. Consultation of the EP by the Council is no exception. Provided that the formal consultation procedure has taken place, there is nothing further the EP can do to press the Council itself to accommodate its views.

Should there be a defect, however, in the formal procedure of consultation then different issues are raised. Such a defect in the procedure by which a legally binding act is passed will call into question the validity of the act itself. This is certainly the position with, for example, delegated legislation in English law and is also the case under Community law. This was confirmed by the ECJ in the *Isoglucose*[6] cases of 1980. The producers of isoglucose - a sugar substitute - had, in a previous case before the ECJ, had a regulation struck down on the grounds that it discriminated against them in relation to sugar. The Commission then produced a draft regulation which imposed a quota system on isoglucose production, similar to the system applying to sugar production, to apply from 1 July 1979. In March 1979 the Council submitted the draft regulation to the EP, as required by Article 43(2), indicating that 'since the regulation is intended to apply as from 1st July 1979, the Council would welcome it if the Parliament would give an opinion on the proposal at its April session'. In fact the regulation was considered by the Budgets and the Agriculture Committee and the latter's resolution was put to the EP, but rejected, on 11 May. It was then referred back to Committee. The May session was the last before Parliament was dissolved for the first direct elections. The President had, however, specifically adverted to the fact that an extraordinary session could be held 'in so far as the Commission or the Council consider it necessary'.

On 25 June, notwithstanding the absence of a reply from the EP, the Council adopted the regulation (1293/79) including in its preamble the words 'having regard to the fact that the European Parliament has been consulted', rather than the usual phrase 'having regard to the opinion of the European Parliament'. The isoglucose producers then applied to the ECJ (under Article 173) to have the regulation annulled on the ground, amongst others, of lack of consultation. The EP decided to avail itself, for the first time ever, of the right given to 'institutions' by Article 37 of the Statute of the Court to intervene in support of one of the parties to a case before the Court. Despite the opposition of the Council, the ECJ ruled that the EP did have such a right of intervention and subsequently struck down the regulation on the grounds that 'consultation ... is the means which allows the Parliament to play an actual part in the legislative process of the Community. Such power represents an essential factor in the institutional balance intended by the Treaty. Although limited it reflects at Community level the fundamental democratic principle that the peoples should take part in the exercise of power, through the intermediary of a representative assembly. Due consideration of the Parliament ... therefore constitutes an essential formality, disregard of which means that the measure concerned is void ... It is impossible to take the view that the requirement is satisfied by the Council's simply asking for an opinion.' The Court was not prepared to accept the view that the EP itself had made consultation impossible, pointing out that an extraordinary session could have been called.

The decision was widely hailed, particularly by MEPs, as evidence that the European Parliament had a delaying power, even a veto, over those Council acts for which an opinion of the EP is necessary. It can, however, be restricted to its facts, so as to argue that it was simply the failure to call the extraordinary session which invalidated the regulation, rather than the lack of opinion *per se*, for the Council had not done all it could to obtain that opinion.[7] The obligation on the Council to consult, must be matched by a corresponding duty on the EP to give its opinion - wilful delay would surely discharge the Council of the obligation to wait for an opinion. In institutional terms, however, the *Isoglucose* judgment has significantly strengthened the EP's hand, and its new rules of procedure, adopted in 1981, incorporate a procedure not unlike the facts of the case itself.

Under Rule 35 of these rules, the EP has permitted itself to delay the adoption of an opinion until the Commission has had an opportunity to comment upon the proposed amendments to its draft.

Should the Commission refuse to accept the EP's amendments then the proposal can be referred back to committee by the plenary session for representation to plenary within a month. Should the Commission still remain unwilling to re-examine the proposal, the procedure does not prevent the proposal being again referred back to committee. When the procedure of Rule 35 was first used in June 1981 in relation to a Commission proposal on the harmonisation of tobacco tax, it was referred back and forth to committee three times until the Commission decided to withdraw the proposal altogether.

The procedure sails very close to the borders of legality. While the proposal is under active consideration it is difficult to say that the Parliament is wilfully delaying or obstructing it (which would be grounds for the Council to proceed without its opinion). But the political intent of the procedure could be said to be precisely that - to put pressure on the Commission to amend or withdraw proposals which the EP finds unacceptable. Moreover, in political terms this institutionalised delay is more efficacious than outright rejection. A resolution rejecting a proposal must be classified as an opinion, thus the formal requirements of the Treaty are met, and the Council can ignore the opinion with legal impunity. Although this must be seen, as Lodge has pointed out, against the background of Parliament's question time (see above) where the Council may be called upon 'to explain publicly why it chooses in a secret meeting to reject ... the views of the EC voters' elected representatives'.[8] If, as seems likely at present, Council ministers are not susceptible to this kind of political embarrassment, the Rule 35 procedure provides an ingenious way of influencing the legislative process by putting pressure not on the Council, but the Commission.

## THE CONCILIATION PROCEDURE

In addition to the procedure of Rule 35, there are two further ways that the views of the EP can be brought to bear upon the Council. The first is through the Conciliation Procedure. Under the 1975 Joint Declaration by the Commission, Council and European Parliament,[9] this can be called into play in relation to Commission proposals for 'Community Acts of general application which have appreciable financial implications'. The Commission decides whether the procedure is applicable to any particular proposal. At the instigation of Parliament a meeting will then take place between representatives of Parliament (usually ten) and members of the

Council. Conciliation discussions will then take place with the aim of reaching agreement within three months (or sooner in cases of urgency - as determined by the Council). It simply provides an opportunity for confrontation and debate and has not been outstandingly successful, for there is no further assistance in compromise or conciliation.[10] The Council has been known to back down in the face of well-prepared and highly technical amendments, but it is rare. MEPs have denounced it as a sham, with the Council unwilling to move its position on any major issue. Significantly in their proposed 'European Act', Genscher and Colombo envisaged that this procedure, which they saw as 'the precursor of Parliament's right to be involved in Council decisions' should be extended. What the 1986 Single European Act has done is to introduce a second procedure - the *Cooperation Procedure* - which is likely to become the most effective method of influencing the Council. (See p. 77)

### Decision-making

Once a Commission proposal has been through the consultation procedure (if applicable) it then comes for consideration by the Council. Before it reaches a full meeting of the Council it will usually go through two preliminary stages of examination within the Council machinery. First by working party, and then by COREPER.

### Working Parties

Council working parties are comprised of representatives of each of the Member States, and are chaired by the representative whose state currently holds the Council Presidency. Council voting rules apply. The representatives are not politicians, but national officials acting under explicit instructions from their governments. There are some 150 of these working parties and they hold up to 40 meetings a week. The Commission representative will introduce the proposal, the representatives then express the view their instructions permit and the chairman sums up. The issues debated at this level tend to be highly technical, so the representatives are often experts in each field, and may even write the instructions which, after higher level approval, they use for the meeting. If agreement is not immediately forthcoming, then the representatives may return to their governments for fresh instructions. This process will continue until there is either agreement or complete deadlock. In the case of agreement the proposal will go forward to COREPER for formal approval before going to the Council under the A procedure (see below). If there is deadlock, it will again be passed up to COREPER which will explore the possibility of agreement at a higher level.

Some preliminary vetting of highly technical proposals is obviously essential, but these working groups have been criticised on two main grounds. First, the number of national experts in the more esoteric areas of activity is limited. Hence the expert at the working group may well have been the expert who initially advised the Commission, and who may also advise COREPER at the higher stage. It may thus be unreal to regard all these processes as permitting new perspectives to be found in controversial areas. Second - and this point was stressed by the Three Wise Men - the working groups can become deadlocked over political issues which represent an outdated view of the political stances of their superiors. To prevent these delays or deadlocks, which result in reference up to COREPER and even the Council, of issues which *should* be decided at the technical level, the Three Wise Men argued for an improved, more flexible, chain of information and instructions between the groups and their political superiors.

## COREPER (THE COMMITTEE OF PERMANENT REPRESENTATIVES)

Unlike the working groups COREPER derives its formal existence from the Treaty, in that the Merger Treaty of 1965 (Article 4), recognising formally what was already in existence, provided that 'a committee consisting of the Permanent Representatives of the Member States shall be responsible for preparing the work of the Council and for carrying out the tasks assigned to it by the Council'. There are in fact two COREPERS, COREPER 1 which is the Deputy Permanent Representatives and COREPER 2 which is the Representatives themselves. There is also a special Committee with exclusive jurisdiction on agricultural questions. These committees are in virtually continuous session, meeting several days each week. At this level, if agreement has been reached below, the matter will not be discussed further. If the working party has not agreed, then discussions will continue until COREPER agrees, or feels that agreement may be reached at higher level, in which case it is referred up to Council. If no agreement seems in prospect then it will be referred back to the working party.

The object at this stage is to filter out matters which can be dealt with at the highest civil servant level, thus leaving the Council agenda clear for the higher policy issues. Again the Three Wise Men pointed out that this is not always what happens. They felt that the Council agenda was often excessively cluttered by matters which, given clearer chains of communication between permanent representatives and their governments, could be settled without resort to discussions at ministerial level.

## THE COUNCIL OF MINISTERS

Once the filtering process of the working groups and COREPER has taken place, the Council will be left with an agenda composed of two sections. Section A represents the items on which there has already been agreement at a lower political level, as well as issues which, having been decided in principle at a previous Council meeting, are now presented in detailed form, the text having been finalised by the Council Secretariat. Section B contains those issues which after progress through the two earlier stages still remain unresolved. The common practice is for Section A to be approved *en bloc* without discussion, so that the working time can be devoted to the outstanding issues in Section B.

The endemic problem all Council meetings face is lack of time. The meetings cannot go on indefinitely if only because of the ministerial responsibilities of the national representatives. At a major Agricultural Council meeting, for example, the British delegation alone may have two ministers and a parliamentary secretary. In the search for agreement meetings may last a number of days going on late into the night. Pressure of time can often be part of the strategy for reaching agreement on major issues. Final agreement will in part depend on the role of the President (who may wish to end his term of presidency with concrete achievements to his credit) and the Commission which, attending as of right in the role of 'honest broker', may promote a compromise 'package deal' of otherwise unrelated issues, placating one state with concessions in return for its consent to another matter. The practice of linking unrelated issues, developed by the Commission, has also been used by ministers themselves, e.g. British insistence in May 1982 that discussions on their contribution to the Community Budget be linked with the annual raising of farm prices. This sort of tactic (although in that case unsuccessful) is only possible because of the decision-making mechanisms used by the Council.

It will be remembered that the Council can use one of three voting procedures, depending on the wording of the Treaty provisions under which it is acting. It can act:

(a) by absolute majority - this is envisaged by Article 148(1) as the norm, but is rarely used;
(b) by qualified majority - where according to the weighting formula decisions must be taken by 54 votes where the Council acts on a proposal from the Commission (or on any other matter by 54 votes drawn from eight states);
(c) unanimously.

The Treaty provides for a large number of decisions to be taken by a majority vote but it is used in less than 5% of Council decisions, largely because of the Luxembourg Compromise (or Accords). After a major constitutional crisis in 1965, between the French and the other Community states, a statement was issued in January 1966 that 'where in the case of decisions which may be taken by majority vote on a proposal of the Commission, very important interests of one or more partners are at stake, the Members of the Council will endeavour within a reasonable time, to reach solutions which can be adopted by all the members of the Council'. The French insisted further, however, that such discussion must continue until 'unanimous agreement is reached'. In practice the French view has prevailed and hence a *de facto* 'veto' has been introduced into Council procedure. As will be remembered from Chapter 2, the Luxembourg Compromise has no formal legal status although it represents the continuing rule of procedure in the Council. Despite attempts by the Genscher-Colombo initiative, and the EP's Draft Treaty on European Union to eliminate the veto from Council proceedings, the Single European Act makes no explicit reference to it even though changes are made to the procedure for passing harmonisation laws (under Article 100) permitting extended use of majority voting.

## THE ROLE OF WESTMINSTER

The meetings of the Council of Ministers are held behind closed doors, and although there is publication in the Official Journal of the acts which are passed, there is no publication of the voting which takes place within the Council.

There is of course vigorous press reporting, sometimes conflicting, of what has taken place, but in the absence of an official public record it is impossible to identify with certainty the role any particular minister has taken in decision-making. It is for this reason that it is certainly true to say that membership of the European Communities has increased the power of national executives.

Community legislation passed by the Council (as discussed in Chapter 2) is often directly applicable in national law in all Community Member States, and superior to national law; yet the secrecy which surrounds these sessions provides a serious obstacle to effective national scrutiny of ministers' behaviour in the Council. It is this sheer lack of information which gives ministers themselves more freedom from supervision or criticism than they are accustomed to in their domestic parliaments.

If the Community is to possess a legislative function, there must inevitably be some surrender or pooling of the legislative powers previously exercised by national parliaments. Parallel to this, there will, of course, be an increase in the scope and content of legislation which can be passed by the central legislative institutions. Nevertheless, the extent to which a national parliament continues to exercise influence, or to make some contribution to the content of Community legislation depends upon the constitutional procedures it adopts to deal with this extra dimension of law making.

At Westminster this has been done, albeit slowly, in two main areas. The first is the extension of the doctrine of ministerial or government accountability to Parliament to include decisions taken within the Community. The second is the scrutiny at Westminster of draft Community legislation at such a stage that Parliament can formulate and, if necessary, express a view on it before the Council makes its decisions.

## Government Accountability to Parliament

The British government has accepted the general principle that the doctrine of parliamentary accountability extends to decisions on Community matters and taken within Community institutions. First, it has undertaken to supply to Parliament all draft proposals submitted by the Commission for the consideration of the Council. It has also undertaken to provide within two weeks - although this has not always been honoured - memoranda explaining the implications of the proposals for the UK. These proposals are then scrutinised by the Select Committees appointed in both houses (see below). If, for example, the Commons Select Committee recommends that a particular proposal should be debated, then the government has indicated that it will not agree to such a proposal at a Council until a debate has taken place 'whenever British interests can be so preserved'. The latitude which this latter limitation gives to ministers to ignore the Select Committee's recommendations led to a reconsideration of the issue in the late 1970s. However, a resolution passed by the Commons in 1980 still accepted that 'for special reasons' a minister may be compelled to agree to a proposal which had not been debated. The resolution does, however, compel him to explain his reasons to the House at the first opportunity. If a debate does take place and the House passes a resolution disapproving of a particular proposal, that resolution is not legally binding upon the government. Nevertheless, the established view is that the government would ignore it 'at its peril'.[11]

Second, ministers have undertaken to make statements to the House after Council meetings have taken place. They have, however, consistently refused to explain to the House in advance of a Council meeting the stance they intend to take, on the grounds that this would compromise their negotiating position. This position contrasts vividly with the approach to ministerial responsibility taken by the Danish Parliament, and the Danish procedures provide an illuminating comparison.[12]

On accession to the Community, the Danish Parliament (the *Folketing*) established a Permanent Parliamentary Commission on European Community matters (the *Folketingets Markedsudvalg*). The Danish government undertook to supply the *Markedsudvalg* with copies of all Commission proposals within four weeks of receipt together with explanatory memoranda. In addition, however, Danish ministers were required to consult the *Markedsudvalg* before Council meetings to set out their negotiating position, in writing if necessary, for their approval. Provided that the *Markedsudvalg* did not reject their position, then the government had a mandate for the Council negotiations. If during the meeting negotiations took an unexpected turn, then the minister would need to seek an amended mandate. He would also be expected to report on the conduct of the meeting to the *Markedsudvalg* on his return. Within this system the *Folketing* has accepted the need for the government to have some flexibility so as to be able to negotiate satisfactorily. Nevertheless Danish ministers were, from the outset, placed on a much tighter leash than their British counterparts. It may be that such a rigorous system of accountability could only work in a small state, with closer links between parliament and government, where there is significant opposition to Community membership, and to consequent surrender of national sovereignty. In Britain too, however, there is strong parliamentary opposition to continued Community membership, but neither of the major political parties has, when in office, been prepared to accept a comparable view of ministerial accountability to Parliament.

Third, the government, through the Foreign Secretary, has undertaken to provide Parliament with a report on developments within the Communities every six months. These reports are published as white papers. Two days per session are allocated for discussion of these reports which cover matters from January to June and July to December. They are clearly important in providing a wider perspective, but for the purposes of detailed review their utility is limited by the time they take to prepare. The January-June 1986 report (Cmnd. 9911), for example, was not discussed until 29 January 1987.

In addition to the formal reports, four days each session are also allocated for debate on Community affairs, and specific times have been allocated on the question time rota for questions on EC matters. Since 1980 the House of Commons has also been able to spend longer dealing with individual reports from its Scrutiny Committee, both on the floor of the House and in Standing Committees. With the new Select Committee structure, which came into operation in 1980, came also the power for them to investigate the *merits* of Commission proposals within their sphere of interest. (The Scrutiny Committee isolates issues of legal and political importance - see below.) Debates on Scrutiny Committee reports are now on substantive motions (e.g. expressing disapproval) rather than the unsatisfactory 'taking note' motion initially permitted.[13]

*The Scrutiny Committees*

The first committees appointed in December 1972 by each House of Parliament to consider the problems caused by accession to the Community held their first meeting early in 1973 when the UK was already a member of the Community. It was the proposals of these two committees - the Foster Committee in the Commons and the Maybray-King Committee in the Lords, which resulted in the appointment in 1974 of Select Committees in both houses, and the guidelines outlined above for the provision of information to Parliament by the government. The two Committees have different terms or 'orders' of reference and it is worth considering each of them separately:

*The House of Lords Select Committee on the European Communities.* The 'order' of reference of the Committee is to consider Community proposals, whether in draft or otherwise, to obtain all necessary information about them, and to make reports on those which, in the opinion of the Committee, raise important questions of policy or principle and on other questions to which the Committee considers that the special attention of the House should be drawn.[14]

In order to fulfil these very wide instructions the Committee has power to appoint sub-committees, of which there are currently six with specialised interests: A, Finance, Economics and Regional Policy; B, Trade and Treaties; C, Health, Employment, Education and Social Affairs; D, Agriculture and Consumer Affairs; E, Law; and F, Energy, Transport, Research and Environment. The Committee (and this is mainly the work of the Chairman) sifts through the mass of Commission proposals referred to them by the government and classifies them primarily into List A proposals - which are the majority and which are thought not to require special attention and List B proposals, the minority thought to require the attention of the relevant sub-committee and maybe the House. The sub-committee then reports back on these proposals and its view is invariably adopted.

The bulk of material meant that in 1985-8 the Committee published 29 reports of its 'sifts' through proposals and to assist in keeping track of the material it now publishes a further three lists: List C, of proposals which, having been referred to sub-committee as List B items, are not thought to be worthy of individual report to the House; List D, of proposals reported to the House during the current and previous session purely for information; and most importantly, List E, of the reports made to the House on which the Committee feels there should be debate. This list includes matters which were so referred during the current and previous session and indicates which reports are still outstanding for debate.

This highly systematic sifting typifies the work of the Lords Committee, and its reports tend to concentrate on the *merits* (or demerits) of particular proposals. In sharp contrast, the Commons committee, with different terms of reference, has often become bogged down in determining the legal or political importance of a proposal.

*The Law Sub-Committee.* In a work of this kind the Law Sub-Committee deserves some special mention. It is composed mainly of lawyers (professionals and academics) and has the power to appoint specialist advisers (which in 1980-1 included Professor Francis Jacobs and Professor John Usher). It has wide terms of reference, and despite criticism that they were already too wide, these were extended in 1980-1, so that they are now:

> To consider and report to the Committee:
> (a) whether any draft regulation or draft directive would, if adopted, impliedly repeal or amend existing UK legislation;
> (b) whether any draft regulation, if adopted, would render legislation in the UK necessary or desirable to facilitate its operation;
> (c) whether any draft directive, if adopted, would necessitate any legislation in the UK to give effect to it;
> (d) upon the merits of such proposals as are referred to them by the Select Committee;
> (e) whether any important developments have taken place in Community law;
> (f) any matters which they consider should be drawn to the attention of the Committee concerning (i) the form which legislation, found to be necessary or desirable under paragraph (a) or (c) above, should take; (ii) the *vires* of any proposal.

Within this wide mandate the sub-committee has investigated such issues as the 'Direct Applicability of Directives' (its famous 10th report[15]) and the legal problems of the accession of the European Community to the European Convention on Human Rights.[16] It will be noted that it has the power not only to consider the legal implications of proposals but also their *vires* - that is whether they are a legitimate exercise of Community powers. Such questions have on occasion been raised, even though there is little that Parliament can do to challenge the legality of a proposal.

The sub-committee has established itself as an adventurous and forthright investigator, and its reports have been of benefit to both Houses as well as to bodies outside Parliament. In fact the work of the Lords Committee as a whole indicates the useful role that a second chamber (however it is constituted) can play in providing more time for the detailed scrutiny of proposals which the Commons cannot adequately deal with, given its greater pressures and different concerns.

*The House of Commons Select Committee on European Legislation etc.* Originally called the Select Committee on European *Secondary* Legislation the word secondary was dropped in the 1977-8 session in line with a general recognition that it is misleading to classify Community legislation as analogous to national secondary legislation.

The Committee's task is to consider draft Community legislation and other documents published by the Commission for submission to the Council, to report their opinion as to whether such proposals or other documents raise questions of legal or political importance, to give their reasons for their opinions, to report what matters of principle or policy may be affected thereby, and to what extent they may affect the law of the UK, and to make recommendations for the further consideration of such documents by the House.

The Committee has only 16 members, with a quorum of five, and no power to coopt (House of Commons Standing Order No.105). Although there are two sub-committees it does not use them to the same extent as the House of Lords Committee in order not to put intolerable burdens on the time of its members. Neither does it make use of specialist advisers in the same way as the Lords Committee.

The mandate of the Committee is primarily to determine issues of legal or political importance. Unlike the Lords Committee it cannot consider the merits of proposals but it does have the power to liaise freely with the Lords. This mandate, together with the political need to balance pro- and anti-marketeers in the composition of the Committee has resulted in a very different approach to its work. St. John Bates, in a very comprehensive review of the early work of the Scrutiny Committees[17], cites as an extreme example the Commons Committee's consideration of a draft directive on the production and marketing of honey. The Committee took the view that this raised a question of political importance, in that the obligation to label and describe honey might give private bee-keepers 'the fear that they were being administratively harassed'. The late John Davies, the Committee's first chairman, is reported as commenting that 'it took a lot of time to eradicate honey from our system'.

The Committees' reports, together with those from the Lords, supply the House with the bulk of the information which it uses to control ministers. (Although since 1980 the new Select Committees have also been able to raise Community matters for debate.) In the 1985-6 session the Committee reported on such matters as fish prices, hormone use in animals, milk production and the accession to the Community of Spain and Portugal.

*Assessment*

The previous discussion will have indicated that the influence which Westminster can exercise over the Community legislative process is indirect - through its influence on government. Three points particularly underline the indirect nature of this role.

First, Parliament is totally dependent for its information on the government honouring its undertaking to supply all proposals within 48 hours of receipt from Brussels. This is very different from the position in the Federal Republic of Germany, where the German act of accession itself obliged the government to supply the *Bundestag* with such documents. Predictably there have in Britain been breaches of this undertaking and on occasion government has also had difficulty in supplying explanatory memoranda within the specified two-week period.

Second, the draft proposals seen by the Scrutiny Committees represent, as we have seen, only one stage in the legislative history of a proposal. It may be amended by the Commission to accommodate the views of the European Parliament or the Council. The government, however, is not prepared to supply amended proposals, nor to indicate its own negotiating positions.

Third, the government has given its assurance it will not ignore either recommendations for debate, or the views of Parliament once a debate has taken place. But Council decisions are taken in secret and sometimes by majority vote. Westminster's power is essentially negative, urging British ministers *not* to vote for or to accept certain proposals - perhaps even to block them, if the 'veto' is applicable. But recent events suggest that even the 'veto' can no longer be relied upon as a guarantee that the British view will always prevail.

It is therefore unrealistic to pretend that membership of the Community has not affected the power of Westminster, as it has affected the power of the other national parliaments. Like the British, other Member States have experienced difficulties in maintaining a balance between acceptable levels of parliamentary scrutiny and adequate ministerial flexibility for Council negotiations. In those areas where Community legislative competence has replaced national competence, the role of national parliaments has become in Kolinsky's words 'protective rather than creative',[18] but no less important.

It has been argued that any increase in the power of the European Parliament is likely to reduce the power of the Council, and hence reduce still further the influence that national parliaments can exercise over their ministers. This view must be a short-sighted one. If the scrutiny of Community proposals at national levels is seen as protective, while the European Parliament is seen as developing a creative role in the legislative process, then both entities have a complementary function. Both would clearly benefit, however, from closer links and the mutual interchange of information and ideas.

After direct elections, the House of Lords Scrutiny Committee published a report[19] on some of the implications of the consequent loss of the automatic 'dual mandate', by which MEPs were also members of national parliaments. It recommended the establishment of a 'European Grand Committee' of the 81 British MEPs and the members of the two Westminster Scrutiny Committees, in order to foster closer relations between the two groups thus 'strengthening MEPs' appreciation of the British factors in European policies' and making 'Westminster more aware of the EEC point of view'. It also recommended mutual participation at each other's meetings and regular exchanges of documents. Unfortunately these proposals were not taken up. The House of Commons, acutely aware of the already overcrowded facilities at the Palace of Westminster, was only prepared to allow British MEPs access to a limited number of areas, so that, in the main, MEPs without the dual mandate are to be treated, like the general public, as 'strangers'. MEPs may not, as yet, have the power or prestige of national MPs, but for the time being the opportunity has been lost of treating them as colleagues, rather than as competitors, in the attempt to introduce direct democratic influence into the Community legislative process.

## THE LEGISLATIVE POWER OF THE COMMISSION

The dominant role of the Council in the legislative process makes it easy to forget that the Commission too has an important legislative role. In numerical terms alone, the Commission's role is larger than that of the Council. In 1986, while the Council approved 473 regulations, 184 decisions and 74 directives, the Commission adopted a total of 12,081 acts. Much of this activity is in the nature of delegated or secondary legislation, implementing policies approved by the Council according to pre-determined principles. This secondary role is envisaged by Article 155 when it requires the Commission to 'exercise the powers conferred on it by the Council for the implementation of rules laid down by the latter'. But Article 155 also insists that the Commission shall 'have its own power of decision' - a form of words remarkably similar to the power 'to take decisions' which is the basis of the Council's legislative power under Article 145. No distinction is made by Article 189 (which sets out the forms of Community legislation - see above Chapter 2) between the Council and the Commission in relation to their powers to enact the full spectrum of legally binding acts. There are indeed a number of areas in the Treaty where the Commission is specifically authorised to enact what might be called 'primary legislation' in the sense that it derives its authority directly from the Treaty and not indirectly from the Council. For example, Article 13(2) empowered the Commission to determine by directive the timetable for the abolition of 'charges having an effect equivalent to customs duties' - the subject of the famous *Grad*[20] decision, discussed above. Article 90 (concerned with the application of the competition rules to nationalised and state-financed industries) empowers the Commission, in order to ensure the application of its provisions, to 'address appropriate directives or decisions to Member States'. This latter provision was, in fact, the subject of a recent decision of the Court of Justice,[21] in which the British government had argued for the annulment of such a directive on the ground, *inter alia*, that the Commission had no right of primary legislation. This argument was firmly dismissed by the Court for the reasons summarised below.

## The Commission's Power of Secondary Legislation and the Management Committees

Despite the above arguments, the overwhelming majority of legal acts passed by the Commission are of a secondary nature, in the sense that the Council has expressly delegated to it the task of detailed implementation of policy. It is now, however, a firmly established practice dating from 1962, that in the implementation of these policies, particularly in the sphere of agriculture, that a 'management committee' should be established to ensure that the implementing legislation is in line with Council guidelines. The first of these committees was appointed to monitor the regulation of cereal products, and there were at the end of 1981 26 'agricultural' management committees each with a specialised sphere of activity: pigmeat, sugar, hops, wine, etc.

These committees are composed of representatives of each of the Member States, but chaired by a (non-voting) Commission official. In brief the procedure is this: the draft legislation from the Commission is presented to the relevant committee, which, after detailed consideration and discussion, can take one of three courses. Using the weighted voting system of the Council, the committee can approve the legislation, or it can express no opinion at all (because, for example, it is unable to gather enough support for a positive endorsement). In either of these cases the Commission drafts will then become law, although in the latter case the Commission can withdraw or amend the proposal if it wishes. If, however, the committee is able to muster a qualified majority (i.e. 54 votes) *against* the proposal, then the draft legislation will not come into force for one month - during which time reference may be made to the Council which can within that period vote to reject the draft. Lasok and Bridge comment that the procedure 'operates as an alarm mechanism and gives a clear indication of a serious problem which can be effectively resolved only by ... the Council'.[22] The appeal to the Council is very rare. In 1981 in the 527 meetings of the agricultural management committees, although 2,165 acts were approved, and 200 were passed without opinion, no unfavourable opinions were expressed at all. This compares with one in 1980.

The management committee procedure received the approval of the Court of Justice in the *Köster* case (1970),[23] when the Court ruled that as the committees only concerned themselves with legislative powers which had been specifically delegated to the

Commission by the Council, they did not detract from the Commission's power of decision. As the committees had no power of decision themselves, the procedure did not distort the administrative structure of the Treaty - which would have been grounds for declaring it illegal.

In the light of the success of the agricultural management committees, similar committees, called variously 'rule-making' or 'advisory', some with different forms of procedure, have been set up to supervise Commission activities in other spheres such as the European Regional Development Fund, energy and data-processing. The increase in the budgetary powers of the European Parliament has brought under renewed scrutiny the legality of these committees and of other procedures whereby the Council can monitor and approve the executive actions of the Commission. The EP is particularly concerned at the use of such procedures to regulate expenditure in areas where it has now acquired the power to allocate funds (i.e. areas of non-obligatory expenditure - for a full discussion see Chapter 5 below). In the field of regional policy, for example, the EP, using its new powers, has a number of times voted extra money into the Budget for regional development, but that money has not been spent because the Council has failed to approve any of the projects proposed to it by the Commission in accordance with one of these supervisory procedures. This, argues the EP, is a distortion of the Treaty regime.[24] If the EP has been given the power to vote money into the Budget in certain areas, and the Commission has an obligation under Article 205 to 'implement' the Budget, then the Council has no authority to assume for itself *de facto* the last word on how the money is to be spent by compelling all projects to be submitted to it for approval. This is, continues the EP's argument, transforming the Council into an executive body and thus radically encroaching on the role of the Commission.

The *Köster* decision, then, can be seen as an endorsement of the management committee procedure in so far as it applies to the common agricultural policy - an area of obligatory expenditure over which Parliament has no direct control. However, in areas of Community expenditure where the Parliament has been given increased power, the use of management-type committees and similar procedures whereby the Council can retain influence over the implementation of policy may well be open to renewed legal challenge.

## NOTES

1. 'Crocodile' - Letter to the Members of the European Parliament. Edited by A. Spinelli and F. Ippolito, No.1, October 1980, p.8.

2. *Twentieth General Report on the Activities of the European Communities in 1986* (Office for Official Publications of the EC, Luxembourg, 1987), p.40.

3. See P. Norton, *The Commons in Perspective* (Martin Robertson, Oxford, 1981), p.101.

4. *European Parliament Working Documents*, 1-207/81, p.14.

5. See e.g. case 9/56, *Meroni v. H.A.* [1957 & 58] E.C.R. 133.

6. Cases 138 and 139/79, *Roquette Frères v. Council* and *Maizena GmbH v. Council* [1980] E.C.R. 3333.

7. See e.g. F.G. Jacobs, 'Isoglucose resurgent' (1981), 18 *C.M.L. Rev* 219.

8. J. Lodge, 'The European Parliament after Direct Elections: Talking Shop or Putative Legislature', *The Journal of European Integration*, Vol.5, 1982, p.259.

9. O.J. 1975, C 89/1.

10. See further J. Forman, 'The Conciliation Procedure' (1979) 16, *C.M.L.Rev.* pp.77-108.

11. Erskine May, *Parliamentary Practice*, 19th edn., ed. Sir D. Lidderdale (Butterworths, London, 1976), p.843.

12. See H. Rasmussen (1975-6) 1 *E.L.Rev.* p.82.

13. See Norton, *The Commons*, p.160ff.

14. Erskine May, *Parliamentary Practice*, p.669 and see T. St John. N. Bates, 'The Scrutiny of European Secondary Legislation at Westminster' (1975-6) 1, *E.L.Rev.* p.22.

15. (1974-5) H.L. 85.

16. (1979-80) H.L. 362.

17. Bates, 'Scrutiny', pp.27-8.

18. M. Kolinsky, 'Parliamentary Scrutiny of European Legislation', *Government and Opposition*, Vol.10, 1975, p.46.

19. 'Relations between the United Kingdom Parliament and the European Parliament after Direct Elections'(1977-8) H.L. 256-I.

20. Case 9/70, *Grad v. Finanzamt Traunstein* [1970] E.C.R. 825; [1971] C.M.L.R. 1.

21. Cases 188-190/80, *France, Italy and the United Kingdom v. Commission* [1982] E.C.R. 2545.

22. D. Lasok and J. Bridge, *Law and Institutions*, p.214.

23. Case 25/70, *EVSt v. Köster Berodt* [1970] E.C.R. 1161; [1972] C.M.L.R. 255.

24. See R. Jackson, 1980 *F.I.D.E. Reports*, Vol.3, p.53.

# 5

# The Budget

The financing of the EC has been a long-standing bone of political contention both between the Member States themselves and between the Community institutions.[1] Disputes between the Member States have generally been about the amounts of national contributions, for as a result largely of the workings of the Common Agricultural Policy (which the Budget classifies as spending under the European Agricultural Guidance and Guarantee Fund - the EAGGF) there have been periods when the poorest European states such as the UK and Italy have been net contributers to the Community, while the richer states of Germany, Denmark and Holland have been net beneficiaries. In the early 1980s the UK was continually pressing for a budgetary rebate to ensure that its contribution more accurately reflected its GNP, while hanging over the whole debate was the prospect that the Community financed at that time principally by a levy of 1% of the VAT raised by each Member State - would simply run out of money.

At an inter-institutional level, the Budget has been at the centre of pressure by the EP to increase its power and influence in Community decision-making. The limited budgetary powers given to the EP by the 1970 Budgetary Provisions Treaty and the 1975 Financial Provisions Treaty[2] were seen by MEPs to give them a 'foot in the door' of the financial decision-making process, which they have sought to use both to change the pattern of Community expenditure (by a swing from agricultural spending to areas such as regional aid and social policy) and also to increase the scale of their participation in Community decision-making. It should become apparent from this chapter that unlike national parliaments, where budgets are usually 'rubber stamped', the EP does play an important part in the budgetary process and can and does *amend* the

Budget which is put to it. In 1979 the first directly elected Parliament made use of its powers under Article 203 to reject the first Budget presented to it. In 1984, the second directly elected Parliament rejected the 1985 Budget, and in December 1985 after changes made by the EP the 1986 Budget was challenged before the ECJ in an action by the Council.[3] Both these latter actions have sprung directly from the financial crisis in which the Community has found itself. Because the Community was running out of money, the 1985 Budget proposed by the Commission did not cover the full year's expenditure; it was for this reason that it was rejected by the EP. In the following year the accumulated deficits of the previous years precipitated action which resulted in the Council alleging that the Budget had been illegally adopted.

It should therefore be apparent that an understanding in general terms at least of the basic principles of Community financing is essential to a proper understanding of the way that the Community functions. The aim of this chapter is to provide only a brief explanation of the budgetary procedure and an outline of some of the main problems to which it has given rise.

## HOW THE COMMUNITY IS FUNDED

The EEC was originally funded by block payments paid direct to it by governments; the actual sums payable by each state were initially set by the Treaty itself.[4] In 1970,[5] however, pursuant to the obligation in Article 201, the Council decided that the EEC should have its 'own resources', that funding should not come from lump-sum contributions negotiated annually, but principally from a percentage of the VAT collected by national authorities on behalf of the Community, and then remitted directly to it. The initial maximum for the amount which could be levied by the EEC on national VAT returns was set at 1%, but as the Community began to run out of money in the 1980s, the Council after protracted debate agreed to raise the ceiling to 1.4%.[6] This direct VAT payment amounts to about two-thirds of EEC revenue (i.e. estimated in 1986 as 20 thousand million ECUs out of a total revenue of 33 thousand million ECUs). The balance comes from common customs tariff duties collected on goods crossing the external customs barrier, and from levies on certain agricultural and other products.

## COMMUNITY EXPENDITURE

The main areas of budgetary expenditure[7] are the following:

1. *Agriculture and Fisheries.* Despite changes in the patterns of EC expenditure over the last few years the predominant area of EC expenditure is still agriculture. In 1983 66.4% of total spending was on agriculture and fisheries, although this compares with 80.6% in 1973, more recently the proportion has been increasing again, and in 1985 the proportion was 72.9%.[8]
2. *Regional policy.* This accounts for some 6% of expenditure.
3. *Social policy.* This accounts for 5.7%.
4. *Research, Energy, Industry and Transport.* Together account for 2.6%.
5. *Overseas Aid, and Cooperation.* About 4%.
6. *Reimbursements to Member States* (for the costs of collecting EEC 'own resources'). About 5%.
7. *Administration.* About 4%.

## THE BUDGETARY PROCESS

As has been said above, the original system of financing the EC was by an annual contribution from each of the Member States calculated according to a formula agreed in Article 200 EEC. This meant that the Community was to some extent dependent upon these sums being promptly paid by governments, which often had to seek the approval of their national parliaments for this remittance. The 1970 'Own Resources' decision of the Council enabled the Community to transfer to an automatic system of financing. This was based principally on an automatic levy, set at a maximum of 1% of all VAT collected in the Member States and paid directly to the Commission, supplemented by other levies and duties described above. The introduction of this system of 'own resources' financing for the Community meant that controls which may previously have been exercised by national parliaments over national lump-sum contributions were lost. The 1970 Budgetary Treaty therefore sought to replace national parliamentary accountability with a similar accountability at Community level, hence the increased budgetary powers vested in the EP. In fact the new budgetary powers could hardly be described as extensive. The Parliament was given a power amounting in effect to the last word on all expenditure which was not 'necessarily arising under the

Treaties',[9] or (as it will be called hereafter 'non-compulsory' expenditure). Thus the vast bulk of the Community Budget which went on financing the Common Agricultural Policy and which was said to be 'compulsory' expenditure was outside the control of the EP.

These powers came fully into effect in 1975, the year that the VAT levy was planned to be fully implemented. At the same time the Council, Commission and Parliament issued a joint declaration[10] establishing a conciliation procedure between the Council and Parliament for the discussion of all acts 'of general application which have appreciable financial implications' and whose adoption 'is not required by virtue of acts already in existence'. However, this procedure, which is discussed in Chapter 4 above, has not been a success. And 1975 was also the year that a further Budgetary Powers Treaty was negotiated. The 1975 Financial Provisions Treaty increased still further the EP's budgetary powers, so that Parliament was given, as Usher has commented, 'the final word on the fate of the whole Budget, if not control over every detail of it'.[11] This Treaty came into force in 1977.[12]

The procedure by which the Parliament and the Council (which together now constitute the Budgetary Authority) adopt the Budget is complicated. However, an understanding in outline of the procedure is necessary for an appreciation of the role of each institution in the process. It is as follows:

### 1. The Preliminary Draft Budget

By 15 June[13] each year the Commission submits to the Budgetary Authority a Preliminary Draft Budget for the following year. This sets out estimates of revenue and expenditure for the following year for all the institutions. In calculating these figures the Commission takes into account the general economic climate as well as existing and past Community commitments, and proposals for new areas of activity. It has to ensure that its planned expenditure on non-compulsory areas does not increase each year by more than a maximum rate (which it also calculates by a set formula) without requesting the agreement of both institutions making up the Budgetary Authority.[14] This maximum rate is calculated from the growth of Community GNP, the growth of central government expenditure and of prices. At the time the Commission is calculating the maximum rate the most up-to-date figures available to it are of the previous complete year, thus the figures will always be two years out of date by the time the Budget comes to be applied. As non-compulsory expenditure represents new areas of development, the Commission usually proposes increases in non-compulsory expenditure which are in excess of this maximum rate of increase.

Although consultation with both the EP and the Council precedes the production of this Preliminary Draft Budget, the Commission has to steer a difficult path of producing a Budget which serves the interests of the Community without being politically unrealistic. As a Commission official has commented 'it is invariably criticised for the way it has done its job. Either by the Council for being irresponsible, or the Parliament for being too timid - often both criticisms appear at the same time'.[15] It should therefore be apparent that the task is not a simple accounting exercise, it involves a strong, and often controversial, policy input, for no new Community spending activities are possible without proper financing being provided by the Budget.

## 2. The Draft Budget

### *Before the Council*

Once the Preliminary Draft Budget has been presented to the Council it is debated at the Budget Council in late July. The Budget Commissioner attends to present Commission views on any proposed changes, and a delegation from the EP usually attends the early part of the meeting to put the views of the EP (elicited from a July debate) on the Preliminary Draft. If the Council feels any changes are necessary to the Preliminary Draft, which it inevitably does, then it will adopt a counter proposal called the Draft Budget. Invariably in this Draft Budget the Council radically reduces all proposed non-compulsory expenditure, but in recent years it has also come under increased pressure to look carefully at compulsory expenditure, particularly on agriculture.

### *Before the Parliament*

The Draft Budget is then sent to the EP for debate in September, prior to being sent back to the Council for further consideration in October. It is at this stage before the Parliament that the distinction between compulsory and non-compulsory expenditure becomes significant, for the EP's powers vary depending upon the type of expenditure proposed.[16] A further distinction to make at this point is between an amendment to the Budget and a proposed modification. If the Budget is compared with the passage of a UK parliamentary bill the significance of this difference may be clearer. When a bill is going through its various readings its text may be changed as it goes, these are amendments which stand unless they are overturned by later counter-amendments. At some stages in the readings, however, proposals for change are made which do not themselves amend the text, they are merely carried forward to be considered by the body with the power to make amendments. Such proposals in the EC Budget are termed *modifications*. In order to make their status clear they will here be called *proposed modifications*. In areas of compulsory expenditure, the EP may (acting by a majority of votes cast) propose modifications. These may later be rejected by the Council which has the ultimate authority over compulsory expenditure.

In areas of non-compulsory expenditure, however, the EP may (acting by a majority of its members) make *amendments*, provided that it does not increase the total expenditure in this area above a certain limit set by the maximum rate of expenditure (see below for detailed discussion). This restriction is known as Parliament's *margin of manoeuvre*. It operates as follows. The maximum rate of increase is set by the Commission (above). Let us say for the sake of simplicity that the maximum rate has been set at 10%. In its Preliminary Draft Budget the Commission may have proposed that for non-compulsory expenditure the full 10% increase be used in the forthcoming year. The Council, anxious as ever to reduce expenditure in non-compulsory areas, then reduces the envisaged expenditure of this type to say 5% (i.e. half the maximum rate of increase). Parliament (which has the final word on non-compulsory expenditure) may then increase the expenditure to 10% (i.e. the full maximum). This will be the final provision in the Budget.

However, complications arise where the Council agrees to spend more than half the proposed maximum rate of increase, say 8%. In such a case Article 203(9) specifically permits the EP a further right to increase expenditure by a sum 'not exceeding half the maximum rate'. This provision is intended to ensure that the Council does not pre-empt all expenditure, thus reducing the Parliament's input. It means, in our example, that Parliament is given the right to increase expenditure by a further 5% (i.e. half of the maximum rate), thus permitting total expenditure in that area to be 13% (i.e. 8% established by the Council, 5% voted by the EP). This procedure does mean that in some cases the maximum rate of increase set by the Commission is not in fact the maximum rate.[17]

*Second reading before the Council*

Once the Parliament has reached decisions on proposed modifications and on amendments, then the Draft is referred back to the Council, usually in mid–November, which then has to make the final decisions on *compulsory* expenditure. The procedure is complex,[18] but briefly it means that if the Parliament's proposed modifications to compulsory expenditure do not involve an overall increase in expenditure (i.e. they propose a cut or they are linked to a corresponding modification proposing a decrease in another area) then the proposed modification will stand unless rejected by a qualified majority of the Council. However, where the proposed modifications do involve an increase in general expenditure they will be automatically rejected unless they command a similar qualified majority. This procedure means that the Parliament's proposals will really only have a chance of adoption at this stage if they have substantial support within the Council of Ministers.

In areas of *non-compulsory* expenditure the position is almost reversed. Council may themselves only propose modifications to the amendments to the Draft Budget already made by the Parliament and can do so only by a qualified majority.

The whole Draft Budget is then sent back to Parliament, which is informed of the action taken by the Council on both the amendments and the proposed modifications which Parliament had made at its first reading.

*Second reading in Parliament*

This is the final stage of the procedure. It is, of course, the Parliament which, acting by a majority of its members and two-thirds of the votes cast, may now reject the Budget *in toto*.[19] Before it decides whether or not to do this, it will have been notified of the actions which the Council has taken on compulsory expenditure, and of the Council proposals in the area of non-compulsory expenditure. Parliament has no further power over compulsory expenditure but, within 15 days, it must vote on the modifications which the Council has proposed in non-compulsory expenditure. Acting by a majority of its members and three-fifths of the votes cast, it may amend or reject these Council proposals. If, however, it fails to reach agreement and to act within this 15-day period the Budget is deemed to have been adopted.[20]

## Implementation of the Budget [21]

Once the Budget has been approved, it is the job of the Commission to implement the policies for which finance has been provided. In doing so it is, of course, accountable to both institutions of the Budgetary Authority. It is generally accountable to the Council of Ministers who may supervise various sectors of activity through the management committee procedure (above), but it is also accountable to the EP (who may, of course, dismiss it *en bloc* by a motion of censure under Article 144, and who discuss its general report, Article 143). Most specifically, however, it is obliged at the end of each financial year to apply to both the institutions which make up the Budgetary Authority for a discharge 'in respect of its implementation of the Budget'. There is no obvious equivalent in British constitutional procedure to the application for a discharge. In commerce a loosely equivalent idea could perhaps be found in the annual financial report made by directors to the shareholders of a public company. Just as the directors must submit their accounts to independent auditors, so the Commission is obliged to submit its accounts to the Court of Auditors. The annual reports which that body produces are intended to be of crucial importance to the task of the Council and the EP. This may be seen from the text of Article 206b (and also from a perusal of the reports themselves). Article 206b says:

> The Assembly, acting on a recommendation from the Council which shall act by qualified majority, shall give a discharge to the Commission in respect of the implementation of the budget. To this end, the Council and the Assembly in turn shall examine the accounts and the financial statement referred to in Art 205a and the annual report of the Court of Auditors together with the replies of the institutions under audit to the observations of the Court of Auditors.

Shortly after the 1975 Treaty came into force in 1977, the then Commissioner of Budgets, Christopher Tugendhat, stated publicly the importance which the Commission attached to this discharge, and suggested that a refusal to grant a discharge would be treated by the Commission as equivalent to a vote of censure, and thus require a resignation *en bloc*. In fact the procedure for discharge operates at a considerable period in arrears and the degree of accountability which Tugendhat envisaged has not manifested itself, as yet, in such a resignation. In January 1983 the EP granted a discharge for the 1980 financial year, after deferring it to enable the Commission to provide more information, which it duly did. In November 1984 the EP refused to grant a discharge for the implementation of the 1982 Budget and passed a resolution making it clear that it regarded this refusal as a political judgment of the Commission's management of the Budget. The reason that no resignations resulted from this refusal was that in 1984 the Commission was about to be replaced in any event, and it was interpreted by the new Commission not as criticism of itself (despite the fact that a number of members of the old Commission remained Commissioners) but rather like a shot across their bows, as a 'signal to the new Commission that they should pay even greater heed to Parliament's wishes'.[22]

## Some Budgetary Problems

### *1. Rejection of the Budget*

If the Parliament votes to reject the Budget, which to date it has done on two occasions, in 1979 and in 1984, then the 'provisional twelfths' arrangements come into operation.[23] The Community is financed each month by sums equivalent to one-twelfth of the preceding year's Budget, until the revised Budget is approved. This may take some time. The 1985 Budget was not finally approved until 13 June 1985. It means that Community activity is considerably restrained as it is functioning at the previous year's levels of expenditure, and if approval is delayed too long it may also mean that the institutions may be compelled to process two budgets simultaneously, an onerous and time-consuming operation.

### *2. The maximum rate of increase*

Some of the problems which result from the fact that the maximum rate of increase can in certain circumstances (under Article 203(9)) be automatically exceeded, have been referred to above. It should also be noted that it is always possible for a new (increased) maximum rate of increase to be set by agreement of the Council and the Parliament (i.e. the Budgetary Authority) and it is, in fact, not uncommon for the Commission to make proposals in its Preliminary Draft Budget for expenditure in excess of the maximum rate. For example, in the 1983 Preliminary Draft the Commission had proposed, in order to permit Community activities to develop, that increases in commitments in non-compulsory areas of expenditure be increased by 33.19%,[24] against a fixed maximum rate of increase of 11.8%. To the Commission's dismay these were reduced by the Council at its first reading to 6.60%. Although some of these cuts were ultimately reversed by the Parliament, non-compulsory expenditure does habitually suffer severely at the hands of the Council. This has led to serious conflicts between the Council and the Parliament, both over the question of which items can legitimately be classified as compulsory (and thus outside the EP's right of amendment) and also over what constitutes agreement to an increase in the maximum rate. On the first issue it is notable that the percentage of the Budget classified as non-compulsory has increased under Parliament's pressure from 3% in 1973 to about 25% in 1986.

The second issue was strikingly illustrated in 1978 when the Parliament approved amendments in its first reading exceeding the maximum rate. The Council was unable to find a qualified majority either to reject Parliament's amendments or to agree on a new maximum rate. In its second reading Parliament refrained from adopting any amendment so that the Council's version of the Budget stood, with Parliament arguing that if Council objected to the resulting Budget, it could take itself to court.[25] The UK, Denmark and France threatened legal action, but a solution was found with a supplementary Budget.[26]

The EP has continued to see its budgetary powers as a lever to gain more influence over the content of Community policy, and in particular to press for a greater share of the Community Budget to be classified as non-compulsory. In an effort to avoid political wrangles each year, the 'conciliation' procedure was developed.[27] This procedure permits representatives of the Council, the Parliament and the Commission to meet to try and reconcile possible conflicts before the Budget procedure begins and formal positions are taken by each institution. The conciliation meetings also consider proposals for new laws with financial implications. These procedures have been reinforced by the 1982 Joint Declaration by those three institutions on various methods to improve the budgetary procedure.[28]

### *3. The Joint Declaration of 30 June 1982 by the European Parliament, the Council and the Commission on various measures to improve the budgetary procedure*

This declaration covers three main issues. First, the parties agree upon a general definition of compulsory expenditure based upon the 1982 Budget. Second, they agree to set up a Tripartite Dialogue under the chairmanship of the Commission to attempt to resolve disagreements about the classification of new budget items as compulsory or non-compulsory expenditure before the Budget is adopted. Third, it formalises inter-institutional collaboration over the Budget, in particular by ensuring that the EP's views on the Commission's Preliminary Draft Budget are made known in time for the Council to take them into account before it adopts the Draft Budget, and also by establishing a procedure whereby both the Parliament and the Council might be able to agree formally to exceed the maximum rate of increase for non-compulsory expenditure if it appears necessary. Finally, the declaration seeks to clarify a number of points which have caused friction in the past, namely that the Parliament's 'margin of manoeuvre' of half the maximum rate of increase will only apply to the Budget adopted by the Council at its first reading; that the same 'margin of manoeuvre' will apply to all Budgets adopted within one financial year, and that if it is not all used on the main Budget, the remainder may be utilised in supplementary Budgets (this is to prevent the margin of manoeuvre being invoked at both the first and the second Parliamentary readings and possibly again in a supplementary Budget). Significant new expenditure will require new legislation (i.e. the approval of such an item in the Budget does not in itself represent a legal authority for spending the money). The Commission will propose any such legislation by January and the Council and Parliament will use their best endeavours for it to be adopted by the end of May at the latest - this will enable Parliament to use its budgetary powers to initiate legislative proposals. The legislation itself should not, however, fix amounts of maximum expenditure so as to circumvent the budgetary process.

Despite the importance of this declaration which addresses the main causes of dispute between the Council and the Commission, there has been no significant diminution in the friction which the budgetary procedure has engendered. Indeed, in December 1985 Parliament adopted the 1986 Budget after voting to increase expenditure above the maximum rate agreed by the Council and in excess of the margin of manoeuvre left by the Council's first reading. In doing this Parliament declared itself to be supporting the legal obligation to take account of the costs of accession of Spain and Portugal and to meet outstanding commitments from the budgetary problems of 1984 and 1985. The Council then decided to challenge the validity of the Parliament's action before the ECJ.[29]

At the time of writing the judgment in this important case is still awaited.

*4. The future*

Following two summit meetings of the European Council in 1984, both virtually devoted to budgetary matters, the Council of Ministers agreed in May 1985 to a solution to two major outstanding problems of the financing of the Communities. The long-standing UK demand for a reduction in its contribution to the Budget, and an increase in the rate of 'own resources' derived from VAT. The Council Decision of 7 May 1985[30] established a mechanism whereby the disproportionate net contribution of the UK to the Community Budget (which arose from the fact that the UK as an island state generates customs duties out of proportion to its GNP and that as it has only a small agricultural sector it benefits to a lesser degree from CAP expenditure) would be 'modulated', with the cost of the correction being borne by the other Member States, and with a downward adjustment of Germany's share. The Decision also imposed important new requirements of budgetary discipline - that spending on the CAP would not exceed the rate of overall increase in spending, and that non-compulsory expenditure would not exceed the maximum rate.

The problem of structural underfunding was met by an agreement that the maximum share of VAT which Member States contribute to the Community Budget rise from 1% to 1.4% with effect from 1 January 1986, and then to 1.6% on 1 January 1988. Before either change could be implemented the change had to be approved by each state according to its normal constitutional procedures. The 1986 change has been so approved. The significance of these agreements which seem to present at least a medium-term solution to the financial problems of the Community should not be underestimated. Whether new financial problems will arise remains to be seen.

## APPENDIX

Since going to press the case between the Council and Parliament concerning the EP's power to increase non-compulsory expenditure in the EC budget has been decided by the ECJ.

Case 34/86 *Council v. European Parliament* [1986] 3 C.M.L.R. 94

In December 1985 the President of the EP declared the 1986 budget adopted following its second reading in the EP. The adopted budget contained an increase in non-compulsory expenditure in excess of the maximum rate fixed by the Commission, and without the agreement of Council having been secured. As indicated above, the main factors motivating the EP to pursue this course of action were the failure of the Council to take into account commitments to expenditure which had been agreed in previous years, and the costs of the accession of the Iberian countries. The Council sought review of the EP President's decision under Article 173. The ECJ held: (1) The Council's application for review was admissable despite the silence of Article 173 concerning the susceptibility of the EP's acts to review. Following much the same line of reasoning as in the case of *Les Verts* (below p. 177) the ECJ held that where the acts of the EP produced legally binding effects on third parties, its acts would be subject to review. (2) The ECJ rejected the EP's argument that because the budgetary process was complete before the President made his declaration of adoption it could not be regarded as an 'act'. The court held that the declaration endowed the budget with binding force vis-à-vis the other institutions and it was therefore an act with a legally objective nature. The ECJ also rejected the EP's argument that the whole budgetary process was a 'combined act' the various parts of which could not be separated. Here, the Court took the view that its power to review acts could not be excluded for two reasons: first, the Court must retain the competence to examine acts which might encroach upon the powers of other institutions or the powers of the Member States; and second, the Treaty itself did not preclude the possibility of review in the area of budgetary activity. (3) On the substance of the case the ECJ found that the EP had acted prematurely in adopting the budget since the Budgetary Authority (i.e. the Council and EP acting in concert) had not reached agreement on a new rate of increase for non-compulsory expenditure. The Court ruled that the EP President's declaration of adoption was a legal act which should be annulled. However, using its powers under Article 174 the ECJ ruled that the whole budgetary procedure did not have to be reopened, but should be resumed at the point in the EP's second reading at which it was considering the question of the maximum rate of increase for non-compulsory expenditure. One week after the ECJ's judgment the budget was agreed. Its cost was 2 billion ECUs more than the annulled budget.

## NOTES

1. For a detailed exposition of the way the Community is financed see D. Strasser, *The Finances of Europe* (Brussels, 1981), and for a still useful political perspective see H. Wallace, *Budgetary Politics: the Finances of the European Communities* (Allen and Unwin, London, 1980). For a useful legal perspective see Sopwith, 'Legal Aspects of the Community Budget' (1980) 17 *C.M.L.Rev.* p.315.

2. U.K.T.S. No.1 (1973), Part II, p.306, Cmnd.5179. U.K.T.S. No.103, (1977); Cmnd.7007.

3. *Nineteenth General Report of the Activities of the European Communities, 1985* (Office for Official Publications of the EC, Luxembourg, 1986), p.52.

4. The relative shares of each of the original six Member States are set out in Article 200 EEC.

5. *Council Decision of 21 April 1970 on the Replacement of Financial Contributions from Member States by the Communities Own Resources,* O.J. (special edition), 1970, L 94/19. The ECSC has always been funded by a direct levy on coal and steel companies.

6. Council Decision of 7 May 1985 on the Communities system of own resources. 85/257/EEC, EURATOM.

7. The Community does have other Budgets. The ECSC Budget represents income at about 2% of the EEC Budget level. The European Development Fund (at about 1,000 million ECUs) is accounted separately, as are Borrowing and Lending operations (about 8,000 million ECUs annually).

8. By excluding fisheries (c.1%), and the structural guidance expenditure (c.3%) and using commitments figures rather than payments, this percentage can be reduced to about 63% which is a more accurate assessment of the cost of the CAP itself.

9. Article 203a EEC. The terms 'non-necessary', 'non-obligatory' and 'non-compulsory' are used interchangeably to describe this type of expenditure.

10. Joint Declaration by the European Parliament, the Council and the Commission on Conciliation Procedures, 4 March 1975, O.J. 1975, C 89/1. See further above pp.118–19.

11. J.A. Usher, 'The Financing of the Community' in *Thirty Years of Community Law* (Luxembourg, 1984), pp.195–217, at 212.

12. Despite this, the procedure it set out was used for the 1977 Budget.

13. This date is part of what is called the 'pragmatic timetable' - designed to give the budgetary procedure more time than the original treaty drafters allowed. The treaty timetable *requires* the preliminary draft to be submitted by 1 September. For a number of reasons the 'pragmatic' timetable has not been used for the 1986 and 1987 Budgets - but will be returned to as soon as possible.

14. Discussed further below pp.123–4.

15. Paper presented by Harry Salter of the Directorate-General for Budgets of the EC Commission. UKAEL Conference, 25 September 1981.

16. Article 203(4).

17. See Article 203(9) and below pp.124–5. Hence the use of the terms maximum maximum rate and minimum maximum rate! Another significant power of the EP over non-compulsory expenditure about which it has reservations is to vote money into the Reserve - known as 'Chapter 100'. This has the effect of freezing the expenditure and the money cannot be spent until it has been transferred at a later date to another specific budget item at which point the Commission may be required to explain its expenditure plans more fully.

18. Article 203(5).

19. Article 203(8). For a discussion of problems of interpretation of Article 203 see Sopwith, 'Community Budget'. Note that no formal note is necessary for *approval* of the Budget - only the EP President's signature.

20. Article 203(6).

21. See D. Strasser, *The Finances of Europe*, 2nd Edn. (Office for Official Publications of the EC, Brussels, 1981), Ch.4.

22. *Eighteenth General Report of the Activities of the European Communities, 1984* (Luxembourg, 1985), p.60.

23. Article 204.

24. *Sixteenth General Report of the Activities of the European Communities, 1982* (Office for Official Publications of the EC, Luxembourg, 1983), p.46. This figure is for commitments, payments were projected at an increase of 24.60%.

25. Ibid (payments were cut to 3.69%).

26. See further e.g. H. Wallace, *Budgetary Politics*, p.88.

27. See above, p.119.

28. Joint Declaration of 30 June 1982 by the European Parliament, the Council and the Commission on various measures to improve the budgetary procedure.

29. See above, note 3.

30. See above, note 6.

BUDGET PROCEDURES

| Which Institution | Date set by Treaty by which to act (note "Pragmatic" timetable see note 13) | Duties and Powers | Empowering Article and Section |
|---|---|---|---|
| Commission | 1 May | After consulting economic policy committee establishes max rate of increase for non-obligatory expenses. | 203(9) |
| All Institutions | 1 July | Draw up own expense estimates and pass to Commission. | 203(2) |
| Commission | 1 September | Consolidate all separate estimates into Preliminary Draft Budget. May also attach opinion containing different draft estimates to those supplied by other institutions. | 203(2) |
| Council | 5 October | After consulting Commission and any other institution from whose estimate it intends to depart, establishes Draft Budget by qualified majority. | 203(3) |
| Parliament | Within 45 days of receipt | Must accept or propose changes. If no action, deemed to be accepted and established after 45 days.<br>Powers to change:<br>*For obligatory expenditure*<br>Acting by absolute majority of votes cast it may propose modifications to Draft Budget.<br>*For non-obligatory expenditure*<br>Acting by majority of members (not votes cast), it may amend Draft Budget. | 203(4) |

| | | | | | |
|---|---|---|---|---|---|
| Council | Within 15 days of receipt | After appropriate discussions with Commission and, where appropriate, other institutions Council may: | | | |
| | | *For obligatory expenditure*: | | *For non-obligatory expenditure* | |
| | | If overall increase: May accept by a qualified majority, otherwise deemed to be rejected. | If overall decrease: May be rejected by qualified majority or deemed to be accepted. | Modify any amendment adopted by Parliament - must be by qualified majority. | 203(5) |
| Parliament | Within 15 days of receipt | *For obligatory expenditure* No power to alter further. | | *For non-obligatory expenditure* May be acting by majority of members and 3/5 of votes cast amend or reject the Council's modifications to its amendments. If not done, deemed to be accepted. | 203(6) |
| | | N.B. Power to reject *in toto* by majority of members and 2/3 votes cast. | | | 203(8) |

# 6

# The Court of Justice

The European Court of Justice (ECJ) plays a unique and crucial role in the functioning of the Community. In a community comprising twelve Member States, 13 legal systems and nine official languages, it has to 'ensure that in the interpretation and application of this [the EEC] Treaty the law is observed' (Article 164). It is given a wide-ranging role, being required by various articles to act as an international court (Article 170), as an administrative court (Articles 173-6, 178, 184), as a civil court (Article 215), as an industrial tribunal (Article 179), and as a transnational constitutional court (Article 177). The work of the ECJ has rightly received a great deal of detailed attention but this chapter will only attempt to present an outline of its composition and organisation, and the main types of work which it performs, together with some assessment of the role it plays in the development of Community law. The chapter concludes with a brief comment on the impact of the ECJ's jurisprudence on the English courts.

## COMPOSITION AND ORGANISATION

The ECJ is made up of 13 judges[1] and six advocates general[2] (whose role is discussed below). They are chosen by the 'common accord' (i.e. unanimous agreement) of the governments of the Member States.[3] They serve for six-year renewable terms, but their elections are staggered so that six or seven judges and three advocates general are replaced or re-elected every three years.[4]

Election to the Court is open to any persons 'whose independence is beyond doubt and who possess the qualifications required for appointment to the highest judicial office in their respective countries, or who are jurisconsults of recognised competence'.[5] In the majority of civil law systems jurisconsults (or legal academics, in practice professors of law) are themselves eligible for appointment to high judicial office, but the drafting of Article 167 does admit the possibility of a professor of law being appointed to the Court from a state (like the UK) where non-practising academic lawyers are not eligible for appointment to the bench. The majority of the bench of the ECJ are former legal practitioners or members of the judiciary from Member States, but many have combined legal practice with a university appointment, or a career in politics. Significantly the ECSC Treaty did not even require a legal qualification as a prerequisite for appointment, and it has been suggested that the ECJ's distinctive judicial style - particularly its teleological approach to interpretation - can be attributed to the wider perspectives of a judiciary whose professional careers, unlike the English (and Scottish) bench, have not been restricted to practice at the bar.

The Treaty does not require that each Member State should have a judge in the Court, but in practice this is what has always happened. The appointment of an extra judge being used to avoid an even number in the Court, and thus the possibility of the ECJ being equally divided, is rotated in turn around the four largest Member States. Similarly the advocates general have always been chosen from these larger states, although on the accession of Greece in 1981 a fifth advocate general was appointed from the Netherlands and on the accession of Spain and Portugal in 1986 a sixth was appointed.

In order to help expedite the work of the Court, Article 165 permits it to form chambers of three or six judges. These chambers are competent either to undertake preparatory work in certain types of case or to determine cases themselves. Generally speaking, when an important issue arises, that is, one in which the Court's jurisprudence is likely to be extended, the ECJ will sit in plenary session. In cases brought before the Court by a Member State or by an institution of the Community the ECJ *must*, however, sit in plenary session. Since the enlargement of the Community in 1986 there have been six chambers: four chambers consisting of three judges and two chambers of six judges.

As a strategy for dealing with the increasing number of time-consuming direct actions coming before the ECJ, Article 11 of the Single European Act, which introduces Article 168A by way of amendment to the EEC Treaty, provides for the creation and attachment of a court to the ECJ with jurisdiction to hear and determine at first instance certain classes of action brought by natural or legal persons. This court would be competent to hear all direct actions seeking review of Community action and actions for damages against Community institutions. It would not, however, be competent to hear actions brought by Member States, or by Community institutions or questions referred for a preliminary ruling under Article 177. The decisions of this court of first instance would be subject to appeal to the ECJ on points of law.

This court is to be brought into being at the request of the ECJ by the Council acting unanimously after consulting the Commission and the Parliament. The Council is also to determine the composition of the court whose judges, like the judges of the ECJ, are to be chosen from persons whose independence is beyond doubt and who possess the ability required for appointment to judicial office. The judges are to be chosen by the common accord of the Member States and are to hold office for a period of six years. At the time of writing no steps have been taken to bring the court into being.

## INDEPENDENCE

The Treaty and the rules of procedure contained in the Statute of the Court (a protocol to the founding Treaties) specifically require impartiality of the members of the ECJ.[6] Indeed on appointment members are required to take an oath to perform their duties 'impartially and conscientiously', and to 'preserve the secrecy of the deliberations of the Court'.[7] This secrecy surrounding the deliberations is also an aspect of independence, for the Court gives only one judgment; separate or dissenting opinions which are a commonplace of most national and international courts, are not permitted. This is intended to protect individual judges, who are, after all, appointed for a relatively short period only with the unanimous approval of the Member States, from being the victim of pressure - whether intentional or unintentional - from Member States to vote in a particular way. There is, however, a price to be paid for this. Judgments are often brief to the point of terseness on controversial issues. Points of considerable interest and debate and of future importance, which are not immediately germane to the case in hand, are frequently left without comment, and not explored *obiter dicta* in the way they are by common law judges.

## Advocates General

The advocates general of the ECJ have no direct counterpart in either common or civil law systems. Although they are members of the Court and thus equal in status to the judges, theirs is an independent position and they are not entitled to participate in the secret deliberations of the judges. The closest analogous office to that of the advocate general is the *commissaire du gouvernement* of the French *Conseil d'Etat*, but unlike the advocates general, the *commissaire* lacks independence and is specifically enjoined to deliberate with the *conseillers* in cases before the *Conseil*.

The functions of the advocates general are set down in Article 166 EEC:

> It shall be the duty of the Advocate-General, acting with complete impartiality and independence, to make, in open court, reasoned submissions on cases brought before the Court of Justice, in order to assist the Court in the performance of the task assigned to it in Article 164.

In practice, however, the main function of the advocate general is to assist the judges of the ECJ by offering a reasoned opinion on the case before it. In the advocate general's opinion, which is purely personal and does not represent the views of either the Community, the Member States or the Court, he or she will advise the Court as to the way in which he or she believes the case ought to be decided. Sometimes the Court will follow the submissions of the advocate general; sometimes it will, at least on the face of the judgment, disregard them. However, the office of advocate general has had a significant impact upon the style of the ECJ and the advocates general's opinions have proved to be a fruitful source for the development of the Court's *jurisprudence*.

## THE POWERS OF THE COURT

The most important powers of the ECJ will be dealt with under four main headings:

A) Judicial Review
B) Actions for Damages
C) Actions against Member States
D) Preliminary Reference Procedure

## A) JUDICIAL REVIEW

Judicial review provides a system of judicial supervision of the legislative system of the Community, and its inclusion in the EEC Treaty reinforces the point that neither the legislature nor the executive are above the law of the Treaty. In exercising its power of review the ECJ is the supreme arbiter of the law. As Brown and Jacobs have pointed out, unlike the UK legal system where decisions of the House of Lords can be reversed by an Act of Parliament even with retroactive effect, 'the decisions of the Court of Justice cannot be reversed by an act of the Council; on the contrary, any measure of the Council having legal effect can be annulled by the Court if contrary to the Treaties'.[8] The powers of the ECJ itself are not, however, unrestricted, for the Treaties set out the circumstances in which it may exercise its powers of review. Nevertheless, the way that it exercises certain of its powers has given rise to controversy.

### A Controversial Strategy?

It will soon become apparent that although Member States and certain institutions (so-called 'privileged plaintiffs') are given wide rights of access to the Court, private individuals have much more limited rights. Indeed such restricted rights as the Treaty gives, the Court has interpreted even more restrictively.

Why a court which usually takes such an expansive view of its powers should seek to restrict the rights of individuals has given rise to a great deal of speculation. Rasmussen[9] points out that individuals may use the doctrine of 'direct effect' to challenge the legality of Community law before national courts and request the national court to refer the issue to the ECJ under Article 177. This indirect access, where the ECJ acts as a form of superior court (although *not* as a court of appeal), does not involve the ECJ in time-consuming fact-finding inquiries, for the facts will have been found by the national court. Is therefore the ECJ, he asks, seeking to change its constitutional role, by encouraging 'appellate' style jurisdiction under Article 177, and restricting its first instance fact-finding role, such as is involved in judicial review cases? In reply it has been pointed out that from an early date the ECJ has stressed the need for certainty in Community legislation, and that a relatively unrestricted access to the Court to challenge the legality of Community legislation might result in a lack of confidence in this new form of legislation.[10] To put the issue into a comparative perspective: if the EEC Treaty is seen as a constitutional document and, as argued above, Community legislation is seen as the equivalent of statutes in national systems then, since very few national constitutions permit individuals to challenge the legality of statutes, by analogy it will only be very rarely that individuals are permitted to challenge Community acts. In the UK, for example, the doctrine of parliamentary supremacy has made such challenge impossible (certainly until the passing of the European Communities Act 1972). In those countries where it is possible (e.g. West Germany) it is only permitted on very restricted grounds of unconstitutionality. In this context it may be understandable why the ECJ does not wish to encourage the challenge of legislation from too many quarters, which would raise uncertainty about the status of much Community legislation.

## REVIEW OF COMMUNITY ACTS: ARTICLE 173

The power of review given by Article 173 permits the Court to annul acts of the Council or Commission which violate Community law. There are restrictions both on those who have the right to bring an action (*locus standi*), and the grounds on which actions may be brought. Furthermore, in order to be admissible, actions must be brought within two months of the publication of the act or within two months of its notification to the plaintiff.

### Locus Standi

Article 173 only gives *locus standi* to specific classes of applicants:

*1. Privileged plaintiffs*

Member States, the Council and the Commission are designated privileged plaintiffs. Although, like individuals, they have to bring their actions within two months, these privileged plaintiffs have no further hurdles to overcome in order to establish the admissibility of their case. It is notable, however, that the EP has no independent right to appear as a plaintiff under Article 173 although it may intervene on behalf of one party in existing proceedings as it did in the *Isoglucose* cases.[11]

*2. Natural or legal persons*

Article 173(2) provides that:

> Any natural or legal person may, under the same conditions, institute proceedings against a decision addressed to that person or against a decision which, although in the form of a regulation or a decision addressed to another person is of direct and individual concern to the former.

From this somewhat complicated drafting there are three situations where such a person may bring an action:

*(a) A decision addressed to that person.* Where a Council or Commission decision is addressed directly to an individual or an undertaking (i.e. any entity which is engaged in commercial activity) then there is a clear right to challenge. In *Prais v. Council*,[12] Prais had applied for a post as legal interpreter with the Council. When the date of the examination for the post was announced it fell on a Jewish holy day and she was unable to attend. She sought an alternative date, but the Council decided that other arrangements could not be made for her. She was able, therefore, to bring an action to challenge that decision. Her case does, however, raise a problem in that the act which the individual is seeking to challenge may not be labelled a 'decision'; it might for example be called an opinion, or simply be contained in a letter. The ECJ has ruled that whatever an act is called, if it affects the legal position of the individual it is in substance a decision. Thus in *Noordwijks Cement Accoord*[13] the Commission wrote to the cement firms, who were parties to an agreement regulating cement prices, to tell them that in its opinion the agreement was contrary to Community competition law. The parties to the agreement sought to challenge this letter as a decision addressed to them. The Commission, however, argued that this was not a decision but an opinion and was thus excluded from review under Article 173. The Court pointed out, however, that as Community law gives the Commission itself

power to decide which agreements do or do not contravene competition law, the effect of the letter was to make parties to the agreement subject immediately to fines. The letter thus affected their position and was a decision.

*(b) A decision addressed to another person which is of direct and individual concern to the former.* The definition of a decision is of course the same as discussed above. Here the decision must be addressed to another person, as in *Metro*[14]. Metro owned a self-service wholesale business for electrical goods which had been refused distribution rights for goods manufactured by SABA - a German electronics firm. Metro complained to the Commission that this refusal by SABA infringed EC competition law. The Commission exonerated SABA from the complaint, but Metro considered that the Commission had erred in making its decision and sought review. In view of Metro's special interest in the case having initiated the original complaint, the ECJ decided that although the decision of the Commission was not addressed to Metro, nevertheless its complaint was admissible under Article 173(2).

It is worth noting that another person may include a Member State (and possibly an institution). So in *Plaumann v. Commission*[15] the applicant was a German importer of clementines affected by a Commission decision addressed to the Federal Government. And in *Töpfer v. Commission*[16] the applicant was one of 27 importers of maize into West Germany. The Commission issued a decision authorising the German government to refuse him an import licence. It was possible for Töpfer (who was also able to prove that he was directly and individually concerned - the problems of this are discussed below) to challenge the legality of this decision addressed to another person - the German government.

*(c) A decision, in the form of a regulation, which is of direct and individual concern to the former.* The first point to consider is how a decision can be in the form of a regulation. As we have seen above in the *Noodrwijks* case the Court will look at the *effect* of an act, rather than what it is called. It is therefore able to examine regulations to see whether they possess the essential qualities of regulations - i.e. that they are of general application. This is linked to the discussion of the requirement of 'direct and individual concern' (below), but basically it can be said that if an act which

calls itself a regulation has such limited application that it cannot in reality be said to be 'of general application', then it may not be a regulation at all, but a decision and thus open to challenge. An example may make this clearer. The *International Fruit Company* case[17] concerned the system by which the Commission controlled the import of apples. Each week companies wishing to import apples applied to their governments, which then passed the applications to the Commission. On the basis of the applications received, the Commission settled the amount of apples which would be imported in the following week, and accordingly a percentage of the amount each importer had requested would be granted. The figures were then enacted by regulation. When a disappointed Dutch company complained about its allocation, the ECJ held that although the Commission had acted by regulation, it was in effect issuing decisions to those who had requested licences, hence it was not a true regulation at all but a 'bundle of decisions'.

*Direct and individual concern.* This is a requirement which is obviously intended to restrict the right of application for annulment to those who have a clear interest in the case; it has been interpreted strictly by the ECJ.

Of the two requirements, the more difficult to establish is individual concern, but direct concern can be an obstacle too. An individual will only be directly concerned if there is a direct link between the decision and the application of that decision to the individual. Rather like the doctrine of direct effect, with which it has been compared, the decision must be complete, there must be no margin of discretion in the way in which it can be applied. In *Alcan v. Commission*[18] the applicants were Belgian aluminium producers who, through their government, had sought an increase in the allocation of low-tariff aluminium allocated to Belgium and thus to them. When they challenged the Commission for refusing this increase, the ECJ held that even if an increased quota had been allotted to Belgium, the Belgian government would then have had a discretion as to which of the firms the quota should go. The chain of the direct link between the companies and the Commission was therefore broken by the discretionary power of the Belgian government. The applicants were only concerned indirectly.

In the majority of cases, however, the ECJ concerns itself primarily, if not exclusively, with the issue of individual concern. This is so difficult to establish that in the history of the EEC less than a dozen applicants have overcome this hurdle. Indeed, if it can be overcome then virtually all the other requirements usually follow in its wake. The classic test for individual concern was laid down in *Plaumann v. Commission*, where the ECJ said:[19]

> Persons other than those to whom a decision is addressed may only claim to be individually concerned if that decision affects them by reason of certain attributes which are peculiar to them, *or* by reason of circumstances in which they are differentiated from all other persons *and* by reason of these factors distinguishes them individually just as in the case of the person addressed. [emphasis added]

The few cases that have been successful show that in order to satisfy this stringent test the applicants need to be members of a closed or a fixed and ascertainable group at the time the decision was passed. In other words, at the time the institution made the decision it must have known, or been able to ascertain, exactly who was affected by it and the decision then adopted must apply to them and to no one else. In practice the only way that this rigorous test can be met is if there is an element of retroactivity in the decision. This can be clearly seen in the first case ever to be found admissable, *Töpfer*.[20] In this case the German authorities had, as a result of an error, set the import levy on maize from outside the EEC at zero. On 1 October 1963 Töpfer together with 25 other German companies applied to import a substantial amount of maize free of levy. Alerted by the substantial increase in applications, the German authorities realised the error and refused to issue licences. On 4 October the Commission authorised the German authorities to raise a normal levy on maize imports 'including those at present and duly pending before the authorities'. The only persons affected by the retrospective application of that decision, indeed the only persons who could be affected by it as a matter of fact and of law, were the applicants. They were therefore individually concerned.

In *Bock v. Commission*[21] the German government had prohibited the import of Chinese mushrooms. While a ban on direct imports from China would have been legal, a ban on imports in free circulation in other Member States constituted an obstruction to the free movement of goods. On 4 September 1970 Bock applied to import a consignment of mushrooms from Holland. He repeated his request on 9 and 11 September. Meanwhile the German authorities had approached the Commission for authorisation to refuse such imports 'including the import envisaged'. On 15 September the

Commission issued a decision authorising such refusal, including applications 'at present and duly pending'. The German authorities then turned down Bock's request. The ECJ found Bock individually concerned by the Commission decision, for those affected by its retrospective character were 'fixed and ascertainable' at the time it was made.

Similarly in *International Fruit Company v. Commission*[22] when the Commission issued its 'bundle of decisions' on licence applications, it knew precisely who the companies were which had applied. The group could not be added to, therefore all were individually concerned. In more recent cases, such as *Metro v. Commission*[23] and the *Japanese Ball Bearing* cases[24] there appears to have been some relaxation of the rule relating to individual concern, but this is probably limited to these particular cases which were in some senses unusual. They do not give a general indication that the ECJ has abandoned its rigorous approach in more usual review actions.

## Grounds for Complaint

Article 173(1) sets out the four grounds on which an act may be annulled. These are loosely based upon the four grounds for judicial review developed by the Supreme French Administrative Court, the *Conseil d'Etat*. However, the ECJ has developed them virtually beyond recognition. When bringing an action an applicant may allege any one or more of the following grounds, but if the ECJ finds for the applicant, it does not always clarify the exact ground which it has found to be satisfied.

### *1. Lack of competence*

Corresponding loosely to the English law concept of substantive *ultra vires*,[25] complaints on this ground will allege that the Council or the Commission have acted outside their authority or the powers attributed to them under the Treaty. A case which demonstrates this, and also shows the interdependence of the grounds of review is *Meroni v. High Authority*.[26] The ECSC High Authority had delegated certain of its powers to take decisions on the assessment of levies on the production of iron from scrap to another body it had established - 'the Scrap Bureau'. The ECJ found that the delegation was a violation of the ECSC Treaty (see ground 3 below) hence decisions of the High Authority simply endorsing those of the Scrap

Bureau were 'improperly taken'.

*2. Infringement of an essential procedural requirement*

Again this ground loosely corresponds with the English law idea of procedural *ultra vires*,[27] but again the approach of the ECJ is more interventionist than the English courts. Two categories of cases have utilised this ground. The first category arises from the requirement to give reasons. In the *Brennwein case*,[28] Germany sought permission from the Commission to import, in 1961, 450,000 hectolitres of cheap non-EEC wine to make into a fortified wine called *brennwein*. The Commission granted permission for only 100,000 hectolitres, pointing out that 'on the basis of the information collected' (which it did not specify) it was satisfied that 'production of wines in question is amply sufficient' within the EC to meet the requirements of the *brennwein* producers, thus the grant of the requested quota might lead to 'serious disturbances in the market'. The ECJ struck the decision down, pointing out that Article 190 required reasons to be given for decisions so that the Court could effectively exercise its powers of review. Here the requirements of Article 190 were not satisfied because of the 'inadequacy, the vagueness and the inconsistency of the statement of reasons'.[29] By suggesting that it is prepared not only to see if there are reasons, but also whether the reasons sustain the decisions they accompany the ECJ has made this more than a simple procedural requirement.

The second group of cases arises from the consultation requirements of the Treaty. Failure to consult as required by the Article upon which the act is based will render that act liable to annulment. The *Isoglucose* cases[30] provide an example, for there the ECJ struck down a regulation which had been passed by the Council without waiting for the opinion of the European Parliament.

*3. Infringement of this Treaty or of any rule of law relating to its application*

This is the most important ground of review. Indeed most of the cases discussed above could be annulled simply on this ground. It is not surprising therefore that it is pleaded in virtually all annulment actions.

Infringement of the Treaty may be alleged where there has been a procedural breach (as in the *Brennwein* or *Isoglucose* cases above) or where there has been a substantive breach (as was alleged by the Luxembourg government in *Luxembourg v. European Parliament* above, p.75).

Infringement of a rule of law relating to the application of the Treaty throws a far wider net than the specific requirements of the Treaty itself. It obviously covers situations where the Council or the Commission has acted in breach of the requirements of Community legislation but the ECJ has used this ground to develop a much broader concept of the 'rule of law'. It has held that there are certain 'general principles of law' which underpin the Community legal order and against which the legality of Community acts must be measured.[31] In developing these 'general principles' the Court has drawn, in an eclectic fashion, upon concepts of various national administrative and constitutional laws and even international law. The result is an emerging, truly European, system of administrative law, created by a court drawing on the strengths of the legal systems of the Member States. An analogy can be drawn here with the development, by the *Conseil d'Etat*, of the ground of *violation de la loi.* Originally this meant violation of a statute, but it was gradually extended to mean violation of general concepts of legality.

There is no theoretical limit to the 'general principles'. The ECJ has found that they cover the generally accepted requirements of due process of law - good faith, fairness. For example in *Transocean Marine Paint Association v. Commission*,[32] the English law rule of *audi alterem partem* was used to strike down a Commission decision which had varied the legal position of the applicants without giving them an opportunity to give their view. Other concepts, less familiar to common lawyers, have also been used; such as the concept derived from German administrative law that administrative action should be proportionate to the ends it seeks to achieve (*Verhaltnismassigkeit*), e.g. the CAP scheme to dispose of powdered milk by requiring it to be fed to dairy cows was struck down on these grounds.[33] Other concepts recognised include respect for legitimate expectations (from the German *Vertrauensschütz*), equality and legal certainty, as well as concepts derived from the Treaty, such as the prohibition of discrimination on the grounds of nationality.[34]

Of particular importance have been developments in the field of human rights. A number of Community Member States, notably Germany and Italy, have entrenched provisions of their constitutions protecting human rights. In an important line of cases the ECJ has ruled that similar protection is an inherent part of

Community law. In *Stauder v. City of Ulm*,[35] in spite of the fact that there are no provisions of the EEC Treaty relating to human rights, the ECJ talked of 'fundamental human rights enshrined in the general principles of Community law and protected by the Court'. And in *Internationale Handelsgesellschaft*,[36] when asked to rule whether a provision of an EEC regulation might violate the human rights provisions of the German constitution, the ECJ forcibly rejected the idea that provisions of Community law could be invalidated by any provision of national law, but pointed out that there was an analogous guarantee of human rights inherent in Community law and that 'respect for human rights forms an integral part of the general principles of law protected by the Court of Justice'.[37] These analogous guarantees are not, however, derived only from provisions of some national constitutions. The shared commitment to the protection of human rights which is to be found in the European Convention of Human Rights (a creation of the other European organisation - the Council of Europe) also represents part of the 'constitutional provisions common to Member States' and in *Nold v. Commission*[38] the Court ruled that it and other such 'treaties for the protection of human rights, on which the Member States have collaborated, or to which they are signatories, can supply the guidelines which should be followed within the framework of Community law'.[39] Since then, the right of respect for religious freedom,[40] and the right of property[41] have been recognised in individual cases, and this theme in the Court's work has been strengthened by the 1977 Joint Declaration of the other three main Community institutions on respect for human rights.[42]

*4. Misuse of powers*

This concept is derived from the French *detournement de pouvoir*. There is no precise analogy in English law, but in brief it involves the use of a legitimate power in an illegitimate manner, or for an illegitimate end. It was of considerable importance under the ECSC Treaty, where it was the sole ground for individual complaint (Article 33(2) ECSC), but in the EEC regime its role has been eclipsed by the importance of infringement of the Treaty (3 above). Indeed it is difficult to find an EEC case decided on this principle, but the *Giuffrida* case[43] provides an illustration. The applicants applied for a post with the Council for which the specifications were so precise that they only fitted the qualifications of one candidate. Giuffrida argued that the specifications were imposed simply to ensure that this candidate obtained the post, and that it was not a free competition. The Court upheld this allegation, finding a misuse of powers had occurred.

## REVIEW OF INACTION: ARTICLE 175

Whereas Article 173 permits review of acts of the Council and the Commission, Article 175 permits review of their failure to act. The two rights of action have been described as the two sides of the same coin, part of the 'same system of review',[44] but this perhaps underplays the differences between the two actions.

In order to sustain an action under Article 175, it is necessary to establish that the Council or the Commission has failed to act 'in infringement of [the] Treaty', i.e. there must be a violation of a provision which imposes an obligation to act; a mere discretionary power, such as that contained in Article 169, is not sufficient. What is not yet clear is whether Article 175 can only be used for infringements of Treaty articles, or whether it might be taken to include infringements of 'any rule of law relating to the application of [the] Treaty' (discussed above). If the ECJ were to take a broader view of legality and thus of the terminology of Article 175, this would permit an action not only for a failure to act which is in infringement of an article of the Treaty itself, but also for an infringement of a rule of Community legislation (perhaps of a regulation or a decision), or even of a 'general principle of law'. Indeed Schermers suggests that the Commission could be held liable for a failure to act which infringed human rights.[45]

### Locus Standi

As under Article 173 Member States have privileged status, but it is also extended to *all* the institutions, so that it includes the EP which in 1985 brought a successful action against both the Council and the Commission for failure to implement a Common Transport Policy.[46] Before such an action may be started the institution complained of must first be called upon to act. If it has not acted within two months, then an action may be brought within a further two-month period.

Natural or legal persons may also bring such an action under the same time constraints, if 'an institution of the Community has failed to address to that person an act other than a recommendation or an opinion'.[47] It seems then that this can be utilised against institutions other than the Council and Commission, but only where the failure has been to address a legally binding act. In addition it seems from *Lord Bethel v. Commission*,[48] that an individual is only likely to be successful in complaining of a failure to act in circumstances in which, if the institution had acted, the act would have been of direct and individual concern to the complainant. So, a plaintiff in a similar situation to *Metro* above, who found that the Commission was not prepared to take any action against suppliers imposing possibly illegal conditions, might be able to use Article 175 to compel it to take action. What is clear, is that Article 175 cannot be used to change a decision, thus seeking to avoid the restricted rights of direct access to judicial review under Article 173, by arguing, for example, that the Commission has 'failed to act' because it has not acted in the manner the complainant wishes, perhaps by refusing the complainant's application for a licence when it should have accepted it.

## THE EXCEPTION OF ILLEGALITY: ARTICLE 184

Article 184 provides a means by which 'any party' may dispute the legality of a regulation when the two-month limitation period has elapsed, but the regulation is invoked against them. In such proceedings, when the regulation is put in issue, the ECJ is empowered to rule that, if it infringes any of the grounds for review set out in Article 173 (see above pp.142-6), it is inapplicable. The classic case is where a regulation is passed, which contains, for example, a procedural irregularity, authorising the imposition of levies on certain classes of importers. Those who might be affected by it fail to realise its significance within the two-month limitation period of 173(3), or more probably are unable to establish *locus standi* to challenge it. A decision is then passed, based upon the regulation, imposing a levy on a particular firm. That firm may challenge the decision under Article 173, but the basis of its complaint is the illegality of the regulation from which the decision derives, and that has become unassailable through the passing of the two-month limitation period. Here the applicant can use Article 184 to put the validity of the basic regulation in issue, and the ECJ may rule that it is 'inapplicable', i.e. it retains its validity against the world at large, but may not be invoked against the applicant.[49]

The issuing institution will then usually withdraw it.

This example shows that Article 184 can only be used when the regulation is put in issue in proceedings which have already begun before the ECJ. It does not provide a means of taking a dispute for the first time to that Court. Two other issues surrounding the use of Article 184 are not so clear. First, whether Member States, or institutions, are able to utilise Article 184. It will be recalled that they have privileged rights of challenge under Article 173, and in addition they will have participated in the making of the regulation. Although there is evidence from a number of cases[50] to suggest that they cannot, the question has yet to be finally resolved. Second, can Article 184 be used only to challenge proper regulations, or, given the fact that the ECJ looks in other situations to the substance of an act rather than its form, can decisions in the form of regulations, or even regulations in the form of decisions be challenged? This too awaits a definitive ruling.

## B) ACTIONS AGAINST THE COMMUNITY FOR DAMAGES

The ECJ is given jurisdiction to hear actions brought by an individual claiming damages against the Community in two circumstances:

### (a) Contractual liability

Where an allegation is made that the Community is in breach of contract, the applicable law will be the law governing the contract, and the case may be heard by the relevant national courts or by the ECJ if the parties so designate.[51]

### (b) Non-contractual liability

In such cases the Community is obliged to 'make good any damage caused by its institutions or by its servants in the performance of their duties' in accordance with 'the general principles common to the laws of the Member States'.[52]

Such cases, which must be brought within five years of the damage being suffered,[53] have the effect of holding the Communities liable for losses suffered. Where the complaint arises from the effects of legislation (e.g. where a plaintiff suffers losses as a result of a regulation which he claims is discriminatory or illegal in some other way), it seemed initially that an action had first to be brought to annul the legal act concerned - by use of either Article 173 or 177 - with the action for damages following after the annulment had been secured.[54] However, in its later case law the ECJ has relaxed this formal requirement, stressing that actions for damages and actions for annulment are distinct and different actions.[55] Nevertheless, the restrictive approach to direct actions which was apparent from the Court's attitude to *locus standi* under Article 173 (see above pp. 137-42) has a parallel in the requirements that a complainant seeking damages must meet. The Community will not be liable for all damages suffered as a result of its actions (or those of its servants), but only for that which can be proved to be the result of Community action where the action was not only unlawful, but seriously unlawful. In fact in *Zuckerfabrik Schoppenstedt v. Council* it was held that before the Community will be liable for damages there must be a sufficiently serious (or 'manifest and grave') violation of a superior rule of law intended for the protection of the individual. It is worth considering each of these requirements in turn.

*(i) Breach of a superior rule of law*

This will be a rule which would normally be a ground for annulment, so that even if annulment is not sought before an action for damages is brought, there must still exist sufficient substantive reasons for an annulment before the ECJ will consider the damages action.[56]

*(ii) A sufficiently serious breach*

The simple fact that there are grounds to annul an act (or indeed if the act complained of *has* been annulled) does not in itself mean that damages will be awarded. The Community must have been guilty of a serious beach of a law - or as it is termed a 'manifest and grave' breach. There is, however, some discussion as to whether the terms 'manifest' and 'grave' relate to the consequences of the breach or to the nature of the conduct of the Community complained of.[57] In the *Quellmehl and Gritz* cases[58] the complainants suffered severe losses as a result of a Council decision to withdraw subsidy from them. The ECJ struck down the decision (in an Article 177 reference) on the grounds that it was discriminatory. In awarding damages for the amount of subsidy lost the Court held that the complainants' losses 'went beyond that inherent in business'. In other words the gravity of the violation seemed to relate to the gravity of the loss suffered.

However, two months later in the *Isoglucose* cases[59] the Court seemed to take a different approach. Isoglucose is a sugar substitute, and in the early 1970s producers had received a subsidy. When the price of sugar fell in the late 1970s the subsidy for isoglucose was stopped and then large levies were imposed on its production. Losses of up to £30 million were suffered by the isoglucose producers who were able to have the regulations imposing the levies struck down and then claimed damages. Here the Court stressed not the extent of the harm, but the degree of the violation of the rule of law, holding that the Community would only be liable if its behaviour 'verged on the arbitrary' - which in this case it did not. This latter conclusion seems highly questionable but the significance of this case for the future is that it seems that a complainant needs to be able to show that both the scale of the loss *and* the degree of the Community's violation of the rule of law were manifest and grave if he is to have any chance of satisfying this requirement.

*(iii) Violation of a rule of law intended for the protection of the individual*

Most of the grounds for review discussed above would seem to be relevant, notably lack of proportionality, breach of legitimate expectation and discrimination, together with violations of human rights.

A further hurdle in the way of a plaintiff seeking damages from the Community, is that the ECJ will decline to hear a case if the substance of the complaint is not EC law itself, but the way that it has been implemented by the national authorities - such a claim must be heard by the national courts. However, the distinction is not always easy to draw, and the ECJ has yet to provide clear guidelines for this 'choice of court' problem.[60]

## C) ACTIONS AGAINST MEMBER STATES: ARTICLES 169 AND 170

The Treaty provides two methods by which actions may be taken against a Member State which 'fails to fulfil an obligation under [the] Treaty'.[61] Such action may be taken either by the

Commission, under Article 169, or by another Member State, under Article 170. The procedure is very similar in both cases. We will deal first with Article 169, which confers a discretionary power on the Commission (discussed above in Chapter 2) and where the Commission can be seen clearly in the exercise of its role as 'Guardian of the Treaty'. The procedure has three stages:

(a) The Commission, having come to an informal view that a state is in default, asks that state for its observations on that view.

(b) After receiving the observations, or in their absence, the Commission delivers a 'Reasoned Opinion'. This sets out the reasons for the allegation of default, and sets a time-limit for its rectification, usually six months, although it may be shorter in urgent cases.

(c) If the defaulting state fails to take remedial action within the specified time, the Commission may then take the matter to the ECJ.

If the Court finds that there has been a failure to fulfil a Treaty obligation, then it will make a ruling to that effect. Its ruling is declaratory. Although the state is 'required to take the necessary measures to comply with the judgment',[62] there is no formal sanction, either for the original breach, or even for failure to comply with the Court's ruling. Nevertheless, the record shows that in the overwhelming majority of cases, Member States comply with Commission opinions either before court proceedings are commenced, or during the course of the proceedings themselves. Although late compliance (i.e. after the expiry of the time limit specified) with a Commission opinion does not entitle the defaulting state to have the proceedings withdrawn - for otherwise it would be difficult for the Commission to obtain a clear legal condemnation of certain practices - nevertheless, in the exercise of its discretion the Commission may withdraw the case once the defaulting state has complied. The ECJ has even been known to permit a case to be withdrawn after the oral hearing. The motive for this is clear. Most cases do not involve novel points, they are predominantly concerned with states' failure to implement the obligations of directives, or the imposition of illegal trade barriers. Once the object of the immediate proceedings has been fulfilled, the Commission is often content to let the matter drop.

It seems then that the declaratory judgment is its own sanction and that states generally seek to avoid a judgment against them, representing as it does, in Everling's vivid phrase, 'a documented record of intrusion upon their sovereignty'.[63] Where such a finding is made, it is very rare for a state to maintain its illegal conduct in the face of a judgment. Should a judgment not be complied with, however, it is then open to the Commission to bring a second action, as it did in the *Second Art Treasures* case,[64] based on Article 171.

Under Article 170, one Member State may take an action against another. However, before such proceedings can be initiated, the matter must be brought before the Commission, which as in Article 169 proceedings then delivers a 'reasoned opinion', after having conducted an initial inquiry into the matter in which both states must have the opportunity to submit their case, and their observations on the other party's case, both orally and in writing. If the opinion is not given within three months, the complainant may press on with proceedings before the Court. However, the procedure is designed to introduce the Commission as 'honest broker' between the two states, and if a complaint is sustainable the Commission may take over the proceedings under Article 169, if not, it may keep a politically damaging dispute out of court. In fact only one such case between France and the UK over fishery legislation has ever got as far as court proceedings.[65]

## D) THE PRELIMINARY REFERENCE PROCEDURE: ARTICLE 177

Article 177 provides the main link between the courts of the Member States and the ECJ. Pescatore has called it an 'instrument of transnational law'[66] for, in so far as it provides a mechanism for national courts to refer problems of interpretation of Community law to the ECJ, the Treaty seeks to ensure that there will be uniformity in the application of Community law in all the national legal systems. The procedure is modelled on the reference to the national constitutional court which many civil law systems possess, and just as the intention of those national procedures is to ensure that all courts interpret the constitution in the same way, Article 177 is intended to ensure that the uniform application of Community law is not disturbed by varying, possibly conflicting, interpretations. It is for this reason that the ECJ's role has been described as a transnational constitutional court, inviting the analogy of the EEC treaty with a written constitution.[67] The importance that the drafters envisaged for the Article 177 procedure can be seen from the fact that the Treaty requires that Article 177 references be heard by the full Court in plenary session, not by a Chamber of the Court (Article 165(2)); and the importance that the procedure has acquired in practice can be seen from the fact that the pressure of work under Article 177 has forced the Court to abandon this requirement and to hear these cases in Chambers.

Article 177 provides that if, before any national court or tribunal, a question arises as to the:

(a) interpretation of [the EEC] Treaty;
(b) validity or interpretation of acts of the institutions of the Community;
(c) interpretations of the statutes of bodies established by the Council, where such statutes so provide

and a decision on that question is necessary to enable it to give judgment, then that court of tribunal may, and indeed must if it is a court of tribunal against whose decisions no judicial remedy is available, make reference to the ECJ.

**Interpretation not Application**

It must be stressed that the role of the ECJ under Article 177 is interpretation and not application. So, if a possible conflict between Community law and national law arises before a national court, and that court refers the issue to Luxembourg, the ECJ will not give any ruling on the validity or otherwise of the national provisions. Its role will be restricted to interpreting the provision of Community law.[68] This does not preclude the Court from indicating the effects that Community law is required to have in national systems, and the duties of the national judge to comply with such requirements. It is, however, the national judge who must take the actual decision in the case, and although the ECJ has ruled that interpretations rendered under Article 177 are legally binding (under Community law) on national courts,[69] it is the national judiciary which, armed with the ECJ's ruling, must then apply that ruling and make a decision in the instant case. Inevitably this has led to accusations that in certain cases the ECJ has exceeded its role,[70] however, if the Court is presented with a reference which asks it to do something impermissible, then it will rewrite the questions to bring it within its constitutional powers.[71]

Paradoxical as it may seem, Article 177 has itself raised a number of questions of interpretation relating both to its meaning and scope of application.

*Any national court or tribunal*

In a number of cases the question has arisen as to whether the body making a reference to the ECJ under Article 177 has been competent to do so. These have generally related to the ability of inferior tribunals to seek preliminary rulings. The ECJ has made it clear that the question of whether a body is a 'court' or 'tribunal' for the purposes of Article 177 is a matter for Community law and not a matter of national law.

In *Vaassen-Göbbels*[72] a preliminary ruling was sought by the *Scheidsgericht* - Arbitration Tribunal of the Mine Employees Fund - in the Netherlands. The Fund claimed that since the Tribunal was primarily of a private character and had extremely limited jurisdiction it was not a court or tribunal for the purposes of Article 177 and thus was not entitled to make a reference. The ECJ upheld the Tribunal's right to so make a reference. Examining the composition and functioning of the Tribunal the ECJ noted that its members were nominated by the Dutch government; its rules of procedure were laid down by the government; cases before the Tribunal were conducted as if it were a court (i.e. with full arguments being heard from both sides) and it was bound by its constitution to apply rules of a public law character. From a functional viewpoint, therefore, the Tribunal was like any other court which was bound to apply rules of law and to exercise a judicial function, i.e. to decide between two competing claims.

The judicial function is clearly the most important element in determining whether or not a body falls within the term 'court or tribunal' in Article 177. In *Jules Borker*,[73] for example, the ECJ held that the Bar Association of Paris was not competent to seek a preliminary ruling on whether a French lawyer was entitled as of right to appear before a German court since the Association was not 'called upon to give judgment in its proceedings intended to lead to a decision of a judicial nature'. Although there has been some dispute as to whether disciplinary or arbitral tribunals fall within Article 177, the ECJ has generally taken an expansive view of such matters relying on the functional nature of the body in question.

*Court or tribunal against whose decisions there is no judicial remedy under national law*

Most courts or tribunals have a discretion whether or not to refer questions of Community law to the ECJ, but where a question of Community law is raised before a court or tribunal 'against whose decisions there is no judicial remedy under national law, that court of tribunal *shall* bring the matter before the Court of Justice' (Article 177(3)) (emphasis added).

Generally, there will be little difficulty in determining which national courts fall within Article 177(3); usually it will be a court from which there is no right of appeal. In England, however, a particular problem is posed by the fact that there is no automatic right of appeal from the Court of Appeal to the House of Lords: leave must either be obtained from the Court of Appeal or from the House of Lords Appeal Committee. If leave is denied, the Court of Appeal becomes the court from which there is no judicial remedy. Questions of Community law raised in the Court of Appeal ought therefore to have been referred to the ECJ under Article 177(3) - although at the time of the hearing the Court of Appeal did not realise it was subject to this obligation and there is thus a possibility that the Community law element in a case may not have been properly determined. Lord Denning in *Bulmer v. Bollinger*[74] suggested it should normally be the Court of Appeal which referred issues to the ECJ and Collins suggests that the court from which there is no appeal *as of right* should be treated as the final court.[75] In England, therefore, it would normally be the Court of Appeal unless the 'leap-frog' procedure to the House of Lords was engaged.

*Whether a question is raised on which a decision is necessary to enable a national court to give judgment*

The question of whether to request a preliminary ruling from the ECJ is an issue solely within the discretion of the national court even if a question is substantially the same as one which has been referred previously.

In *Da Costa*,[76] for example, the facts were substantially the same as those in *Van Gend en Loos* and the questions put to the ECJ by the Dutch tribunal were the same. The ECJ affirmed the right of the Dutch tribunal to seek the ruling, but was content to refer the tribunal to the *Van Gend en Loos* judgment pointing out that it will usually be unnecessary to refer a question 'materially identical with a question which has already been the subject of a preliminary ruling in a similar case'. This approach is similar to the doctrine of *acte clair*, the exercise of which has been claimed by a number of national courts in a variety of circumstances involving Community law. The *acte clair* doctrine derives from French constitutional law. Under the French constitution the courts are obliged to seek guidance from the *Quai d'Orsay* (the French Foreign Ministry) when a question of interpretation of a treaty to which France is a party arises in the French courts. The French courts have used the doctrine of *acte clair*, i.e. that the treaty provisions are clear and freely susceptible to interpretation, to evade the need to refer.

The unregulated use of this doctrine by national courts in relation to the interpretation of Community law would undermine the effectiveness of the Article 177 procedure and the uniformity of interpretation of Community law which it facilitates and thus, understandably, the ECJ has never explicitly sanctioned the use of this doctrine in relation to Community law. However, it gave qualified approval to the idea in *CILFIT*.[77] In this case the ECJ identified three conditions which, if fulfilled, rendered it unnecessary for a court of last resort within the meaning of Article 177(3) to refer a question of Community law to the ECJ:

First, where the national court, exercising its discretion, did not think that it was necessary for the ECJ to give a ruling in order to enable it to give judgment.

Second, where the question raised was materially identical to one on which the ECJ had already given a ruling.

Third, and this is the closest to a sanctioning of the doctrine of *acte clair* the ECJ has come, where the correct application of Community law may be so obvious as to leave no scope for any reasonable doubt as to the way in which the question raised should be resolved.

However, the ECJ added a number of cautionary checks which a national court ought to carry out before coming to such a conclusion. First, it should note that Community law is drafted in several equally authentic languages which make linguistic comparisons difficult. Second, even where a degree of linguistic consistency is identifiable, Community law has several concepts and terminology which are peculiar to it, and these concepts and terms may not have the same meaning in the law of the Member States. Finally, Community law must be placed in its context and interpreted in the light of Community law as a whole, bearing in mind its objectives and state of evolution at the time the question arises. Thus the limitations on the exercise of this highly modified version of *acte clair* seem to suggest that national courts should proceed only with the utmost caution. As Dashwood and Arnull point out:[78]

> A court which has been systematically taken through the 'CILFIT' checklist by counsel should be in no danger of jumping to rash conclusions.

The issue of whether the ECJ had the power to refuse to give a ruling at the request of a national court was raised in *Foglia v. Novello*,[79] where the ECJ refused to give a ruling, declaring that no question of Community law was raised which had to be answered before the trial judge could decide the case. In *Foglia* Mrs Novello ordered a consignment of wine from Foglia in Italy which was to be despatched to her in France. The contract between Novello and Foglia provided that Novello would not be liable for any French taxes which were contrary to Community law as did the agreement with the shipping company - Danzas - under which Foglia undertook to indemnify Danzas against any illegally levied French taxes. When Danzas shipped the wine to France it was required to pay a tax on it corresponding to its alcohol content. This was in violation of Article 95 EEC (prohibiting internal taxes discriminating against goods from another Member State). Foglia indemnified Danzas in accordance with the terms of their contract and then sued Novello in the Italian courts for a refund of the illegally levied tax.

Novello refused to pay the tax to Foglia on the basis that since it was illegal, it was covered by the clause in the contract relating to taxes levied by France in contravention of Community law. The Italian judge referred the question of whether the French tax based on the alcohol content of wine was contrary to Article 95 EEC.

The ECJ, following Advocate General Warner, refused to give a ruling because it considered that there was no genuine dispute between the parties. This was, in fact, quite true. Foglia was acting for a group of Italian viniculturalists who were concerned with unlawful French action which was designed to restrict the sale of foreign wines in France, and the indemnity clause had been included in the contract in an attempt to persuade the Italian courts to give a ruling on the legality or otherwise of the French measures. Furthermore, relying on the direct effect of Article 95, Danzas would have been able to challenge the legality of the French tax in the French courts, but had chosen not to do so. The ECJ in refusing to give a ruling in this case where the 'dispute' had clearly been artificially created, commented that its duty under Article 177 was 'not that of delivering advisory opinions on general or hypothetical questions but of assisting the administration of justice in the Member States'.[80]

The ruling in *Foglia v. Novello* has been criticised as an abdication of the ECJ's responsibility under Article 177 which jeopardises the relationship of mutual respect and cooperation which exists between the national courts and the ECJ.[81] *Foglia*, however, was a very special case arising during a period of tension between two Member States, and the ECJ has not hesitated before nor since *Foglia* to give rulings in friendly and no doubt contrived actions where there has been a genuine issue of Community law requiring interpretation. However, the ECJ must surely have a residual power to control its own jurisdiction so as to prevent abuses.[82]

*Appeals against a decision to refer to the ECJ*

When an inferior court or tribunal decides to refer a question to the ECJ, a party opposed to the reference may often appeal to a higher national court against the order seeking a ruling. Whether such an appeal precludes a reference to the ECJ until the appeal is heard is a matter regulated by national rather than Community law. For example, in the Netherlands a reference to the ECJ will stand despite an appeal to the contrary, whereas in the UK by the terms of Rules of the Supreme Court (RSC) Order 114(5)[83] a reference will not be sent on to Luxembourg until the time for appeal has elapsed or if an appeal against the reference has been lodged, that appeal has been heard.

As might be expected, the ECJ has not considered itself constrained by national procedural rules. Once the ECJ is seised of a question of Community law, even if the reference is subject to an appeal in the national courts, it may still proceed to a ruling. In the early case of *De Geus v. Bosch*[84] the Court commented that[85]

> ... the Treaty subjects the jurisdiction of the Court of Justice solely to the existence of a request within the meaning of article 177, without requiring the Community judge to examine whether the decision of the domestic judge is appealable under the provisions of its domestic law.

There is, however, little point in the ECJ insisting on giving a ruling in a case where the decision of the referring judge has been quashed on appeal and the reference has lost its purpose. Provided therefore that the Court is satisfied that the national appeal procedures are not being used to fetter the discretion of inferior courts to refer questions of Community law, then it will simply suspend the hearing of a case subject to appeal - and remove it from its list if the national authorities inform it that the ruling is not longer needed.[86]

**Interpretation and Application**

In addition to the powers of interpretation of the EEC Treaty and acts of the Community institutions conferred by Article 177, the ECJ is also empowered under the Article 177 reference procedure to rule on the validity of Community legislation. There is, however, inherent in Article 177 a division of competence between the ECJ and the national courts; while it is the ECJ which interprets Community law, it is the national courts which apply it. The ECJ has always been at pains to emphasise this distinction yet in practice it has found it virtually impossible not to trespass on occasions into the area of application of Community law.

In *Costa v. ENEL*,[87] the ECJ, when requested to give a ruling on the constitutionality of an Italian law nationalising the supply of electricity, held that 'Article 177 gives the Court no jurisdiction either to apply the Treaty to a specific case or to decide upon the validity of a provision of domestic law in relation to the Treaty ...'

Similarly in *Van Gend en Loos*[88] the ECJ referring to the second question put to it by the Dutch *Tariefcommissie* said:

> The question clearly does not call for an interpretation of the Treaty but concerns the application of Netherlands customs legislation to the classification of aminoplasts, which is outside the jurisdiction, conferred upon [the ECJ by Article 177(1)(a)]. The Court has therefore no jurisdiction to consider the reference made by the Tariefcommissie.

Nevertheless, the ECJ was prepared to reformulate the question to enable it to give a ruling. As the Court said in similar circumstances in *Costa* 'the Court has power to extract from a question imperfectly formulated by the national court those questions which alone pertain to the interpretation of the Treaty'.[89]

The dividing line between interpretation and application is, however, very fine. In a number of cases the ECJ's judgment has been so precise and detailed that virtually no leeway has been left to the national courts in implementing it. For example, in *Minister of Finance v. Simmenthal*[90] the Court imposed a *duty* on a national court to apply Community law in preference to national law.

And in *Macarthys Ltd v. Smith*[91] when faced with the question of whether the scope of Article 119 proscribed sex discrimination over pay in situations of sequential employment as well as situations of contemporaneous employment, the ECJ replied with such precision that the mode of application of Article 119 by the English courts was left in no doubt whatsoever. On other occasions, however, the Court has produced rulings which have been so abstract as to require further interpretation[92].

### Validity

The ECJ's second function under Article 177, that of pronouncing upon the validity of Community legislation by way of a preliminary ruling, provides an increasingly significant form of protection for the individual under the Treaty. A request for a ruling on the validity of a Community measure emanating from a national court is not subject to the two-month limitation period applicable to applications under Article 173 for judicial review, nor is it subject to the problems of *locus standi* referred to earlier in this chapter. What is notable, however, is the effect of a finding by the ECJ under Article 177 that a Community act is invalid. Initially it was thought that the effect of such a finding was limited to the instant case before the Court - without impugning the validity of the measure as far as the rest of the world was concerned.

From the ECJ's ruling in the *International Chemical Corporation* case,[93] it seems that although a declaration of invalidity in the preliminary ruling procedure applies formally only to the case in question, the *de facto* effect is to establish the invalidity of the act *erga omnes* (against the whole world).

In this case, the ECJ declared invalid a Council regulation on the compulsory purchase of skimmed milk. ICC therefore sought the return of a deposit which it had been required to pay under the regulation by way of security. The ECJ in declaring the act void for the case in question acknowledged that in so doing it affected an essential element of the measure, namely its legal certainty. Thus, said the Court, 'it is sufficient reason for any other national court to regard that act as void for the purposes of a judgment which it has to give'. Nevertheless, the ECJ noted that this ruling did not preclude a national court from making a reference if it thought it necessary to do so, commenting that 'there may be such a need in particular if questions arise as to the grounds, the scope and possibly the consequences of the invalidity established earlier'.

The overall effect of the *ICC* judgment is that a Community act which is declared void in the course of a preliminary ruling is for all practical purposes void *erga omnes*. It seems clear also that the ECJ uses the term 'void' advisedly since the purpose of the Article 177 procedure is to obtain a declaration of what the law is and thus what it always has been. As we have seen in the *Defrenne* case this means that a ruling by the ECJ tends to have a retroactive quality and therefore where the validity of a Community act is in question this must mean that the act is void *ab initio* (i.e. from the date of its passing) and not voidable (i.e. from the date of the judgment).[94]

## THE RECEPTION OF COMMUNITY LAW BY THE UK COURTS

Since the UK joined the Communities in 1973, many cases involving Community law have come before the domestic courts. The judiciary has therefore had to deal with a number of legal concepts which had, prior to 1973, been alien to it. Steeped in the doctrine of parliamentary supremacy and the strong dualistic tradition of the British constitution, the judges have found that questions of Community law which arise before the domestic courts do not fall happily within these traditional concepts. Consequently, cases involving Community law before the English courts have produced a welter of uncertain and conflicting dicta. Commentators too have struggled to reconcile the conflicting pronouncements of the judiciary in this field. The problem has often been how to reconcile traditional legal theory with the political and constitutional realities of the UK's Community membership. The nub of the question which has arisen directly or indirectly in a number of English cases is whether, given a conflict between Community law and a domestic statute, the former or the latter should prevail. The question has a number of variations such as whether a distinction ought to be drawn between statutes passed prior to UK accession and statutes passed subsequently, but the underlying theoretical issue is whether the principle of unbridled parliamentary sovereignty has been affected in any way by UK membership of the EEC.

Early judicial points of view on the question of whether parliamentary legislative supremacy was likely to remain intact following the UK's accession to the Communities were at variance. In *Blackburn v. Attorney-General*[95] a declaration was sought that accession to the Treaty of Rome would result in a surrender of parliamentary sovereignty and would thus be unconstitutional and hence unlawful. Although the application was rejected as disclosing no cause of action, Lord Denning MR and Salmon, LJ offered opinions *obiter dicta* on the question of whether Parliament could, if it wished, repeal the European Communities Act in the future. Lord Denning, observing that legal theory did not always march with political reality, preferred to leave open the question of the power of Parliament to repeal the European Communities Act until the courts were actually faced with the issue. He seemed, therefore, to be implying that the matter was not soluble by reference to traditionally accepted doctrine. Salmon, LJ inclined, however, to the traditional view saying:[96]

> As to Parliament, in the present state of the law, it can enact, amend and repeal any legislation it pleases.

Despite Lord Denning's earlier statement in which he indicated that he was prepared to adopt a flexible approach to the question of parliamentary legislative supremacy, it became clear in subsequent cases that he too was approaching the Treaty of Rome according to traditional constitutional theory. In *Bulmer v. Bollinger*,[97] a case which concerned an action by the respondent against the appellant for allegedly attempting to 'pass off' Babycham, a 'champagne' perry, as champagne, Lord Denning said that 'Parliament has decreed that the Treaty [of Rome] is henceforward to be part of our law. It is equal in force to any statute.' Similarly in *Felixstowe Dock and Railway Company v. British Transport Docks Board*[98] in which the applicant claimed that a private bill promoted by the Board for the purposes of nationalising Felixstowe Docks being contrary to the Community's competition rules - notably Article 86 - should be set aside, Lord Denning made the following observation:[99]

> It seems to me that once the Bill is passed by Parliament and becomes a Statute, that will dispose of all this discussion about

> the Treaty. These courts will then have to abide by the Statute without regard to the Treaty at all.

These views appeared to cast the Treaty of Rome squarely in the mould of any other treaty and hence subject to the traditional doctrine of Parliament's legislative supremacy. They also seemed to place the EEC Treaty, as transformed by the European Communities Act, on an equal footing to any other statute with the implied assumption that it could be repealed either expressly or impliedly at any time. Certainly neither Lord Denning nor Salmon, LJ adverted to the requirement of EC law of the supremacy of Community law over conflicting domestic law which would have entailed a recognition by them of Community law as a *sui generis* form of law and not just a rather novel branch of English law.

Some clarification of the English judges' attitude towards the relationship between Community law and English law has, however, been forthcoming in a line of cases involving issues of sex discrimination. It will be recalled that Article 119 of the Treaty of Rome requires that men and women 'should receive equal pay for equal work'. The UK had purported to give effect to this obligation in the Equal Pay Act 1970 and in the Sex Discrimination Act 1975, but a number of issues not specifically dealt with by the legislation arose for judicial determination.

In *Shields v. Coomes*[100] the applicant, a woman, was employed as a betting shop counterhand but she was paid less than her male colleague on the grounds that he might have to perform a 'protective function' should the betting shop clientele get out of hand. The Court of Appeal found that there had, in fact, been clear discrimination. The significance of this case in the present context, however, is that the Court of Appeal produced varying dicta on the question of the significance of Community law. Lord Denning was prepared to acknowledge the supremacy of Community law should any ambiguity or inconsistency emerge in a statute, saying that it was the duty of a court or tribunal to resolve such ambiguity or inconsistency 'by giving primacy to Community law'. Bridge, LJ, however, took a rather more conventional view arguing that the Treaty and any implementing directives could be used to assist in interpreting an ambiguous UK statute. Orr, LJ, on the other hand, was of the opinion that no question of Community law arose in this case and that it was therefore unnecessary to make a pronouncement upon it.

In *Macarthys v. Smith*[101] the question arose as to whether the relevant UK legislation on sex discrimination covered a situation in which a woman was employed subsequently to a man and paid at a lower rate, or whether it covered only situations in which the man and the woman were employed contemporaneously at different pay. Lawton, LJ and Cumming-Bruce, LJ when invited to apply Article 119 declined to do so on the grounds that the UK legislation was perfectly clear and that it did not apply to situations embracing sequential employment but covered only cases of contemporaneous employment. Lord Denning thought differently arguing that 'If on close investigation it should appear that our legislation is deficient - or is inconsistent with Community law - by some oversight of our draftsmen - then it is our bounden duty to give priority to Community law'.[102] Nevertheless, he made it clear that he was only talking about non-intentional inconsistencies; a statute which was intended to repudiate the Treaty or any provision of it would have to be followed by the English courts.

Reference to the ECJ for a preliminary ruling on the question of whether Article 119 covered sequential as well as contemporaneous employment resulted in an affirmative response.[103] The case therefore fell for determination by the Court of Appeal on the basis that Article 119 gave more rights to individuals than domestic legislation. Lord Denning reiterated that Community law was supreme:[104]

> It is important now to declare ... that the provisions of article 119 of the EEC Treaty take priority over anything in our English statute on equal pay which is inconsistent with article 119. That priority is given by our own law. It is given by the European Communities Act 1972 itself ... Community law is part of our law by our own statute, the European Communities Act 1972. In applying it, we should regard it in the same way as if we found an inconsistency between two English Acts of Parliament; and the court had to decide which had to be given priority.

Despite Lord Denning's assertion of the primacy of Community law, it is clear that the framework which he was using was still that of conventional constitutional principles in which matters relating to statute are primarily issues of construction. There is nothing in Lord Denning's judgment which questions the overriding principle of parliamentary supremacy, thus suggesting that in cases of deliberate inconsistency between English law and Community law, the courts will follow the will of Parliament by giving effect to the former.

It is arguable that this position remains unaffected by the most recent of the equal pay cases - *Garland v. British Rail Engineering.*[105] Here, Mrs Garland, a retired British Rail employee, claimed that she did not enjoy the same concessionary travel rights as her retired male colleagues. The main issue arising from the case was whether Article 119 embraced such matters. On a reference back from the ECJ which indicated that concessionary travel rights did indeed fall within the scope of Article 119, Lord Diplock giving judgment for the House of Lords dealt with the issue primarily as one of statutory construction. He said:[106]

> ...it is a principle of construction of United Kingdom statutes, now too well established to call for a citation of authority, that the words of a statute passed after the Treaty has been signed and dealing with the subject matter of the international obligation of the United Kingdom are to be construed, if they are reasonably capable of bearing such a meaning, as intended to carry out the obligation and not be inconsistent with it. *A fortiori* this is the case where the treaty obligation arises under one of the Community treaties to which section 2 of the European Communities Act 1972 applies.

Lord Diplock left open the question of whether an express statement of Parliament's intention to legislate contrary to the EEC Treaty was necessary before the question of inconsistency could not be resolved by the courts simply applying techniques of interpretation. Nevertheless, it seems clear that Lord Diplock was impliedly giving continued support to the theory of unrestricted parliamentary legislative supremacy in his *dictum* in *Garland.*

Although, therefore, the *dicta* in the relevant cases appear to leave the issue in an uncertain position, it seems clear that the English courts still feel themselves constrained by traditional principles of parliamentary supremacy. The best that can be said is that if a conflict between statute and Community law arises, then as long as the legislature has not stated expressly that it is seeking to abrogate the EEC Treaty, the courts will construe a statute to accord as closely as possible to the UK's Community law obligations. It can hardly be said, however, that this position is satisfactory in view of the rulings of the ECJ concerning the supremacy of Community law and the correlative obligation to 'set aside' inconsistent domestic laws. Perhaps the true response to the theoretical difficulties lies in political reality. As Bradley suggests:[107]

> a very strong constitutional convention will evolve that Westminster will refrain from seeking to legislate to the full extent of its legal capacity; and in the fullness of time it may come to seem absurd that it should ever wish to do so.

Despite these theoretical arguments concerning the place of Community law within the UK's constitutional context, it is nevertheless apparent that courts have been employing Community law as a matter of course in a number of situations. The predominant use to which it has been put has been as defences of various kinds in criminal cases. Article 48 concerning the free movement of workers has been used as a defence to deportation[108] as well as a cause of action to secure admission to the UK.[109] Article 30 prohibiting Member States from applying quantitative restrictions or similar measures to the import and export of goods has been used as a defence in criminal cases concerning the importation of pornography,[110] gold coins[111] and inflatable rubber dolls.[112]

In civil cases the use of directly effective Community provisions has been somewhat restricted, but in one case the House of Lords has held that damages may be recoverable relying on Community law as a cause of action. In *Garden Cottage Foods Ltd v. Milk Marketing Board*[113] the Board, the only supplier of bulk butter in the UK, decided to change its marketing strategy by selling bulk butter to only four outlets. Garden Cottage Foods (GCF), who had previously bought bulk butter direct from the Board repackaged it and exported it to Holland, was not one of the nominated outlets. GCF argued that if the Board persisted with its strategy, then GCF would be forced out of business. GCF claimed therefore that the Board was abusing its dominant position (monopoly position) contrary to Article 86 of the Treaty and was thereby injuring GCF. GCF therefore sought an interlocutory injunction to restrain the Board from acting unlawfully. The House of Lords holding that on a balance of convenience it was not appropriate to grant GCF an injunction held that damages would be an appropriate remedy if it was found that loss had been suffered when the main issue came to trial. The cause of action which was to be employed was the tortious remedy of breach of statutory duty. The House of Lords was reluctant to follow Lord Denning's lead in *Application des Gaz*[114] and hold that the EEC's competition rules (Articles 85 and 86) created 'new torts' in English law. Nevertheless, there was clear recognition that by using domestic procedures the English courts were able to give adequate protection to a violation of directly effective Community law.

## ARTICLE 177 AND THE UK COURTS

At an early stage in the UK's membership of the EEC, Lord Denning in the case of *Bulmer v. Bollinger*[115] sought to establish the conditions under which the English courts should make reference to the ECJ. Observing that the House of Lords was the only English court which was bound to make a reference under Article 177(3), a matter of some considerable doubt as we have seen, Lord Denning then went on to enunciate four guidelines which courts having a discretion to refer a question to the ECJ ought to follow. The Master of the Rolls' observations here were conditioned by the phrase in Article 177(2) 'if it [the court] considers that a decision on the question is *necessary* to enable it to give judgment' [emphasis added].

The four guidelines which ought to be followed in deciding whether a decision was necessary were: first, the question referred should be conclusive in the sense that once a decision is reached it should resolve the dispute one way or the other; second, where a similar or substantially similar question had already been decided by the ECJ there was no need for an English court to make a reference unless the court wished to have the question reconsidered; third, where the question was 'reasonably clear and free from doubt' there was no need to refer since the court would be competent to decide it; and fourth, a reference should only be made once all the material facts had been determined.

The Denning guidelines have attracted substantial criticism on several grounds. First, that they impose undue restrictions upon the domestic courts if those courts decide to adhere to them rigidly. There is, however, no substantial evidence to suggest that English courts or tribunals have been unduly restrained by the guidelines since they are only of persuasive force and were not, in the event, endorsed by the other members of the Court of Appeal. Second, the enunciation of the *acte clair* doctrine in the third of the guidelines was, and remains, highly contentious. The brand of *acte clair* adopted by the ECJ in *CILFIT*[116] applies only to questions which fall broadly within the category of cases previously decided by the ECJ itself. Lord Denning appeared to be suggesting that if the point raised was clear and free from doubt then, despite the fact that the ECJ had not previously ruled on the question, the English courts were nevertheless competent to decide it for themselves. This was not what the ECJ had in mind in *CILFIT*. Finally, the injuction by the Master of the Rolls that the court making the reference should determine the material facts first raises, as Jacobs points out,[117] difficulties of legal logic since it is often difficult to determine which facts are material until one knows what the relevant law is.

Few English courts or tribunals seem to have complied explicitly with the Denning guidelines in deciding whether to refer questions to the ECJ. References under Article 177 have been made by Magistrates Courts, Crown Courts, the National Insurance Commissioner and the Employment Appeals Tribunal and none of these courts or tribunals appears to have felt itself to be at all restricted in making references of their own volition.[118] It is also clear that the House of Lords has not hesitated to seek rulings from the ECJ even in cases such as *R v. Henn & Darby*,[119] and in *Garland*[120] where it was felt that the issue did not raise real doubts as to the correct interpretation of Community law. Here, therefore, there seems to be an implicit rejection of at least one of the Denning guidelines by the highest English court.

Nevertheless, it is clear that the English courts have demonstrated a certain reluctance to make references to the ECJ. Collins[121] suggests that this is because the training of English judges inculcates in them the view that questions of fact must be decided before it can be properly ascertained that a question of law arises. References from the UK have, therefore, generally been in cases in which there was no dispute of the facts. Dashwood and Arnull[122] prefer a less 'legalistic' view of the relative paucity of references to the ECJ from the UK suggesting that two factors may be of significance: first, that UK businessmen are reluctant to litigate questions relating to customs law whereas their continental European counterparts are not; and second, that 'the first generation of young legal practitioners to have benefitted from an academic training in Community law is only now coming to the fore in the [legal] professions'.

Whatever the reasons for the failure of the English courts to refer questions to the ECJ under Article 177 when it would be in the interests of the proper administration of justice to do so, it cannot be doubted that either the unwillingness or the failure to see a need to refer results in a breakdown of the essential cooperation between the national courts and the ECJ. This has two effects: first, it can lead to a denial of justice in individual cases; and second, it inhibits the development of Community law itself. As Arnull[123] points out, the predilection of the English High Court to resolve commercial cases involving a Community law element itself, especially those concerning intellectual property, without referring them to the ECJ does not bode well for the healthy development of Community law. Furthermore, he argues that the tendency of the High Court not to refer questions to the ECJ but to decide cases itself shows unwelcome signs of spreading to other areas of law.

The procedure for making references by the High Court is set down in Order 114 of the Rules of the Supreme Court. Similar rules exist for all other courts in the UK. Order 114 is, however, of such practical importance that it deserves some detailed attention. It provides:

**RULES OF THE SUPREME COURT. ORDER 114.**

**References to the European Court**

*1. Interpretation*

In this Order:

'the Court' means the court by which an order is made and includes the Court of Appeal;

'the European Court' means the Court of Justice of the European Communities; and

'order' means an order referring a question to the European Court for a preliminary ruling under Art. 177 of the Treaty establishing the European Economic Community, Art. 150 of the Treaty establishing the European Atomic Energy Community or Art. 41 of the Treaty establishing the European Coal and Steel Community.

*2. Making of Order*

(1) An order may be made by the Court of its own motion at any stage in a cause or matter, or on application by a party before or at the trial or hearing thereof.

(2) Where an application is made before the trial or hearing, it shall be made by motion.

(3) In the High Court no order shall be made except by a judge in person.

*3. Schedule to Order to set out Request for Ruling*
An order shall set out in a schedule the request for the preliminary ruling of the European Court, and the Court may give directions as to the manner and form in which the schedule is to be prepared.
*4. Stay of Proceedings Pending Ruling*
The proceedings in which an order is made shall, unless the Court otherwise orders, be stayed until the European Court has given a preliminary ruling on the question referred to it.
*5. Transmission of Order to the European Court*
When an order has been made, the Senior Master shall send a copy thereof to the Registrar of the European Court; but in the case of an order made by the High Court, he shall not do so, unless the Court otherwise orders, until the time for appealing against the order has expired or, if an appeal is entered within that time, until the appeal has been determined or otherwise disposed of.
*6. Appeals from Orders made by High Court*
An order made by the High Court shall be deemed to be a final decision, and accordingly an appeal against it shall lie to the Court of Appeal without leave; but the period within which a notice of appeal must be served under O.59, r.4(1), shall be 14 days.

Several points may be made as regards Order 114:

First: An order referring a question to the ECJ for a preliminary ruling under Article 177 may be made by the High Court *at any time* during the hearing of the case either of its own motion or at the request of any party to the case (Rule 2(1)). This therefore recognises that the High Court judge has a wide discretion in deciding whether to refer a question to the ECJ.

Second: Where an order is made, the proceedings before the Court are stayed until the ECJ has ruled (Rule 4).

Third: An appeal lies against an order to refer but notice of appeal must be served within 14 days (Rule 6). It should be noted that in order to avoid complications as regards appeals against an order to refer, the Senior Master of the Supreme Court will not remit the order to the Registrar of the ECJ until the expiration of 14 days or until any appeal has been determined (Rule 5). This device clearly serves to obviate some of the difficulties in which the Dutch courts have found themselves and which have been discussed above.[124]

Since preliminary rulings are generally viewed as a step in judicial proceedings before a national court, the costs of a reference are normally determined by the national court. This will not usually take place until after the case has been decided. Since, however, the preliminary ruling procedure is only part of the total proceedings, it is clear that the ruling which is given by the ECJ must, at some stage, be applied by the national courts. The view of the ECJ is that its rulings are binding on the national court requesting the reference but that it is the duty of the national court to give effect to the ruling.[125] This view maintains the somewhat artificial distinction between the ECJ's function of interpretation and the national courts' function of application. What, however, would be the position if the national court is unable to understand the ECJ's ruling? In such cases the ECJ has said that it is always open to the national court to seek clarification by a further ruling.[126]

It has been observed that the UK courts have generally applied rulings of the ECJ faithfully, but there have been deviations as, for example, in *Santillo*[127] in which the Divisional Court and Court of Appeal concluded that an order for deportation made some four years earlier was still a valid order according to Article 9 of Directive 64/221 despite a contrary ruling by the ECJ. Nevertheless, the English courts have, on the whole, been aided in the application of a ruling by the ECJ by Section 3(1) of the European Communities Act which provides:

> in any legal proceedings questions concerning the Community Treaties or Community acts should be treated as questions of law and if not referred to the ECJ then they should be determined in accordance with the principles laid down by the ECJ.

## APPENDIX

Since going to press a number of cases have been reported which appear to indicate that the ECJ's strict approach to the question of *locus standi* in direct actions under Article 173(2) may have been further relaxed.

Case 294/83 *Les Verts – Parti Ecologiste v. European Parliament* Judgment of 23 April 1986, not yet reported.

*Les Verts*, a political grouping in the EP, brought an action under Article 173(2) to challenge disbursements made by the Bureau of the EP for the conduct of information campaigns by political groups during the 1984 election campaign. The tenor of *Les Verts'* complaint was that since no uniform electoral procedure had been established in accordance with the Treaty, electoral practices remained governed by domestic law under which the Bureau's disbursements represented a reimbursement of political campaign costs. The important question in this case was whether the acts of the EP were subject to review under Article 173 and if so, whether *Les Verts* were 'directly and individually concerned' within the meaning of Article 173(2). The ECJ held (1) It was necessary to take a functional view of reviewable acts under Article 173. In the case of the EP, the Treaty was silent about the reviewability of its acts because, since the drafting of the Treaty, the EP had acquired the power to adopt legally binding acts in certain areas. The Court therefore declared that 'An interpretation of Article 173 of the Treaty which would exclude measures adopted by the EP from those which could be attacked would lead to a result which is contrary both to the spirit of the treaty as expressed in Article 164 and to its overall structure.' Since, however, *Les Verts* were not privileged plaintiffs, they still had the problems of direct and individual concern to overcome. The ECJ held that *Les Verts* were directly concerned because they had an interest in the way in which the Bureau made the disbursements, and also because the Bureau's decision required payments to be made according to a strict formula without the exercise of any discretion. The Court also ruled that *Les Verts* were individually concerned because they represented members of a discernible class which fell squarely within the *Plaumann* test. *Les Verts'* application was therefore admissable. On the question of the substance of the complaint, the ECJ found that the reimbursement of electoral expenses remained a matter within the domestic competence of the Member States pending the entry into force of a uniform electoral procedure. The decision of the Bureau was therefore annulled.

Two further cases appear to demonstrate a relaxation of the Court's attitude towards private plaintiffs: Case 169/84 *Compagnie Française de l'Azote (Cofaz) v. Commission*, judgment of 28 January 1986, not yet reported; and Case 11/82 *Piraiki-Patraiki v. Commission* [1985] E.C.R. 207. For comment see J. Flynn, 'Who may challenge a Commission decision?' (1987) 12 *E.L.Rev.* pp. 127-31. Note also that a proposal has been made by the ECJ, in accordance with Articles 4, 11 and 26 of the Single European Act, for the establishment of an EC court of first instance. The proposal takes the form of a draft decision which has been remitted to the Council for approval and implementation. See the editorial in (1987) 12 *E.L.Rev.* pp. 77-8.

## NOTES

1. Article 165.
2. Article 166.
3. Article 167.
4. *Ibid.*
5. *Ibid.*
6. Article 167 provides:

The Judges and Advocates-General shall be chosen from persons whose independence is beyond doubt ...

7. Protocol on the Statute of the Court of Justice of the European Economic Community, Article 2.

8. L.N. Brown and F.G. Jacobs, *The Court of Justice of the European Communities,* 2nd edn. (Sweet and Maxwell, London, 1983), pp.32-4.

9. H. Rasmussen, 'Why is Article 173 interpreted against Private Plaintiffs?' (1980) *E.L.Rev.* p.112.

10. See C. Hording, 'The Private Interest in Challenging Community Action' (1980) 5 *E.L.Rev.* p.354.

11. See above pp.115-18.

12. Case 130/75 [1976] E.C.R. 1589; [1976] 2 C.M.L.R. 708.

13. Cases 8-11/66 [1967] E.C.R. 75; [1967] C.M.L.R. 77.

14. Case 26/76 *Metro-SB-Grossmarkte GmbH & Co. K.G. v. Commission* [1977] E.C.R. 1875; 2 C.M.L.R. 1.

15. Case 25/62 [1963] E.C.R. 95; [1964] C.M.L.R. 29.

16. Case 112/77 [1978] E.C.R. 1019.

17. Cases 41-44/70 [1971] E.C.R. 411; [1975] 2 C.M.L.R. 515.

18. Case 69/69 [1970] E.C.R. 385; [1970] C.M.L.R. 337.

19. Case 25/62 [1963] E.C.R. 95 at 107.

20. Above, note 16.

21. Case 62/70 [1971] E.C.R. 897; C.M.L.R. 160.

22. Above, note 17.

23. Above, note 14.

24. Cases 113, 118-121/77 [1979] E.C.R. 1185; [1979] 2 C.M.L.R. 257.

25. See e.g. E.C.S. Wade and A.W. Bradley, *Constitutional and Administrative Law,* 10th edn. by A.W. Bradley (Longman, London and New York, 1985), pp.626-38.

26. Case 9.56 [1957-58] E.C.R. 133.

27. See Wade and Bradley, *Constitutional and Administrative Law,* p.630.

28. Case 24/62 *Germany v. Commission* [1963] E.C.R. 63; [1963] C.M.L.R. 347.

29. [1963] E.C.R. 63 at 69; [1963] C.M.L.R. 347 at 368.

30. Case 138/79 *Roquette Frères v. Council* [1980] E.C.R. 3333 and Case 139/79 *Maizena GmbH v. Council* [1980] E.C.R. 3393.

31. See Case 29/69 *Stauder v. City of Ulm* [1969] E.C.R. 419; [1970] C.M.L.R. 112.

32. Case 17/74 [1974] E.C.R. 1063; [1974] 2 C.M.L.R. 459.

33. See C. Schmittoff, 'The Doctrines of Proportionality and Non-Discrimination' (1977) 2 *E.L.Rev.* p.329.

34. This is a fundamental principle of Community law which is enshrined in Article 7 of the Treaty.

35. Case 29/69 [1969] E.C.R. 419; [1970] C.M.L.R. 112.

36. Case 11/70 *Internationale Handelsgesellschaft v. Einfuhr und Vorratsstelle fur Getreide und Futtermittel* [1970] E.C.R. 1125; [1972] C.M.L.R. 255.

37. [1970] E.C.R. 1125 at 1134.

38. Case 4/73 [1974] E.C.R. 491; [1974] 2 C.M.L.R. 338.

39. [1974] E.C.R. 491 at 507.

40. Case 130/75 *Prais v. Council* [1976] E.C.R. 1589; [1976] 2 C.M.L.R. 708.

41. Case 44/79 *Hauer v. Land Rheinland-Pfalz* [1979] E.C.R. 3727; [1980] 3 C.M.L.R. 42.

42. O.J. 1977, C103/1. There has also been some debate as to whether the Communities should become a party to the European Convention on Human Rights.

43. Case 64/80 *Giuffrida and Campogrande v. Council* [1981] E.C.R. 693.

44. See e.g. Hartley, *Foundations*, pp.386-91.

45. Schermers, *Judicial Protection*, para.336.

46. Case 13/83 *Parliament v. Council* [1985] 1 C.M.L.R. 138.

47. Article 175(3).

48. Case 246/81 [1982] E.C.R. 2277; [1982] 3 C.M.L.R. 500.

49. See e.g. Cases 31 & 33/62 *Milchwerke Wohrman v. Commission* [1962] E.C.R. 501 and Case 92/78 *Simmenthal v. Commission* [1979] E.C.R. 777. The exception of illegality (which is derived from the French *exception d'illegalité*) is similar to the English administrative law rule permitting the collateral challenge of delegated legislation. The difference is, of course, that the primary instrument (statute) on which the unlawful delegated legislation is based cannot be challenged.

50. Case 32/65 *Italy v. Commission* [1966] E.C.R. 389; Case 156/77 *Commission v. Belgium* [1978] E.C.R. 1881.

51. See Articles 181 and 215(1).

52. Article 215(2).

53. Statute of the Court, Article 43.

54. See Case 25/62 *Plaumann v. Commission* [1963] E.C.R. 95 at 108 where the Court held that 'An administrative act which has not been annulled cannot of itself constitute a wrongful act on the part of the administration'.

55. See e.g. Case 4/69 *Lutticke v. Commission* [1971] E.C.R. 325 and Case 5/71 *Zuckerfabrik Schoppenstedt v. Council* [1971] E.C.R. 975.

56. See e.g. Case 74/74 *CNTA v. Commission* [1975] E.C.R. 533; [1976] E.C.R. 797; [1977] 1 C.M.L.R. 171.

57. See further Hartley, *Foundations*, pp.471-81.

58. Case 90/78 *Granaria v. Council and Commission* [1979] E.C.R. 1081; Case 238/78 *Ireks-Arkady v. Council and Commission* [1979] E.C.R. 2955; Cases 261-262/78 *Interquell Starke v. Council and Commission* [1979] E.C.R. 3045; Cases 241, 242 and 245-250/78 *DGV v. Council and Commission* [1979] E.C.R. 3017; Cases 64 and 113/76 *Dumortier Frères v. Council* [1979] E.C.R. 3091.

59. Cases 116 and 124/77 *Amylum v. Council and Commission* [1979] E.C.R. 3497; Case 143/77 *Koninklijke Scholten-Honig v. Council and Commission* [1979] E.C.R. 3583.

60. See Cases 5, 7, 13-24/66 *Kampffmeyer v. Commission* [1967] E.C.R. 245; Case 96/71 *Blaegman v. Commission* [1972] II E.C.R. 1005; Case 43/72 *Merkur v. Commission* [1973] E.C.R. 1055; Case 99.74 *Grands Moulins de Antilles* [1975] E.C.R. 1531; Case 46/75 *IBA v. Commission* [1976] E.C.R. 65; Cases 67-85/75 *Cotelle v. Commission* [1976] E.C.R. 391; Case 26/74 *Roquette v. Commission* [1976] E.C.R. 677; Case 34/74 *Roquette v. France* [1974] E.C.R. 1217. See also C.S.P. Harding, 'The choice of court problem in cases of non-contractual liability under EEC Law' (1979) 16 *C.M.L.Rev*. p.389.

61. Article 169.

62. Article 171.

63. V. Everling, 'The Member States of the European Community before their Court of Justice' (1984) 9 *E.L.Rev*. 215 at 222.

64. Case 48/71 *Commission v. Italy* [1972] E.C.R. 532; [1972] C.M.L.R. 699.

65. Case 141/78 *France v. UK* [1979] E.C.R. 2923; [1980] 1 C.M.L.R. 6.

66. P. Pescatore, 'Interpretation of Community Law and the Doctrine of "Acte Clair"', in M.E. Bathurst, et al (eds), *Legal Problems of an Enlarged European Community* (Stevens, London, 1972), p.27.

67. E. Stein, 'Lawyers, Judges and the making of a Transnational Constitution' (1981) 75 *A.J.I.L*. 1.

68. See Case 26/62 *Van Gend en Loos v. Nederlandse Administratie der Belastingen* [1963] E.C.R. 1; [1963] C.M.L.R. 105 and Case 6/64 *Costa v. ENEL* [1964] E.C.R. 585; [1964] C.M.L.R. 425.

69. See Case 29/68 *Milchkontor v. Hauptzollamt Saarbrucken* [1969] E.C.R. 165; [1969] C.M.L.R. 390 and Case 52/76 *Benedetti v. Munari Fratelli* [1977] E.C.R. 163.

70. See e.g. J. Hamson, 'Methods of Interpretation - A Critical Assessment of the Results', *Reports of the Judicial and Academic Conference*, (Luxembourg, 1976), p.II-3.

71. See e.g. Case 22/80 *Boussac Saint-Frères SA v. Gerstenmeier* [1980] E.C.R. 3427; [1982] 1 C.M.L.R. 202.

72. Case 61/65 *Vaassen-Göbbels v. Beamtenfonds Mijnbedrijf* [1966] E.C.R. 261; [1966] C.M.L.R. 508.

73. Case 138/80R [1980] E.C.R. 1975; [1980] 3 C.M.L.R. 638.

74. [1974] Ch 1 401; [1974] A11 ER 1226.

75. L. Collins, *European Community Law in the United Kingdom*, 3rd edn. (Butterworths, London, 1984), pp.113-14.

76. Case 28-30/62 *Da Costa en Schaake v. Nederlandse Administratie der Belastingen* [1963] E.C.R. 31; [1963] C.M.L.R. 224.

77. Case 283/81 *CILFIT Srl v. Ministry of Health* [1982] E.C.R. 3415; [1983] 1 C.M.L.R. 472.

78. A. Dashwood and A. Arnull, 'English Courts and Article 177 of the EEC Treaty' (1984) 4 *Y.E.L.* 255 at 261.

79. Case 104/79 *Foglia v. Novello* [1980] E.C.R. 745; [1981] 1 C.M.L.R. 45.

80. [1980] E.C.R. 745 at 760.

81. See A. Barav, 'Preliminary Censorship? The Judgment of the European Court in *Foglia v. Novello*' (1980) 5 *E.L.Rev.* p.443.

82. For an elaboration of this point see D. Wyatt, 'Following up Foglia: Why the Court is right to stick to its guns' (1981) 6 *E.L.Rev.* p.447.

83. See below pp.169-70.

84. Case 13/61 [1962] E.C.R. 45; [1962] C.M.L.R. 1.

85. [1962] E.C.R. 45 at 50.

86. See e.g. Case 166/73 *Rheinmuhlen-Dusseldorf v. Einfuhr und Voratsstelle für Getreide* [1974] E.C.R. 33; [1974] 1 C.M.L.R. 523.

87. Case 6/64 [1964] E.C.R. 585 at 592-3; [1964] C.M.L.R. 425 at 454-5.

88. Case 26/62 [1963] E.C.R. 1 at 14; [1963] C.M.L.R. 105 at 118.

89. [1964] E.C.R. 585 at 593.

90. Case 106/77 [1978] 629; [1978] 3 C.M.L.R. 263. See D. Freestone, 'The Supremacy of Community Law in National Courts' (1979) *M.L.R.* p.220.

91. Case 129/79 [1980] E.C.R. 1275; [1980] 2 C.M.L.R. 205. See D. Freestone, 'Equal Pay in the European Court' (1982) 45 *M.L.R.* p.81.

92. See e.g. Case 12/71 *Henck v. Hauptzollamt Emerid* [1971] E.C.R. 743.

93. Case 66/80 *International Chemical Corporation SpA v. Amministrazione delle Finanzo dello Stato* [1981] E.C.R. 1191; [1983] 2 C.M.L.R. 593.

94. See above pp.36-7.

95. [1971] 2 A11 ER 1380; [1971] 1 W.L.R. 1037; [1971] 1 C.M.L.R. 784.

96. [1971] 2 A11 ER 1380 at 1041.

97. [1974] Ch. 401 at 418; [1974] 2 A11 ER 1226 at 1243.

98. [1976] 2 C.M.L.R. 655.

99. At 664-5.

100. [1979] 1 A11 ER 456; [1978] 1 W.L.R. 1408. See Freestone, 'Equal Pay', p.81.

101. [1979] 3 A11 ER 325.

102. Ibid. at 329.

103. Case 129/79 [1980] E.C.R. 1275; [1980] 2 C.M.L.R. 205.

104. [1981] QB 180 at 200-1; [1981] 1 A11 ER 111 at 120. See Freestone, 'Equal Pay', p.81.

105. [1983] 2 AC 751.

106. Ibid. at 771.

107. A.W. Bradley, 'The Sovereignty of Parliament - in Perpetuity?', in J. Jowell and D. Oliver (eds), *The Changing Constitution* (Clarendon Press, Oxford, 1985), p.23 at p.40.

108. See *R v. Secchi* [1975] C.M.L.R. 383; Case 157/79 *R v. Pieck* [1980] E.C.R. 2171; [1980] 3 C.M.L.R. 220; Case 131/79 *R v. Secretary of State for Home Affairs ex parte Santillo* [1980] E.C.R. 1585; [1980] 3 C.M.L.R. 212 (Divisional Court); [1981] C.M.L.R. 569 (Court of Appeal).

109. Case 41/74 *Van Duyn v. Home Office* [1974] E.C.R. 1337; [1975] 1 C.M.L.R. 1.

110. *Henn and Darby v. DPP* [1981] AC 850.

111. *R v. Thompson, Johnson and Woodiwiss* [1978] 1 C.M.L.R. 390 (Court of Appeal); Case 7/78 [1978] E.C.R. 2247; [1979] 1 C.M.L.R. 47.

112. Case 121/85 *Conegate v. Commissioners of Customs and Excise* [1986] 1 C.M.L.R. 739.

113. [1984] AC 130; [1983] 2 A11 ER 770. See also S. Davidson, 'Actions for Damages in the English Courts for Breach of EEC Competition Law' (1985) 34 *I.C.L.Q.* 178.

114. [1974] 2 A11 ER 1226; [1974] 3 W.L.R. 202.

115. *Loc. cit.*, above, note 97.

116. See above, p.156.

117. F.G. Jacobs, 'When to Refer to the European Court' (1974) 90 *LQR* p.486 at p.491.

118. For a very full analysis of the English courts' attitude to Article 177 see A. Dashwood and A. Arnull, 'English Courts and Article 177 of the EEC Treaty' (1984) 4 *Y.E.L.* p.255.

119. [1980] 2 A11 ER 166.

120. *Garland v. British Rail Engineering* [1982] 2 C.M.L.R. 174.

121. Collins, *European Community Law*, p.142.

122. Dashwood and Arnull, 'English Courts and Article 177', p.302.

123. A. Arnull, 'Article 177 and The Retreat from Van Duyn' (1983) 8 *E.L.Rev.* 365.

124. See above, pp.158-9.

125. See above, pp.152-3 and note 69.

126. Ibid.

127. *R v. Secretary of State for Home Affairs, ex parte Santillo* [1981] 1 C.M.L.R. 569.

# Appendix

**Treaty Establishing the European Economic Community: Selected Articles**

Rome, 25 March 1957 (as amended by the Merger Treaty 1965 and the Single European Act 1986)

**PART ONE. PRINCIPLES**

*Article 1.* By this Treaty, the High Contracting Parties establish among themselves a European Economic Community.
*Article 2.* The Community shall have as its task, by establishing a common market and progressively approximating the economic policies of Member States, to promote throughout the Community a harmonious development of economic activities, a continuous and balanced expansion, an increase in stability, an accelerated raising of the standard of living and closer relations between the States belonging to it.
*Article 3.* For the purpose set out in Art. 2, the activities of the Community shall include, as provided in this Treaty and in accordance with the timetable set out therein:

(a) the elimination, as between Member States, of custom duties and of quantitative restrictions on the import and export of goods, and of all other measures having equivalent effect;
(b) the establishment of a common customs tariff and of a common commercial policy towards third countries;
(c) the abolition, as between Member States, of obstacles to freedom of movement for persons, services and capital;
(d) the adoption of a common policy in the sphere of agriculture;
(e) the adoption of a common policy in the sphere of transport;
(f) the institution of a system ensuring that competition in the common market is not distorted;
(g) the application of procedures by which the economic policies of Member States can be coordinated and disequilibria in their balances of payments remedied;
(h) the approximation of the laws of Member States to the extent required for the proper functioning of the common market;

(i) the creation of a European Social Fund in order to improve employment opportunities for workers and to contribute to the raising of their standard of living;

(j) the establishment of a European Investment Bank to facilitate the economic expansion of the Community by opening up fresh resources;

(k) the association of the overseas countries and territories in order to increase trade and to promote jointly economic and social development.

*Article 4.* 1. The tasks entrusted to the Community shall be carried out by the following institutions: an Assembly, a Council, a Commission, a Court of Justice.

Each institution shall act within the limits of the powers conferred upon it by this Treaty.

2. The Council and the Commission shall be assisted by an Economic and Social Committee acting in an advisory capacity.

3. The audit shall be carried out by a Court of Auditors acting within the limits of the powers conferred upon it by this Treaty.

*Article 5.* Member States shall take all appropriate measures, whether general or particular, to ensure fulfilment of the obligations arising out of this Treaty or resulting from action taken by the institutions of the Community. They shall facilitate the achievement of the Community's tasks.

They shall abstain from any measure which would jeopardise the attainment of the objectives of this Treaty.

*Article 6.* 1. Member States shall, in close cooperation with the institutions of the Community, coordinate their respective economic policies to the extent necessary to attain the objectives of this Treaty.

2. The institutions of the Community shall take care not to prejudice the internal and external financial stability of the Member States.

*Article 7.* Within the scope of application of this Treaty, and without prejudice to any special provisions contained therein, any discrimination on grounds of nationality shall be prohibited.

The Council may, on a proposal from the Commission and in cooperation with the European Parliament, adopt, by a qualified majority, rules designed to prohibit such discrimination.

*Article 8.* 1. The common market shall be progressively established during a transitional period of twelve years.

This transitional period shall be divided into three stages of four years each; the length of each stage may be altered in accordance with the provisions set out below.

2. To each stage there shall be assigned a set of actions to be initiated and carried through concurrently.

3. Transition from the first to the second stage shall be conditional upon a finding that the objectives specifically laid down in this Treaty for the first stage have in fact been attained in substance and that, subject to the exceptions and procedures provided for in this Treaty, the obligations have been fulfilled.

This finding shall be made at the end of the fourth year by the Council, acting unanimously on a report from the Commission. A Member State may not, however, prevent unanimity by relying upon the non-fulfilment of its own obligations. Failing unanimity, the first stage shall automatically be extended for one year.

At the end of the fifth year, the Council shall make its finding under the same conditions. Failing unanimity, the first stage shall automatically be extended for a further year.

At the end of the sixth year, the Council shall make its finding, acting by a qualified majority on a report from the Commission.

4. Within one month of the last-mentioned vote any Member State which voted with the minority or, if the required majority was not obtained, any Member State shall be entitled to call upon the Council to appoint an arbitration board whose decisions shall be binding upon all Member States and upon the institutions of the Community. The arbitration board shall consist of three members appointed by the Council acting unanimously on a proposal from the Commission.

If the Council has not appointed the members of the arbitration board within one month of being called upon to do so, they shall be appointed by the Court of Justice within a further period of one month.

The arbitration board shall elect its own Chairman.

The board shall make its award within six months of the date of the Council vote referred to in the last subparagraph of paragraph 3.

5. The second and third stages may not be extended or curtailed except by a decision of the Council, acting unanimously on a proposal from the Commission.

6. Nothing in the preceding paragraphs shall cause the transitional period to last more than fifteen years after the entry into force of this Treaty.

7. Save for the exceptions or derogations provided for in this Treaty, the expiry of the transitional period shall constitute the

latest date by which all the rules laid down must enter into force and all the measures required for establishing the common market must be implemented.

*Article 8A.* The Community shall adopt measures with the aim of progressively establishing the internal market over a period expiring on 31 December 1992, in accordance with the provisions of this Article and of Articles 8B, 8C, 28, 57(2), 59, 70(1), 84, 99, 100A and 100B and without prejudice to the other provisions of this Treaty.

The internal market shall comprise an area without internal frontiers in which the free movement of goods, persons, services and capital is ensured in accordance with the provisions of this Treaty.

*Article 8B.* The Commission shall report of the Council before 31 December 1988 and again before 31 December 1990 on the progress made towards achieving the internal market within the time limit fixed in Article 8A.

The Council, acting by a qualified majority on a proposal from the Commission, shall determine the guidelines and conditions necessary to ensure balanced progress in all the sectors concerned.

*Article 8C.* When drawing up its proposals with a view to achieving the objectives set out in Article 8A, the Commission shall take into account the extent of the effort that certain economies showing differences in developments will have to sustain during the period of establishment of the internal market and it may propose appropriate provisions.

If these provisions take the form of derogations, they must be of a temporary nature and must cause the least possible disturbance to the functioning of the common market.

## PART TWO. FOUNDATIONS OF THE COMMUNITY

### Title I. Free Movement of Goods

*Article 9.* 1. The Community shall be based upon a customs union which shall cover all trade in goods and which shall involve the prohibition between Member States of customs duties on imports and exports and of all charges having equivalent effect, and the adoption of a common customs tariff in their relations with third countries.

2. The provisions of Chapter 1, Section 1, and of Chapter 2 of

this Title shall apply to products originating in Member States and to products coming from third countries which are in free circulation in Member States.

*Chapter 1. The Customs Union*

*Section 1. Elimination of Customs Duties Between Member States*

*Article 12.* Member States shall refrain from introducing between themselves any new customs duties on imports or exports or any charges having equivalent effect, and from increasing those which they already apply in their trade with each other.

*Article 16.* Member States shall abolish between themselves customs duties on exports and charges having equivalent effect by the end of the first stage at the latest.

*Chapter 2. Elimination Of Quantitative Restrictions Between Member States*

*Article 30.* Quantitative restrictions on imports and all measures having equivalent effect shall, without prejudice to the following provisions, be prohibited between Member States.

*Article 34.* 1. Quantitative restrictions on exports, and all measures having equivalent effect shall be prohibited between Member States.

2. Member States shall, by the end of the first stage at the latest, abolish all quantitative restrictions on exports and any measures having equivalent effect which are in existence when this Treaty enters into force.

*Article 36.* The provisions of Arts. 30 to 34 shall not preclude prohibitions or restrictions on imports, exports or goods in transit justified on grounds of public morality, public policy or public security; the protection of health and life of humans, animals or plants; the protection of national treasures possessing artistic, historic or archaeological value; or the protection of industrial and commercial property. Such prohibitions or restrictions shall not, however, constitute a means of arbitrary discrimination or a disguised restriction on trade between Member States.

**Title III. Free Movement of Persons, Services and Capital**

*Chapter 1. Workers*

*Article 48.* 1. Freedom of movement for workers shall be secured within the Community by the end of the transitional period at the latest.

2. Such freedom of movement shall entail the abolition of any discrimination based on nationality between workers of the Member States as regards employment, remuneration and other conditions of work and employment.

3. It shall entail the right, subject to limitations justified on grounds of public policy, public security or public health:

(a) to accept offers of employment actually made;

(b) to move freely within the territory of Member States for this purpose;

(c) to stay in a Member State for the purpose of employment in accordance with the provisions governing the employment of nationals of that State laid down by law, regulation or administrative action;

(d) to remain in the territory of a Member State after having been employed in that State, subject to conditions which shall be embodied in implementing regulations to be drawn up by the Commission.

4. The provisions of this Article shall not apply to employment in the public service.

*Chapter 2. Right of Establishment*

*Article 52.* Within the framework of the provisions set out below, restrictions on the freedom of establishment of nationals of a Member State in the territory of another Member State shall be abolished by progressive stages in the course of the transitional period. Such progressive abolition shall also apply to restrictions on the setting up of agencies, branches, or subsidiaries by nationals of any Member State established in the territory of any Member State.

Freedom of establishment shall include the right to take up and pursue activities as self-employed persons and to set up and manage undertakings, in particular companies or firms within the meaning of the second paragraph of Art. 58, under the conditions laid down for its own nationals by the law of the country where such establishment is effected, subject to the provisions of the Chapter relating to capital.

*Chapter 3. Services*

*Article 59.* Within the framework of the provisions set out below, restrictions on freedom to provide services within the Community shall be progressively abolished during the transitional period in respect of nationals of Member States who are established in a State of the Community other than that of the person for whom the services are intended.

The Council may, acting by a qualified majority on a proposal from the Commission, extend the provisions of this Chapter to nationals of a third country who provide services and who are established within the Community.

## PART THREE. POLICY OF THE COMMUNITY

### Title I. Common Rules

*Chapter 1. Rules on Competition*

*Section 1. Rules Applying to Undertakings*

*Article 85.* 1. The following shall be prohibited as incompatible with the common market: all agreements between undertakings, decisions by associations of undertakings and concerted practices which may affect trade between Member States and which have as their object or effect the prevention, restriction or distortion of competition within the common market, and in particular those which:

(a) directly or indirectly fix purchase or selling prices or any other trading conditions;

(b) limit or control production, markets, technical development, or investment;

(c) share markets or sources of supply;

(d) apply dissimilar conditions to equivalent transactions with other trading parties, thereby placing them at a competitive disadvantage;

(e) make the conclusion of contracts subject to acceptance by the other parties of supplementary obligations which, by their nature or according to commercial usage, have no connection with the subject of such contracts.

2. Any agreements or decisions prohibited pursuant to this Article shall be automatically void.

3. The provisions of paragraph 1 may, however, be declared inapplicable in the case of:

- any agreement or category of agreements between undertakings;
- any decision or category of decisions by associations of undertakings;

- any concerted practice or category of concerted practices;

which contributes to improving the production or distribution of goods or to promoting technical or economic progress, while allowing consumers a fair share of the resulting benefit, and which does not:

(a) impose on the undertakings concerning restrictions which are not indispensable to the attainment of these objectives;

(b) afford such undertakings the possibility of eliminating competition in respect of a substantial part of the products in question.

*Article 86.* Any abuse by one or more undertakings of a dominant position within the common market or in a substantial part of it shall be prohibited as incompatible with the common market in so far as it may affect trade between Member States. Such abuse may, in particular, consist in:

(a) directly or indirectly imposing unfair purchase or selling prices or unfair trading conditions;

(b) limiting production, markets or technical development to the prejudice of consumers;

(c) applying dissimilar conditions to equivalent transactions with other trading parties, thereby placing them at a competitive disadvantage;

(d) making the conclusion of contracts subject to acceptance by the other parties of supplementary obligations which, by their nature or according to commercial usage, have no connection with the subject of such contracts.

*Chapter 2. Tax Provisions*

*Article 95.* No Member State shall impose, directly or indirectly, on the products of other Member States any internal taxation of any kind in excess of that imposed directly or indirectly on similar domestic products.

Furthermore, no Member State shall impose on the products of other Member States any internal taxation of such a nature as to afford indirect protection to other products.

Member States shall, not later than at the beginning of the second stage, repeal or amend any provisions existing when this Treaty enters into force which conflict with the preceding rules.

# PART FIVE. INSTITUTIONS OF THE COMMUNITY

## Title I. Provisions Governing the Institutions

*Chapter 1. The Institutions*

*Section 1. The Assembly*

*Article 137.* The Assembly, which shall consist of representatives of the peoples of the States brought together in the Community, shall exercise the advisory and supervisory powers which are conferred upon it by this Treaty.

*Article 138.* 1. The Assembly shall consist of delegates who shall be designated by the respective Parliaments from among their members in accordance with the procedure laid down by each Member State.

2. The number of these delegates shall be as follows:

| | | | |
|---|---|---|---|
| Belgium | 14 | Italy | 36 |
| Denmark | 10 | Luxembourg | 6 |
| Germany | 36 | Netherlands | 14 |
| France | 36 | United Kingdom | 36 |
| Ireland | 10 | | |

3. The Assembly shall draw up proposals for elections by direct universal suffrage in accordance with a uniform procedure in all Member States.

The Council shall, acting unanimously, lay down the appropriate provisions which it shall recommend to Member States for adoption in accordance with their respective constitutional requirements.

*Article 139.* The Assembly shall hold an annual session. It shall meet, without requiring to be convened, on the second Tuesday in March.

The Assembly may meet in extraordinary session at the request of the majority of its members or at the request of the Council or of the Commission.

*Article 140.* The Assembly shall elect its President and its officers from among its members.

Members of the Commission may attend all meetings and shall, at their request, be heard on behalf of the Commission.

The Commission shall reply orally or in writing to questions put to it by the Assembly or by its members.

The Council shall be heard by the Assembly in accordance with the conditions laid down by the Council in its rules of procedure.

*Article 141.* Save as otherwise provided in this Treaty, the Assembly shall act by an absolute majority of the votes cast.

The rules of procedure shall determine the quorum.

*Article 142.* The Assembly shall adopt its rules of procedure, acting by a majority of its members.

The proceedings of the Assembly shall be published in the manner laid down in its rules of procedure.

*Article 143.* The Assembly shall discuss in open session the annual general report submitted to it by the Commission.

*Article 144.* If a motion of censure on the activities of the Commission is tabled before it, the Assembly shall not vote thereon until at least three days after the motion has been tabled and only by open vote.

If the motion of censure is carried by a two-thirds majority of the votes cast, representing a majority of the members of the Assembly, the members of the Commission shall resign as a body. They shall continue to deal with current business until they are replaced in accordance with Art. 158.

*Section 2. The Council*

*Article 145.* To ensure that the objectives set out in this Treaty are attained, the Council shall, in accordance with the provisions of this Treaty:

- ensure coordination of the general economic policies of the Member States;
- have power to take decisions;
- confer on the Commission, in the acts which the Council adopts, powers for the implementation of the rules which the Council lays down. The Council may impose certain requirements in respect of the exercise of these powers. The Council may also reserve the right, in specific cases, to exercise directly implementing powers itself. The procedures referred to above must be consonant with principles and rules to be laid down in advance by the Council, acting unanimously on a proposal from the Commission and after obtaining the opinion of the European Parliament.

[Arts. 146 and 147 were repealed by the Merger Treaty.]

## MERGER TREATY

*Article 1.* A Council of the European Communities (hereinafter called the 'Council') is hereby established. This Council shall take the place of the Special Council of Ministers of the European Coal and Steel Community, the Council of the European Economic Community and the Council of the European Atomic Energy Community.

It shall exercise the powers and jurisdiction conferred on those institutions in accordance with the provisions of the Treaties establishing the European Coal and Steel Community, the European Economic Community and the European Atomic Energy Community, and of this Treaty.

*Article 2.* The Council shall consist of representatives of the Member States. Each Government shall delegate to it one of its members.

The office of President shall be held in turn by each Member State in the Council for a term of six months, in the following order of Member States:

- for a first cycle of six years: Belgium, Denmark, Germany, Greece, Spain, France, Ireland, Italy, Luxembourg, Netherlands, Portugal, United Kingdom;
- for the following cycle of six years: Denmark, Belgium, Greece, Germany, France, Spain, Italy, Ireland, Netherlands, Luxembourg, United Kingdom, Portugal.

*Article 3.* The Council shall meet when convened by its President on his own initiative or at the request of one of its members or of the Commission.

*Article 148.* Save as otherwise provided in this Treaty, the Council shall act by a majority of its members.

2. Where the Council is required to act by a qualified majority, the votes of its members shall be weighted as follows:

| | | | |
|---|---|---|---|
| Belgium | 5 | Iceland | 3 |
| Denmark | 3 | Italy | 10 |
| Germany | 10 | Luxembourg | 2 |
| Greece | 5 | Netherlands | 5 |
| Spain | 8 | Portugal | 5 |
| France | 10 | United Kingdom | 10 |

For their adoption, acts of the Council shall require at least:

54 votes in favour where this Treaty requires them to be adopted on a proposal from the Commission,

54 votes in favour, cast by at least eight members, in other cases.

3. Abstentions by members present in person or represented shall not prevent the adoption by the Council of acts which require unanimity.

*Article 149.* 1. Where, in pursuance of this Treaty, the Council acts on a proposal from the Commission, unanimity shall be required for an act constituting an amendment to that proposal.

2. Where, in pursuance of this Treaty, the Council acts in cooperation with the European Parliament, the following procedure shall apply:

(a) The Council, acting by a qualified majority under the conditions of paragraph 1, on a proposal from the Commission and after obtaining the opinion of the European Parliament, shall adopt a common position.

(b) The Council's common position shall be communicated to the European Parliament. The Council and the Commission shall inform the European Parliament fully of the reasons which led the Council to adopt its common position and also of the Commission's position.

If, within three months of such communication, the European Parliament approves this common position or has not taken a decision within that period, the Council shall definitively adopt the act in question in accordance with the common position.

(c) The European Parliament may within the period of three months referred to in point (b), by an absolute majority of its component members, propose amendments to the Council's common position. The European Parliament may also, by the same majority, reject the Council's common position. The result of the proceedings shall be transmitted to the Council and the Commission.

If the European Parliament has rejected the Council's common position, unanimity shall be required for the Council to act on a second reading.

(d) The Commission shall, within a period of one month, re-examine the proposal on the basis of which the Council adopted its common position, by taking into account the amendments proposed by the European Parliament.

The Commission shall forward to the Council, at the same time as its re-examined proposal, the amendments of the European Parliament which it has not accepted, and shall express its opinion

on them. The Council may adopt these amendments unanimously.
(e) The Council, acting by a qualified majority, shall adopt the proposal as re-examined by the Commission.

Unanimity shall be required for the Council to amend the proposal as re-examined by the Commission.
(f) In the cases referred to in points (c), (d) and (e), the Council shall be required to act within a period of three months. If no decision is taken within this period, the Commission proposal shall be deemed not to have been adopted.
(g) The periods referred to in points (b) and (f) may be extended by a maximum of one month by common accord between the Council and the European Parliament.

3. As long as the Council has not acted, the Commission may alter its proposal at any time during the procedures mentioned in paragraphs 1 and 2.

*Article 150.* Where a vote is taken, any member of the Council may also act on behalf of not more than one other member.

**MERGER TREATY**

*Article 4.* A committee consisting of the Permanent Representatives of the Member States shall be responsible for preparing the work of the Council and for carrying out the tasks assigned to it by the Council.

*Article 5.* The Council shall adopt its rules of procedure.

*Article 152.* The Council may request the Commission to undertake any studies which the Council considers desirable for the attainment of the common objectives, and to submit to it any appropriate proposals.

*Article 153.* The Council shall, after receiving an opinion from the Commission, determine the rules governing the committees provided for in this Treaty.

[Article 154 was repealed by the Merger Treaty.]

**MERGER TREATY**

*Article 6.* The Council shall, acting by a qualified majority, determine the salaries, allowances and pensions of the President and members of the Commission, and of the President, Judges, Advocates-General and Registrar of the Court of Justice. It shall also, again by a qualified majority, determine any payment to be made instead of remuneration.

*Section 3. The Commission*

*Article 155.* In order to ensure the proper functioning and development of the common market, the Commission shall:

- ensure that the provisions of this Treaty and the measures taken by the institutions pursuant thereto are applied;
- formulate recommendations or deliver opinions on matters dealt with in this Treaty, if it expressly so provides or if the Commission considers it necessary;
- have its own power of decision and participate in the shaping of measures taken by the Council and by the Assembly in the manner provided for in this Treaty;
- exercise the powers conferred on it by the Council for the implementation of the rules laid down by the latter.

[Articles 156-63 were repealed by the Merger Treaty.]

## MERGER TREATY

*Article 9.* A Commission of the European Communities (hereinafter called the 'Commission') is hereby established. This Commission shall take the place of the High Authority of the European Coal and Steel Community, the Commission of the European Economic Community and the Commission of the European Atomic Energy Community.

It shall exercise the powers and jurisdiction conferred on those institutions in accordance with the provisions of the Treaties establishing the European Coal and Steel Community, the European Economic Community and the European Atomic Energy Community, and of this Treaty.

*Article 10.* 1. The Commission shall consist of 17 members, who shall be chosen on the grounds of their general competence and whose independence is beyond doubt.

The number of members of the Commission may be altered by the Council, acting unanimously.

Only nationals of Member States may be members of the Commission.

The Commission must include at least one national of each of the Member States, but may not include more than two members having the nationality of the same State.

2. The members of the Commission shall, in the general interests of the Communities, be completely independent in the performance of their duties.

In the performance of these duties, they shall neither seek nor take instructions from any Government or from any other body. They shall refrain from any action incompatible with their duties. Each Member State undertakes to respect this principle and not to seek to influence the members of the Commission in the performance of their tasks.

The members of the Commission may not, during their term of office, engage in any other occupation, whether gainful or not. When entering upon their duties they shall give a solemn undertaking that, both during and after their term of office, they will respect the obligations arising therefrom and in particular their duty to behave with integrity and discretion as regards the acceptance, after they have ceased to hold office, of certain appointments of benefits. In the event of any breach of these obligations, the Court of Justice may, on application by the Council or the Commission, rule that the member concerned be, according to the circumstances, either compulsorily retired in accordance with the provisions of Art. 13 or deprived of his right to a pension or other benefits in its stead.

*Article 11.* The members of the Commission shall be appointed by common accord of the Governments of the Member States.

Their term of office shall be four years. It shall be renewable.

*Article 12.* Apart from normal replacement, or death, the duties of a member of the Commission shall end when he resigns or is compulsorily retired.

The vacancy thus caused shall be filled for the remainder of the member's term of office. The Council may, acting unanimously, decide that such a vacancy need not be filled.

Save in the case of compulsory retirement under the provision of Art. 13, members of the Commission shall remain in office until they have been replaced.

*Article 13.* If any member of the Commission no longer fulfils the conditions required for the performance of his duties or if he has been guilty of serious misconduct, the Court of Justice may, on application by the Council or the Commission, compulsorily retire him.

*Article 14.* The President and the six Vice-Presidents of the Commission shall be appointed from among its members for a term of two years in accordance with the same procedure as that laid down for the appointment of members of the Commission. Their appointments may be renewed.

Save where the entire Commission is replaced, such appointments shall be made after the Commission has been consulted.

In the event of retirement or death, the President and the Vice-Presidents shall be replaced for the remainder of their term of office in accordance with the preceding provisions.

The Council, acting unanimously, may amend the provisions concerning Vice-Presidents.

*Article 15.* The Council and the Commission shall consult each other and shall settle by common accord their methods of cooperation.

*Article 16.* The Commission shall adopt its rules of procedure so as to ensure that both it and its departments operate in accordance with the provisions of the Treaties establishing the European Coal and Steel Community, the European Economic Community and the European Atomic Energy Community, and of this Treaty. It shall ensure that these rules are published.

*Article 17.* The Commission shall act by a majority of the number of members provided for in Art. 10.

A meeting of the Commission shall be valid only if the number of members laid down in its rules of procedure is present.

*Article 18.* The Commission shall publish annually, not later than one month before the opening of the session of the Assembly, a general report on the activities of the Communities.

*Section 4. The Court of Justice*

*Article 164.* The Court of Justice shall ensure that in the interpretation and application of this Treaty the law is observed.

*Article 165.* The Court of Justice shall consist of 13 Judges.

The Court of Justice shall sit in plenary session. It may, however, form chambers, each consisting of three or five Judges, either to undertake certain preparatory inquiries or to adjudicate on particular categories of cases in accordance with rules laid down for these purposes.

Whenever the Court of Justice hears cases brought before it by a Member State or by one of the institutions of the Community or, to the extent that the chambers of the court do not have the requisite jurisdiction under the Rules of Procedure, has to give preliminary rulings on questions submitted to it pursuant to Art. 177, it shall sit in plenary session.

Should the Court of Justice so request, the Council may, acting unanimously, increase the number of Judges and make the necessary adjustments to the second and third paragraphs of this Article and to the second paragraph of Art. 167.

*Article 166.* The Court of Justice shall be assisted by six Advocates-General.

It shall be the duty of the Advocate-General, acting with complete impartiality and independence, to make, in open court, reasoned submissions on cases brought before the Court of Justice, in order to assist the Court in the performance of the task assigned to it in Art. 164.

Should the Court of Justice so request, the Council may, acting unanimously, increase the number of Advocates-General and make the necessary adjustments to the third paragraph of Art. 167.

*Article 167.* The Judges and Advocates-General shall be chosen from persons whose independence is beyond doubt and who possess the qualifications required for appointment to the highest judicial offices in their respective countries or who are jurisconsults of recognised competence; they shall be appointed by common accord of the Governments of the Member States for a term of six years.

Every three years there shall be a partial replacement of the Judges. Seven and six Judges shall be replaced alternately.

Every three years there shall be a partial replacement of the Advocates-General. Three Advocates-General shall be replaced on each occasion.

Retiring Judges and Advocates-General shall be eligible for re-appointment.

The Judges shall elect the President of the Court of Justice from among their number for a term of three years. He may be re-elected.

*Article 168.* The Court of Justice shall appoint its Registrar and lay down the rules governing his service.

*Article 168A.* 1. At the request of the Court of Justice and after consulting the Commission and the European Parliament, the Council may, acting unanimously, attach to the Court of Justice a court with jurisdiction to hear and determine at first instance, subject to a right of appeal to the Court of Justice on points of law only and in accordance with the conditions laid down by the Statutes, certain classes of action or proceeding brought by natural or legal persons. That court shall not be competent to hear and determine actions brought by Member States or by Community institutions or questions referred for a preliminary ruling under

Article 177.

2. The Council following the procedure laid down in paragraph 1, shall determine the composition of that court and adopt the necessary adjustments and additional provisions to the Statute of the Court of Justice. Unless the Council decide otherwise, the provisions of this Treaty relating to the Court of Justice, in particular the provisions of the Protocol on the Statute of the Court of Justice, shall apply to that court.

3. The members of that court shall be chosen from persons whose independence is beyond doubt and who possess the ability required for appointment to judicial office; they shall be appointed by common accord of the Governments of the Member States for a term of six years. The membership shall be partially renewed every three years. Retiring members shall be eligible for reappointment.

4. That court shall establish its rules of procedure in agreement with the Court of Justice. Those rules shall require the unanimous approval of the Council.

*Article 169.* If the Commission considers that a Member State has failed to fulfil an obligation under this Treaty, it shall deliver a reasoned opinion on the matter after giving the State concerned the opportunity to submit its observation.

If the State concerned does not comply with the opinions within the period laid down by the Commission the latter may bring the matter before the Court of Justice.

*Article 170.* A Member State which considers that another Member State has failed to fulfil an obligation under this Treaty may bring the matter before the Court of Justice.

Before a Member State brings an action against another Member State for an alleged infringement of an obligation under this Treaty, it shall bring the matter before the Commission.

The Commission shall deliver a reasoned opinion after each of the States concerned has been given the opportunity to submit its own case and its observations on the other party's case both orally and in writing.

If the Commission has not delivered an opinion within three months of the date on which the matter was brought before it, the absence of such opinion shall not prevent the matter from being brought before the Court of Justice.

*Article 171.* If the Court of Justice finds that a Member State has failed to fulfil an obligation under this Treaty, the State shall be required to take the necessary measures to comply with the judgment of the Court of Justice.

*Article 172.* Regulations made by the Council pursuant to the provisions of this Treaty may give the Court of Justice unlimited jurisdiction in regard to the penalties provided for in such regulations.

*Article 173.* The Court of Justice shall review the legality of acts of the Council and the Commission other than recommendations or opinions. It shall for this purpose have jurisdiction in actions brought by a Member State, the Council or the Commission on grounds of lack of competence, infringement of an essential procedural requirement, infringement of this Treaty or of any rule of law relating to its application, or misuse of powers.

Any natural or legal person may, under the same conditions, institute proceedings against a decision addressed to that person or against a decision which, although in the form of a regulation or a decision addressed to another person, is of direct and individual concern to the former.

The proceedings provided for in this Article shall be instituted within two months of the publication of the measure, or of its notification to the plaintiff, or, in the absence thereof, of the day on which it came to the knowledge of the latter, as the case may be.

*Article 174.* If the action is well-founded, the Court of Justice shall declare the act concerned to be void.

In the case of a regulation, however, the Court of Justice shall, if it considers this necessary, state which of the effects of the regulation which it has declared void shall be considered as definitive.

*Article 175.* Should the Council or the Commission, in infringement of this Treaty, fail to act, the Member States and the other institutions of the Community may bring an action before the Court of Justice to have the infringement established.

The action shall be admissible only if the institute concerned has first been called upon to act. If, within two months of being so called upon, the institution concerned has not defined its position, the action may be brought within a further period of two months.

Any natural or legal person may, under the conditions laid down in the preceding paragraphs, complain to the Court of Justice that an institution of the Community has failed to address to that person any act other than a recommendation or an opinion.

*Article 176.* The institution whose act has been declared void or whose failure to act has been declared contrary to this Treaty shall be required to take the necessary measures to comply with the judgment of the Court of Justice.

This obligation shall not affect any obligation which may result from the application of the second paragraph of Art. 215.

*Article 177.* The Court of Justice shall have jurisdiction to give preliminary rulings concerning:

(a) the interpretation of this Treaty;

(b) the validity and interpretation of acts of the institutions of the Community;

(c) the interpretation of the statutes of bodies established by an act of the Council, where those statutes so provide.

Where such a question is raised before any court or tribunal of a Member State, that court or tribunal may, if it considers that a decision on the question is necessary to enable it to give judgment, request the Court of Justice to give a ruling thereon.

Where any such question is raised in a case pending before a court or tribunal of a Member State, against whose decisions there is no judicial remedy under national law, that court or tribunal shall bring the matter before the Court of Justice.

*Article 178.* The Court of Justice shall have jurisdiction in disputes relating to the compensation for damage provided for in the second paragraph of Art. 215.

*Article 179.* The Court of Justice shall have jurisdiction in any dispute between the Community and its servants within the limits and under the conditions laid down in the Staff Regulations or the Conditions of Employment.

*Article 180.* The Court of Justice shall, within the limits hereinafter laid down, have jurisdiction in disputes concerning:

(a) the fulfilment by Member States of obligations under the Statute of the European Investment Bank. In this connection, the Board of Directors of the Bank shall enjoy the powers conferred upon the Commission by Art. 169;

(b) measures adopted by the Board of Governors of the Bank. In this connection, any Member State, the Commission or the Board of Directors of the Bank may institute proceedings under the conditions laid down in Art. 173;

(c) measures adopted by the Board of Directors of the Bank. Proceedings against such measures may be instituted only by Member States or by the Commission, under the conditions laid down in Art. 173, and solely on the grounds of non-compliance with the procedure provided for in Art. 21(2), (5), (6) and (7) of the Statute of the Bank.

*Article 181.* The Court of Justice shall have jurisdiction to give judgment pursuant to any arbitration clause contained in a contract concluded by or on behalf of the Community, whether that contract be governed by public or private law.

*Article 182.* The Court of Justice shall have jurisdiction in any dispute between Member States which relates to the subject matter of this Treaty if the dispute is submitted to it under a special agreement between the parties.

*Article 183.* Save where jurisdiction is conferred on the Court by this Treaty, disputes to which the Community is a party shall not on that ground be excluded from the jurisdiction of the courts or tribunals of the Member States.

*Article 184.* Notwithstanding the expiry of the period laid down in the third paragraph of Art. 173, any party may, in proceedings in which a regulation of the Council or of the Commission is in issue, plead the grounds specified in the first paragraph of Art. 173, in order to invoke before the Court of Justice the inapplicability of that regulation.

*Article 185.* Actions brought before the Court of Justice shall not have suspensory effect. The Court of Justice may, however, if it considers that circumstances so require, order that application of the contested act be suspended.

*Article 186.* The Court of Justice may in any cases before it prescribe any necessary interim measures.

*Article 187.* The judgments of the Court of Justice shall be enforceable under the conditions laid down in Art. 192.

*Article 188.* The Statute of the Court of Justice is laid down in a separate Protocol.

The Council may, acting unanimously at the request of the Court of Justice and after consulting the Commission and the European Parliament, amend the provisions of Title III of the Statute.

The Court of Justice shall adopt its rules of procedure. These shall require the unanimous approval of the Council.

*Chapter 2. Provisions Common to Several Institutions*

*Article 189.* In order to carry out their task the Council and the Commission shall, in accordance with the provisions of this Treaty, make regulations, issue directives, take decisions, make recommendations or deliver opinions.

A regulation shall have general application. It shall be binding in its entirety and directly applicable in all Member States.

A directive shall be binding, as to the result to be achieved, upon each Member State to which it is addressed, but shall leave to the national authorities the choice of form and methods.

A decision shall be binding in its entirety upon those to whom it is addressed.

Recommendations and opinions shall have no binding force.

*Article 190.* Regulations, directives and decisions of the Council and of the Commission shall state the reasons on which they are based and shall refer to any proposals or opinions which were required to be obtained pursuant to this Treaty.

*Article 191.* Regulations shall be published in the Official Journal of the community. They shall enter into force on the date specified in them or, in the absence thereof, on the twentieth day following their publication.

Directives and decisions shall be notified to those to whom they are addressed and shall take effect upon such notification.

*Article 192.* Decisions of the Council or of the Commission which impose a pecuniary obligation on persons other than States shall be enforceable.

Enforcement shall be governed by the rules of civil procedure in force in the State in the territory of which it is carried out. The order for its enforcement shall be appended to the decision, without other formality than verification of the authenticity of the decision, by the national authority which the Government of each Member State shall designate for this purpose and shall make known to the Commission and to the Court of Justice.

When these formalities have been completed on application by the party concerned, the latter may proceed to enforcement in accordance with the national law, by bringing the matter directly before the competent authority.

Enforcement may be suspended only by a decision of the Court of Justice. However, the courts of the country concerned shall have jurisdiction over complaints that enforcement is being carried out in an irregular manner.

### *Chapter 3. The Economic and Social Committee*

*Article 193.* An Economic and Social Committee is hereby established. It shall have advisory status.

The Committee shall consist of representatives of the various categories of economic and social activity, in particular, representatives of producers, farmers, carriers, workers, dealers, craftsmen, professional occupations and representatives of the general public.

*Article 194.* The number of members of the Committee shall be as follows:

| | | | |
|---|---|---|---|
| Belgium | 12 | Ireland | 9 |
| Denmark | 9 | Italy | 24 |
| Germany | 24 | Luxembourg | 5 |
| Greece | 12 | Netherlands | 12 |
| Spain | 21 | Portugal | 12 |
| France | 24 | United Kingdom | 24 |

The members of the Committee shall be appointed by the Council, acting unanimously, for four years. Their appointments shall be renewable.

The members of the Committee shall be appointed in their personal capacity and may not be bound by any mandatory instructions.

*Article 195.* 1. For the appointment of the members of the Committee, each Member State shall provide the Council with a list containing twice as many candidates as there are seats allotted to its nationals.

The composition of the Committee shall take account of the need to ensure adequate representation of the various categories of economic and social activity.

2. The Council shall consult the Commission. It may obtain the opinion of European bodies which are representative of the various economic and social sectors to which the activities of the Community are of concern.

*Article 196.* The Committee shall elect its chairman and officers from among its members for a term of two years.

It shall adopt its rules of procedure and shall submit them to the Council for its approval, which must be unanimous.

The Committee shall be convened by its chairman at the request of the Council or of the Commission.

*Article 197.* The Committee shall include specialised sections for the principal fields covered by this Treaty.

In particular, it shall contain an agricultural section and a transport section, which are the subject of special provisions in the Titles relating to agriculture and transport.

These specialised sections shall operate within the general terms of reference of the Committee. They may not be consulted independently of the Committee.

Sub-committees may also be established within the Committee to prepare, on specific questions or in specific fields, draft opinions to be submitted to the Committee for its consideration.

The rules of procedure shall lay down the methods of composition and the terms of reference of the specialised sections and of the sub-committees.

*Article 198.* The Committee must be consulted by the Council or by the Commission where this Treaty so provides. The Committee may be consulted by these institutions in all cases in which they consider it appropriate.

The Council or the Commission shall, if it considers it necessary, set the Committee, for the submission of its opinion, a time-limit which may not be less than ten days from the date on which the chairman receives notification to this effect. Upon expiry of the time-limit, the absence of an opinion shall not prevent further action.

The opinion of the Committee and that of the specialised section, together with a record of the proceedings, shall be forwarded to the Council and to the Commission.

**Title II. Financial Provisions**

*Article 199.* All items of revenue and expenditure of the Community, including those relating to the European Social Fund, shall be included in estimates to be drawn up for each financial year and shall be shown in the budget.

The revenue and expenditure shown in the budget shall be in balance.

*Article 200.* 1. The budget revenue shall include, irrespective of any other revenue, financial contributions of Member States on the following scale:

| | | | |
|---|---|---|---|
| Belgium | 7.9 | Italy | 28 |
| Germany | 28 | Luxembourg | 0.2 |
| France | 28 | Netherlands | 7.9 |

2. The financial contributions of Member States to cover the expenditure of the European Social Fund, however, shall be determined on the following scale:

| | | | |
|---|---|---|---|
| Belgium | 8.8 | Italy | 20 |
| Germany | 32 | Luxembourg | 0.2 |
| France | 32 | Netherlands | 7 |

3. The scales may be modified by the Council, acting unanimously.

*Article 201.* The Commission shall examine the conditions under which the financial contributions of Members States provided for in Art. 200 could be replaced by the Community's own resources, in particular by revenue accruing from the common customs tariff when it has been finally introduced.

To this end, the Commission shall submit proposals to the Council.

After consulting the Assembly on these proposals the Council may, acting unanimously, lay down the appropriate provisions, which it shall recommend to the Member States for adoption in accordance with their respective constitutional requirements.

*Article 202.* The expenditure shown in the budget shall be authorised for one financial year, unless the regulations made pursuant to Art. 209 provide otherwise.

In accordance with conditions to be laid down pursuant to Art. 209, any appropriations, other than those relating to staff expenditure, that are unexpended at the end of the financial year may be carried forward to the next financial year only.

Appropriations shall be classified under different chapters grouping items of expenditure according to their nature or purpose and subdivided, as far as may be necessary, in accordance with the regulations made pursuant to Art. 209.

The expenditure of the Assembly, the Council, the Commission and the Court of Justice shall be set out in separate parts of the budget, without prejudice to special arrangements for certain common items of expenditure.

*Article 203.* 1. The financial year shall run from 1 January to 31 December.

2. Each institution of the Community shall, before 1 July, draw up estimates of its expenditure. The Commission shall consolidate these estimates in a preliminary draft budget. It shall attach thereto an opinion which may contain different estimates.

The preliminary draft budget shall contain an estimate of

revenue and an estimate of expenditure.

3. The Commission shall place the preliminary draft budget before the Council not later than 1 September of the year preceding that in which the budget is to be implemented.

The Council shall consult the Commission and, where appropriate, the other institutions concerned whenever it intends to depart from the preliminary draft budget.

The Council acting by a qualified majority, shall establish the draft budget and forward it to the Assembly.

4. The draft budget shall be placed before the Assembly not later than 5 October of the year preceding that in which the budget is to be implemented.

The Assembly shall have the right to amend the draft budget, acting by a majority of its members, and to propose to the Council, acting by an absolute majority of the votes cast, modifications to the draft budget relating to expenditure necessarily resulting from this Treaty or from acts adopted in accordance herewith.

If, within 45 days of the draft budget being placed before it, the Assembly has given its approval, the budget shall stand as finally adopted. If within this period the Assembly has not amended the draft budget nor proposed any modifications thereto, the budget shall be deemed to be finally adopted.

If within this period the Assembly has adopted amendments or proposed modifications, the draft budget together with the amendments or proposed modifications shall be forwarded to the Council.

5. After discussing the draft budget with the Commission and, where appropriate, with the other institutions concerned, the Council shall act under the following conditions:

(a) The Council may, acting by a qualified majority, modify any of the amendments adopted by the Assembly;

(b) With regard to the proposed modifications: where a modification proposed by the Assembly does not have the effect of increasing the total amount of the expenditure of an institution, owing in particular to the fact that the increase in expenditure which it would involve would be expressly compensated by one or more proposed modifications correspondingly reducing expenditure, the Council may, acting by a qualified majority, reject the proposed modification. In the absence of a decision to reject it, the proposed modification shall stand as accepted; where a modification proposed by the Assembly has the effect of increasing the total amount of the expenditure of an institution, the Council may, acting by a qualified majority, accept this proposed modification. In the absence of a decision to accept it, the proposed modification shall stand as rejected; where in pursuance of one of the two preceding sub- paragraphs, the Council has rejected a proposed modification, it may, acting by a qualified majority, either retain the amount shown in the draft budget or fix another amount.

The draft budget shall be modified on the basis of the proposed modifications by the Council.

If, within 15 days of the draft budget being placed before it, the Council has not modified any of the amendments adopted by the Assembly and if the modifications proposed by the latter have been accepted, the budget shall be deemed to be finally adopted. The Council shall inform the Assembly that it has not modified any of the amendments and that the proposed modifications have been accepted.

If, within this period the Council has modified one or more of the amendments adopted by the Assembly or if the modifications proposed by the latter have been rejected or modified, the modified draft budget shall again be forwarded to the Assembly. The Council shall inform the Assembly of the results of its deliberations.

6. Within 15 days of the draft budget being placed before it, the Assembly, which shall have been notified of the action taken on its proposed modifications, may, acting by a majority of its members and three-fifths of the votes cast, amend or reflect the modifications to its amendments made by the Council and shall adopt the budget accordingly. If, within this period the Assembly has not acted, the budget shall be deemed to be finally adopted.

7. When the procedure provided for in this Article has been completed, the President of the Assembly shall declare that the budget has been finally adopted.

8. However, the Assembly, acting by a majority of its members and two-thirds of the votes cast, may if there are important reasons reject the draft budget and ask for a new draft to be submitted to it.

9. A maximum rate of increase in relation to the expenditure of the same type to be incurred during the current year shall be fixed annually for the total expenditure other than that necessarily resulting from this Treaty or from acts adopted in accordance therewith.

The Commission shall, after consulting the Economic Policy Committee, declare what this maximum rate is as it results from: the trend, in terms of volume, of the gross national products within the Community; the average variation in the budgets of the Member

States; and the trend of the cost of living during the preceding financial year.

The maximum rate shall be communicated, before 1 May, to all the institutions of the Community. The latter shall be required to conform to this during the budgetary procedure, subject to the provisions of the fourth and fifth subparagraphs of this paragraph.

If, in respect of expenditure other than that necessarily resulting from this Treaty or from acts adopted in accordance therewith, the actual rate of increase in the draft budget established by the Council is over half the maximum rate, the Assembly may, exercising its right of amendment, further increase the total amount of that expenditure to a limit not exceeding half the maximum rate.

Where the Assembly, the Council or the Commissions consider that the activities of the Communities require that the rate determined according to the procedure laid down in this paragraph should be exceeded, another rate may be fixed by agreement between the Council, acting by a qualified majority, and the Assembly, acting by a majority of its members and three-fifths of the votes cast.

10. Each institution shall exercise the powers conferred upon it by this Article, with due regard for the provisions of the Treaty and for acts adopted in accordance therewith, in particular those relating to the Communities' own resources and to the balance between revenue and expenditure.

*Article 203a.* By way of derogation from the provisions of Art. 203, the following provisions shall apply to budgets for financial years preceding the financial year 1975:

1. The financial year shall run from 1 January to 31 December.

2. Each institution of the Community shall, before 1 July, draw up estimates of its expenditure. The Commission shall consolidate these estimates in a preliminary draft budget. It shall attach thereto an opinion which may contain different estimates.

The preliminary draft budget shall contain an estimate of revenue and an estimate of expenditure.

3. The Commission shall place the preliminary draft budget before the Council not later than 1 September of the year preceding that in which the budget is to be implemented.

The Council shall consult the Commission and, where appropriate, the other institutions concerned whenever it intends to depart from the preliminary draft budget.

The Council shall, acting by a qualified majority, establish the draft budget and forward it to the Assembly.

4. The draft budget shall be placed before the Assembly not later than 5 October of the year preceding that in which the budget is to be implemented.

The Assembly shall have the right to propose to the Council modifications to the draft budget.

If, within 45 days of the draft budget being placed before it, the Assembly has given its approval or has not proposed any modifications to the draft budget, the budget shall be deemed to be finally adopted.

If, within this period the Assembly has proposed modifications, the draft budget together with the proposed modifications shall be forwarded to the Council.

5. The Council shall, after discussing the draft budget with the Commission and, where appropriate, with the other institutions concerned, adopt the budget, within 30 days of the draft budget being placed before it, under the following conditions.

Where a modification proposed by the Assembly does not have the effect of increasing the total amount of the expenditure of an institution, owing in particular to the fact that the increase in expenditure which it would involve would be expressly compensated by one or more proposed modifications correspondingly reducing expenditure, the Council may, acting by a qualified majority, reject the proposed modifications. In the absence of a decision to reject it, the proposed modification shall stand as accepted.

Where a modification proposed by the Assembly has the effect of increasing the total amount of the expenditure of an institution, the Council must act by a qualified majority in accepting the proposed modification.

Where, in pursuance of the second or third subparagraph of this paragraph, the Council has rejected or has not accepted a proposed modification, it may, acting by a qualified majority, either retain the amount shown in the draft budget or fix another amount.

6. When the procedure provided for in the Article has been completed, the President of the Council shall declare that the budget has been finally adopted.

7. Each institution shall exercise the powers conferred upon it by this Article, with due regard for the provisions of this Treaty and for acts adopted in accordance therewith, in particular those relating to the Communities' own resources and to the balance between revenue and expenditure.

*Article 204.* If, at the beginning of a financial year, the budget has not yet been voted, a sum equivalent to not more than one-twelfth of the budget appropriations for the preceding financial year may be spent each month in respect of any chapter or other subdivision of the budget in accordance with the provisions of the regulations made pursuant to Art. 209; this arrangement shall not, however, have the effect of placing at the disposal of the Commission appropriations in excess of one-twelfth of those provided for in the draft budget in course of preparation.

The Council may, acting by a qualified majority, provided that the other conditions laid down in the first subparagraph are observed, authorise expenditure in excess of one-twelfth.

If the decision relates to expenditure which does not necessarily result from this Treaty or from acts adopted in accordance therewith, the Council shall forward it immediately to the Assembly; within 30 days the Assembly, acting by a majority of its members and three-fifths of the votes cast, may adopt a different decision on the expenditure in excess of the one-twelfth referred to in the first subparagraph. This part of the decision of the Council shall be suspended until the Assembly has taken its decision. If within the period the Assembly has not taken a decision which differs from the decision of the Council, the latter shall be deemed to be finally adopted.

The decisions referred to in the second and third subparagraphs shall lay down the necessary measures relating to resources to ensure application of this Article.

*Article 205.* The Commission shall implement the budget, in accordance with the provisions of the regulations made pursuant to Art. 209, on its own responsibility and within the limits of the appropriations.

The regulations shall lay down detailed rules for each institution concerning its part in effecting its own expenditure.

Within the budget, the Commission may, subject to the limits and conditions laid down in the regulations made pursuant to Art. 209, transfer appropriations from one chapter to another or from one subdivision to another.

*Article 205a.* The Commissions shall submit annually to the Council and to the Assembly the accounts of the preceding financial year relating to the implementation of the budget. The Commission shall also forward to them a financial statement of the assets and liabilities of the Community.

*Article 206.* 1. A Court of Auditors is hereby established.

2. The Court of Auditors shall consist of twelve members.

3. The members of the Court of Auditors shall be chosen from among persons who belong or have belonged in their respective countries to external audit bodies or who are especially qualified for this office. Their independence must be beyond doubt.

4. The members of the Court of Auditors shall be appointed for a term of six years by the Council, acting unanimously after consulting the Assembly.

However, when the first appointments are made, four members of the Court of Auditors, chosen by lot, shall be appointed for a term of office of four years only.

The members of the Court of Auditors shall be eligible for re-appointment.

They shall elect the President of the Court of Auditors from among their number for a term of three years. The President may be re-elected.

5. The members of the Court of Auditors shall, in the general interest of the Community, be completely independent in the performance of their duties.

In the performance of these duties, they shall neither seek nor take instructions from any Government or from any other body. They shall refrain from any action incompatible with their duties.

6. The members of the Court of Auditors may not, during their term of office, engage in any other occupation, whether gainful or not. When entering upon their duties they shall give a solemn undertaking that, both during and after their term of office, they will respect the obligations arising therefrom and in particular their duty to behave with integrity and discretion as regards the acceptance, after they have ceased to hold office, of certain appointments of benefits.

7. Apart from normal replacement, or death, the duties of a member of the Court of Auditors shall end when he resigns, or is compulsorily retired by a ruling of the Court of Justice pursuant to paragraph 8.

The vacancy thus caused shall be filled for the remainder of the member's terms of office.

Save in case of compulsory retirement, members of the Court of Auditors shall remain in office until they have been replaced.

8. A member of the Court of Auditors may be deprived of his office or of his right to a pension or other benefits in its stead only if the Court of Justice, at the request of the Court of Auditors, finds that he no longer fulfils the requisite conditions or meets the obligations arising from his office.

9. The Council, acting by a qualified majority, shall determine the conditions of employment of the President and the members of the Court of Auditors and in particular their salaries, allowances and pensions. It shall also, by the same majority, determine any payment to be made instead of remuneration.

10. The provisions of the Protocol on the Privileges and Immunities of the European Communities applicable to the Judges of the Court of Justice shall also apply to the members of the Court of Auditors.

*Article 206a.* 1. The Court of Auditors shall examine the accounts of all revenue and expenditure of the Community. It shall also examine the accounts of all revenue and expenditure of all bodies set up by the Community insofar as the relevant constituent instrument does not prelude such examination.

2. The Court of Auditors shall examine whether all revenue has been received and all expenditure incurred in a lawful and regular manner and whether the financial management has been sound.

The audit of revenue shall be carried out on the basis both of the amounts established as due and the amounts actually paid to the Community.

The audit of expenditure shall be carried out on the basis both of commitments undertaken and payments made.

These audits may be carried out before the closure of accounts for the financial year in question.

3. The audit shall be based on records and, if necessary, performed on the spot in the institutions of the Community and in the Member States. In the Member States the audit shall be carried out in liaison with the national audit bodies or, if these do not have the necessary powers, with the competent national departments. These bodies or departments shall inform the Court of Auditors whether they intend to take part in the audit.

The institutions of the Community and the national audit bodies or, if these do not have the necessary powers, the competent national departments, shall forward to the Court of Auditors, at its request, any document or information necessary to carry out its task.

4. The Court of Auditors shall draw up an annual report after the close of each financial year. It shall be forwarded to the institutions of the Community and shall be published, together with the replies of these institutions to the observations of the Court of Auditors, in the Official Journal of the European Communities.

The Court of Auditors may also, at any time, submit

observations on specific questions and deliver opinions at the request of one of the institutions of the Community.

It shall adopt its annual reports or opinions by a majority of its members.

It shall assist the Assembly and the Council in exercising their powers of control over the implementation of the budget.

*Article 206b.* The Assembly, acting on a recommendation from the Council which shall act by a qualified majority, shall give a discharge to the Commission in respect of the implementation of the budget. To this end, the Council and the Assembly in turn shall examine the accounts and the financial statement referred to in Art. 205a and the annual report by the Court of Auditors together with the replies of the institutions under audit to the observations of the Court of Auditors.

*Article 207.* The budget shall be drawn up in the unit of account determined in accordance with the provisions of the regulations made pursuant to Art. 209.

The financial contributions provided for in Art. 200(1) shall be placed at the disposal of the Community by the Member States in their national currencies.

The available balances of these contributions shall be deposited with the Treasuries of Member States or with bodies designated by them. While on deposit, such funds shall retain the value corresponding to the parity, at the date of deposit, in relation to the unit of account referred to in the first paragraph.

The balances may be invested on terms to be agreed between the Commission and the Member State concerned.

The regulations made pursuant to Art. 209 shall lay down the technical conditions under which financial operations relating to the European Social Fund shall be carried out.

*Article 208.* The Commission may, provided it notifies the competent authorities of the Member States concerned, transfer into the currency of one of the Member States its holdings in the currency of another Member State, to the extent necessary to enable them to be used for purposes which come within the scope of this Treaty. The Commission shall as far as possible avoid making such transfers if it possesses cash or liquid assets in the currencies which it needs.

The Commission shall deal with each Member State through the authority designated by the State concerned. In carrying out financial operations the Commission shall employ the services of the bank of issue of the Member State concerned or of any other

financial institution approved by that State.
*Article 209*. The Council, acting unanimously on a proposal from the Commission and after consulting the Assembly and obtaining the opinion of the Court of Auditors, shall:
(a) make financial regulations specifying in particular the procedure to be adopted for establishing and implementing the budget and for presenting and auditing accounts;
(b) determine the methods and procedures whereby the budget revenue provided under the arrangements relating to the Communities' own resources shall be made available to the Commission, and determine the measures to be applied, if need be, to meet cash requirements;
(c) lay down rules concerning the responsibility of authorising officers and accounting officers and concerning appropriate arrangements for inspection.

# Index